The A4 Pacifics After Gresley

The Late L N E R and British Railways Periods, 1942–1966

The A4 Pacifics
After Gresley

The Late L N E R and British Railways Periods, 1942–1966

TIM HILLIER-GRAVES

**PEN & SWORD
TRANSPORT**

AN IMPRINT OF PEN & SWORD BOOKS LTD.
YORKSHIRE – PHILADELPHIA

First published in Great Britain in 2023 by
Pen and Sword Transport
An imprint of Pen & Sword Books Ltd.
Yorkshire - Philadelphia

Copyright © Tim Hillier-Graves, 2023

ISBN 978 1 39907 343 1

Typeset in Palatino by SJmagic DESIGN SERVICES, India.
Printed and bound in India by Replika Press Pvt. Ltd.

Pen & Sword Books Ltd incorporates the imprints of Pen & Sword
Books Archaeology, Atlas, Aviation, Battleground, Discovery, Family
History, History, Maritime, Military, Naval, Politics, Railways, Select,
Transport, True Crime, Fiction, Frontline Books, Leo Cooper, Praetorian
Press, Seaforth Publishing, Wharncliffe and White Owl.

For a complete list of Pen & Sword titles please contact

PEN & SWORD BOOKS LIMITED
47 Church Street, Barnsley, South Yorkshire, S70 2AS, England
E-mail: enquiries@pen-and-sword.co.uk
Website: www.pen-and-sword.co.uk

or

PEN AND SWORD BOOKS
1950 Lawrence Rd, Havertown, PA 19083, USA
E-mail: Uspen-and-sword@casematepublishers.com
Website: www.penandswordbooks.com

CONTENTS

ACKNOWLEDGEMENTS

I have been privileged to meet many people who worked on the railways and were happy to paint vivid pictures of the time when steam dominated their lives – engineers, designers, footplate crew, managers and many more. Their number grows thinner each year, but luckily many have been moved to reminisce or write about their experiences. This has created a bank of information for future generations to enjoy and so increase their understanding of a time of which many can have no personal knowledge.

To this we can add many other individuals who have made a huge commitment, personal and financial, to preserve and record so many aspects of railway history. Amongst them I number my late uncle, Ronald Hillier, whose work has helped me write about railway-related subjects, but particularly the A4s and the LNER. Here his extensive research proved invaluable and made this two volume history of the 'Streaks' possible, hence joint authorship.

The principal sources of material are listed in the reference section of this book. Occasionally I have quoted directly from them, mostly because I couldn`t improve on what they have written. In addition, I believe that using contemporary accounts, wherever possible, captures the spirit of the time in which these events took place much more effectively than I could ever do. There is an immediacy about their words, untainted by beneficial hindsight. I thank the authors or holders of this material for permission to use it to enliven this book and give it greater authenticity.

To all the people who have helped me, I give my thanks and hope I have done justice to all that they have contributed. Ultimately though, all an historian can do is to sift and consider all material and reach a judgement that he or she thinks honestly represents history. There will, undoubtedly,

King's Cross was always the best place to see the A4s in action, as this picture of No. 60013 *Dominion of New Zealand* clearly demonstrates. (THG)

be other views or conclusions and even some omissions that someone thinks may be crucial to a story, but that is as it should be. I don`t think there is ever a final word on any subject and new material may be found to allow fresh interpretations to be made.

In producing photographs for this book some preservation work has been necessary. In some cases, their sepia finish, foxing and dilapidated condition could not be entirely overcome. However, because they are often rare pictures or have some historic significance they have been included despite their condition. I hope this doesn't spoil your enjoyment of the book.

The changing face of life at King's Cross and a sign that the railways and Britain are rapidly modernising. These two photos taken only a few years apart, which Bert Spencer kept, sum these changes up very effectively (Above) 60008 *Dwight D Eisenhower* makes ready to pull the Yorkshire Pullman northwards, while (left) Class 55 Deltic No. D9020 *Nimbus* takes on the prestigious Flying Scotsman very early in her career. This engine, which entered service in February 1962, had a fairly short life, being scrapped in 1980 when replaced by Inter City 125s. (BS)

PROLOGUE

The war is becoming a distant memory, though its many scars were far from being healed. By the mid-1950s, when this photo was taken, Britain's railway network had returned to something near normal after many difficult years and steam still dominated its schedules. Yet times and attitudes were changing and soon diesels will begin to make their appearance and their long period of domination will start. As a result, steam will be consigned to scrapyards and all signs of its existence soon disappear; although soot stains on station buildings, bridges and tunnels will provide a fading trace of these lost engines for many decades to come. For those who lived through these last days, this picture of 60029 Woodcock, waiting at King's Cross to be turned, will evoke many memories. (THG)

Almost 30 years after my uncle stood on the platform at King's Cross watching *Silver Link* pull away for the first time, I found myself near the same spot, at virtually the same age witnessing the last of the A4s in action. I was drawn, like others, by the sight of these fast-disappearing behemoths and wanted to savour soon to vanish scenes before they were gone forever. Yet, beside the new Deltic diesels then beginning to dominate the East Coast Mainline, they looked rather fragile and I again marvelled at their ability to pull massive loads over long distances without difficulty for all those years. By any standard they were remarkable engines and continued to be so until the end, even without *Mallard's* memorable world speed record of 1938. But soon they were gone from BR's service as though they had never been, their great deeds slipping into memory, occasionally discussed and remembered to become a postscript in railway history.

Looking back, it is surprising to think that steam lasted as long as it did. But for Britain's reliance on cheap coal from its collieries and the bankrupting effect of two world wars, it may well have gone sooner. So in many ways these engines were something of a throwback by the 1950s, let alone the 1960s, when many other countries had taken a leap into the future with electric and diesel power. Did nostalgia, and a desire to hold on to the past, play a part in delaying these changes? Or was it simply a practical issue decided by hard-headed businessmen and politicians with limited resources to play with? A mixture of both probably. But the end result was that steam had a second wind and the A4s continued to ply

their trade on a network that for them quickly shrank to nothing. By the early 1960s, withdrawals from service had begun and those engines that remained were relegated to the northern areas of Britain and seen only very rarely on their old, more famous stamping ground between King's Cross and Edinburgh.

Sadly, I saw little of them after 1964, though my Hornby Dublo *Sir Nigel Gresley* and *Silver Link* continued to act as a pleasing reminder of the part they played in my early life. Sadly, it was not until 1990 that I came across one in action again and then by surprise. I was 'standing by' a ship in refit at Smith's Yard on the Tyne but based, with my crew, at Rosyth while she was stripped, rebuilt and

returned to me. My deputy and I were accommodated in a small guest house in Inverkeithing, the wardroom in HMS *Caledonian* being full at the time, with a view over the Firth of Forth bridge, the line curving past my window. It was 100 years since the bridge opened and commemorations were in full swing. I woke late one Saturday morning to find 60009 *Union of South Africa*, renamed *Osprey* for the occasion, trundling back and forth over the bridge. With nothing better to do, I sat watching this reminder of my childhood and later in the day caught up with her at Waverley, gently simmering in the sunshine, her crew having a brief rest. Being in BR green she was exactly as I remembered the A4s at King's Cross in the 1950s and '60s; a coat

The graceful. unforgettable lines of an A4 caught beautifully in 1990 when 60009 *Union of South Africa*, named *Osprey* at the time, was captured by the author waiting patiently near Waverley Station in Edinburgh. She was there as part of the 100th anniversary celebrations for the Firth of Forth rail bridge. (THG)

The only too familiar shape of an A4 captured in the last few weeks of its active service. No. 60032 *Gannet* still looks in fine fettle but in October 1963 will be condemned and then cut up at Doncaster shortly afterwards. (THG)

of soot giving her an appealing, slightly grimy, workmanlike look.

I found all this very thought provoking and in the days that followed found my mind going back to the days when steam locomotives were an everyday sight and dominated many aspects of our lives. To be honest, I hadn't thought about these things for many years and had come to regard the railways as a necessary evil. They had simply become a means to an end as I dragged myself around Britain's network in the service of Queen and Country, barely registering anything I was seeing or riding on. Now, this sudden rush of memories revived my interest and with it a desire to learn more about the people who

designed, built, maintained and worked Britain's evolving fleet of locomotives. And at the top of my list sat the LNER's imperious A4s, but many years would pass before the opportunity to write about them came my way. Then, thanks to Pen and Sword, the moment came and with it a commission for two books.

In the first volume, *Gresley's Silver Link,* I described the design history of the A4s, focussing on all the elements that came together to promote and encourage their development. This second book, which begins after Gresley's death, continues their story, taking it through the cruellest of wars to a pauper's peace, where a near bankrupt nation struggled to make

ends meet. Then government, seeing the parlous state of the network, decided that massive change was necessary and adopted nationalisation as its panacea. And, with that, the railways passed into Westminster's hands for good or bad. As Bert Spencer, Gresley's technical assistant later wrote, 'and no one, least of all the politician's, knew where that would lead as the Ministry of Transport and the British Transport Commission struggled to make sense of all they had inherited and produce a workable plan for the future.'

During these difficult years, the A4s kept running, despite their heavy workload, minimal maintenance at times, a gradual drift of trade to the roads and staff to less demanding, much less strenuous jobs in other industries. In this rapidly modernising world, steam became something of an anachronism, a welcome relic of the past, but increasingly looking out of place when other forms of transport were cleaner, faster and more efficient. Nevertheless, they clung on through the 1950s and into the 1960s until BR finally brought other types of motive power in sufficient numbers to cope with all the railway's needs. It was a long goodbye, but a final goodbye nonetheless and in 1966 the last of the A4s disappeared from service for good. Most were scrapped, but six survived into preservation where they provide a reminder of all that was and now is gone.

This book celebrates these final years.

Chapter 1

WAR AND PEACE

When a leader of such stature as Gresley dies, it inevitably creates a huge void that needs to be filled quickly if an organisation is to continue to function effectively. With war raging this becomes even more important. In most businesses of the LNER's size and complexity there is usually a deputy who can step in and fill the vacancy, being coached and prepared for such a task along the way. Mostly, but not always, this is the most experienced manager available and for the LNER's Chairman, Ronald Matthews, and Chief General Manager, Charles Newton, this meant Edward Thompson, then Mechanical Engineer at Doncaster. For reasons that aren't entirely clear, Gresley preferred not to name him or anyone else as a deputy after Arthur Stamer, who filled this role for ten years, retired in 1933. With the CME's health visibly in decline for some time, this was a mistake which the company's senior managers did little to correct while Gresley was still in post.

Some personal antipathy between Gresley and Thompson has been suggested for this lack of action and there is some evidence to support this view. The CME's daughter

Edward Thompson enjoying a rare moment away from Doncaster during the war. The demands placed on him and his staff were excessive and it stands to his great credit that he kept the railway running and met all the tasks placed on him by the War Ministry and the Ministry of Supply in producing military equipment of many different types. (ET/AP)

In the early months of the war, it was unclear how profoundly the conflict would affect life in Britain. With a substantial army in France, it was thought that this would deter an attack. Until May 1940 this proved to be the case and the evacuation from Dunkirk was soon followed by mass bombing and the threat of invasion. By this stage, the railways began to lose many thousands of men to the services and the general appearance of locomotives and rolling stock rapidly declined and the A4s found themselves undertaking far from glamorous duties. By 1941, although still showing traces of their pre-war glow, their condition, internally and externally, had begun to deteriorate as these pictures bear witness. (Top) 4901 *Capercaillie* passing through Doncaster. (Bottom left) 4487 *Sea Eagle* captured early in the war relegated to freight work. (Bottom right) Some effort made to clean 4485 *Kestrel*, but far from complete before her next turn of duty. (BS)

Violet later recalled that her father described Thompson as being disloyal, though gave no other information about time, place or circumstance to explain this strong feeling. Then Eric Bannister, a junior member of Gresley's HQ team in London, recalled that Thompson's occasional visits to King's Cross were a far from welcome event. 'The only time that he [Gresley] was likely to be solemn and silent was when a certain engineer was visiting and Harper would warn us "Don't go near Gresley – Thompson is coming!"'

It is true that many found Thompson a difficult man to deal with, but he and Gresley had worked together since 1913 so it was a long well-established relationship that seemed to work. And, perhaps more tellingly, the CME had on a number of occasions approved Thompson's promotion until, in 1938, he stood as Gresley's deputy in all but name.

For his part, Thompson, on the rare occasions when speaking on the subject, simply stated that 'Gresley was the greatest British locomotive engineer since Churchward'. Bearing in mind Gresley's great admiration for Churchward, this is high praise indeed.

We will never know the truth about this relationship and what made it tick. In the event, speculation and conjecture have taken root. If each man did indeed harbour doubts about the other, the true reasons for this are lost to time. It may simply have been that they were both strong ambitious men who saw in each other some threat to their position, which led to distrust. If this is true Thompson, at least, still greatly respected Gresley

and was prepared to praise him for his achievements. The feeling may have been reciprocated, as witnessed by Thompson's gradual promotion to senior rank, but Gresley did not live long enough to express a clearer view either way.

If profound differences did exist between the two men, they do not seem to have had an adverse effect on the way the CME's Department was run; quite the opposite in fact. This may be due to the nature of their engineering skills. Gresley was first and foremost a design engineer, fired up by the scientific challenge research and development tasks offered. In contrast, Thompson was a production engineer of great repute who understood how to make workshops operate at

peak efficiency – something he proved time and time again as his career progressed. Design and production are essential bedfellows in any industry. If a very advanced locomotive or carriage is developed, its value can only be realised if workshops can produce them on time, on budget and to the highest quality, then maintain them in a satisfactory condition. This is what Thompson did best, applying all he had learnt in a long career to these essential processes. And in wartime, when developing new products had to take a back seat to maintaining a fleet in good working order, experienced production managers were worth their weight in gold.

Bert Spencer, who observed Gresley and Thompson work at

The decline continues. Staff shortages and heavier usage take their toll. The once high standard of finish applied to the A4 and the other Pacifics in normal times by cleaners has now all but gone. Changed priorities soon saw these engines become more workmanlike in their appearance. A4 No. 4486 *Merlin* is just such a case as she is captured crossing the Firth of Forth. (BS)

In July 1941 A4 No. 4462 *Great Snipe* was renamed *William Whitelaw* at York in honour of the LNER's first chairman. Here, a gust of wind threatens to take over the ceremony before Whitelaw can pull the cord. Left to right – the new Chairman Ronald Matthews, an unidentified director, Edward Thompson and Whitelaw. One of Thompson's first acts was to approve the removal of the A4s' side valances as an aid to maintenance in sheds and workshops where staff shortages were having a profound affect. In this case, 4462 has only lost the valancing over the driving wheels. The section over the front bogie will be removed when the engine arrives at Haymarket towards the end of July. (ET/DN)

close quarters, probably got closest to the truth when he wrote:

He [Thompson] always had the good of the department at heart and could be ruthless in the execution of his duties when necessary. But there was another side to him which was considerate and accommodating. He appeared to think deeply about the future and introduced many changes to improve productivity and working conditions. These were aspects to which Sir Nigel and Bulleid gave little attention, preferring questions of locomotive design to the day to day tasks undertaken in the workshops. Thompson was a good forward-thinking manager and a good workshop manager. However, he was [by comparison to Gresley] also an average, well intentioned engineer who relied upon Windle [the LNER's Chief Draughtsman], in particular, for guidance when it came to locomotive design.

Together these two men made a remarkable team, no matter what their differences. But in 1941, the skills Thompson possessed, plus his extensive military service as a senior officer in the Great War, were considerably more important than an ability to design locomotives.

It was probably in recognition of his well developed production skills that ensured that Matthews and Newton chose him over any other candidate they may have had in mind. A memo written by the Chairman shortly after Gresley's death, when considering who his successor might be, made all this very clear:

His [Thompson's] outstanding qualities as an efficient organiser have been amply testified by the improvements he has effected in the methods of production and the progressive systems of repairs he has introduced at the various works with which he has been connected, which have

contributed in no small measure to the high efficiency and fine quality of workmanship to be found in our modern locomotives and rolling stock built in these works.

And in a press release announcing Thompson's appointment Matthews added a little more detail:

There is a general feeling of satisfaction that the directors have chosen for this very important post one who has been associated with the activities of the CME's Department since amalgamation, and who is fitted by training and ability to carry out the tradition of progress created by his predecessor, having had, at one time or another, charge of the company's locomotive, carriage and wagon works in England.

His new responsibilities, covering as they do locomotive, carriage and wagon work, road motor engineering and docks machinery, together with the Chief Chemist's Department, come at a time of considerable difficulty, but he is assured of the loyal support and co-operation of the staff under him who wish him good health so that his energies may be unimpaired by the strenuous task he has been called upon to undertake.

So, in many ways it was a seamless transfer of power, but with one element carefully stripped away. Gresley had been responsible for developing electrification projects on the LNER and had set up a small team led by Henry Richards to further these aims. Immediately prior to the war, two proposals – Sheffield to Manchester and Liverpool Street Station to Shenfield – had been pursued with some vigour, buoyed up by central government subsidies and a strong desire to modernise the network. Inevitably, the rapidly deteriorating international situation put paid to this work, though planning continued for the day when the war ended. And now the Chairman and General Manager decided to remove oversight of this development work, but not the construction of its motive power, from Thompson and set up Richards as Chief Electrical Engineer. At the same time, they expanded the electrical team with a number of draughtsmen under Tom Street, who had led in producing designs for the A4 as Chief Draughtsman. His place was taken by the experienced Edward Windle, who had been his deputy for many years.

These changes were not thought to be a reflection on Thompson's abilities, more a recognition of the immense burden that was falling on his shoulders, as the company sought to meet many pressing wartime demands. They had seen

The first A4 to have its valences removed entirely was 4487 *Sea Eagle*. The work took place in June/July 1941 during a period of light repair at Doncaster necessitated by a 'superheater header that had cracked'. The engine returned to traffic on 5 July when this photograph was taken. (BS)

A photo that sums up the problems faced by railways in war – a hard to identify streamlined B17 (possibly No. 2859 *East Anglian*) making its way through serious bomb damage that often threatened to bring the network to a halt. By this stage of the war, the A4s and the two streamlined B17s had begun to be painted black overall and have LNER on their tenders shortened to NE. (BS)

how Gresley had struggled with excessive pressure over the years and may have suspected that this had contributed to his early death. So with the 60-year-old Thompson, they probably did not want to repeat this mistake.

Ever conscious of the stress he seemed likely to endure, the new CME soon appointed a deputy in the form of the talented and versatile Arthur Peppercorn, who also became Mechanical Engineer at Doncaster. In the circumstances, it was a wise move and an even wiser choice. Peppercorn, like Thompson was a very experienced

production engineer, who, like his new CME, knew how to extract maximum effort from his staff without taking them to the point of collapse. Together they would make an exceptional team and, in due course, would choose subordinates more than capable of doing their bidding. In most cases, they would be drawn from trusted and talented subordinates already resident in the vast organisation they controlled.

In the LNER's *Journal,* Thompson highlighted the changes made:

In future there will be five Mechanical Engineers. In

addition to Mr Peppercorn at Doncaster, who will also supervise the 'outdoor' carriage and wagon work on the Great Northern Section and the Great Central Section between Sheffield and Marylebone, there will be an ME to supervise Gorton locomotive works, who will report directly to the CME. Mr T. Heywood will continue to be styled ME (Scotland). Mr F.W. Carr remains in charge at Stratford. Mr R.A. Smeddle becomes ME Darlington (on promotion from Locomotive

Works Manager at Darlington), to replace Mr Peppercorn. Mr J.F. Harrison has been appointed to the new post of ME at Gorton.

Mr Harper will remain in charge of the HQ Office with the title of Assistant to the CME (Clerical). Mr Windle will be in charge of both locomotive and carriage/wagon drawing offices. Mr F. Day will continue as Head Carriage Draughtsman and Mr D.D. Gray has been appointed Head Locomotive Draughtsman.

He then added a short note which set his stall out for the future, but also paid due respect to the part played by his predecessor:

It will be appreciated that something like a revolution has been made in the methods of conducting work of the department, but there is every reason to think that

the departures from the old-established practice will put fresh vigour into the establishment which Sir Nigel Gresley has built up since 1923. He left a great example to his successor and the object of all the arrangements

described above is to revitalise the mechanical engineering branch of our railway work and keep the LNER in the forefront as an exponent of modern development, calculated to secure economy and efficiency.

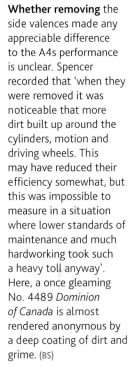

Whether removing the side valences made any appreciable difference to the A4s performance is unclear. Spencer recorded that 'when they were removed it was noticeable that more dirt built up around the cylinders, motion and driving wheels. This may have reduced their efficiency somewhat, but this was impossible to measure in a situation where lower standards of maintenance and much hardworking took such a heavy toll anyway'. Here, a once gleaming No. 4489 *Dominion of Canada* is almost rendered anonymous by a deep coating of dirt and grime. (BS)

Some A4s kept their valancing for a while as it was usually removed when an engine returned to the Works for maintenance. Here No. 4903 *Peregrine* is photographed at Doncaster in August 1942, shortly to undergo a General Repair and be painted black. For the moment, though, she still has her valances intact. In 1948 this engine will be renamed *Lord Faringdon*. (BS)

Finally, when taking up the reins of his new post, Thompson called his senior managers together and, in a short but telling speech, is reported as saying, 'I have a lot to do, gentlemen, and little time to do it in.'

These words are open to different interpretations and some detractors later translated them as meaning that he fully intended to undo Gresley's legacy as recompense for some unspecified slight or grudge. A more rational, fair-minded interpretation is that he was simply referring to the war and the huge amount of work they all had to do if disaster were to be averted and victory secured. At the time he was appointed, the war was going badly for Britain and defeat seemed more than likely, so these encouraging, resolute words were essential. Whatever interpretation is placed on them, though, there was little doubt that

he and his department faced a daunting task.

In the years that followed, Thompson and Peppercorn managed all that was expected of them and more with great energy and skill, so justifying the trust placed in them by Matthews and Newton. But in one area of work, they could not demonstrate their prowess to any great extent – the design of new locomotives. From the beginning, Thompson was limited in what he could do by the instruction that 'the war precluded the introduction of new designs, but I had the freedom to build more engines of existing classes should the need arise'. The need was presumably subject to the closest scrutiny by the LNER's Locomotive Committee and, more importantly, the Ministry of Supply, which became all-powerful when the government took control of the railways in 1939/40.

So, what did this mean in reality? The simple answer seems to be that a newly built engine would have to meet any criteria set out by the two ministries, Supply and War. Inevitably this meant that these locomotives would have to have a warlike purpose. So priority was given to freight over everything else, with high speed passenger work barely registering on this list of requirements. With so many Pacifics already available, this probably did not matter unduly, but any serious problems they encountered in service, or even losses due to enemy action, could not be dealt with by building new. So, goods and mixed traffic engines were all that seemed likely to be allowed for the foreseeable future.

With so many pressing demands placed on the LNER's fleet, anything that reduced availability had to be flagged up very quickly. With this in mind, Thompson soon felt the need to highlight the ever-worsening condition of engines with three-cylinders and conjugated valve gear, their increasing downtime and the cost of maintaining them making this unavoidable. In 1941 when he took over, the three Divisional General Managers were often expressing their concerns about the Gresley engines and the problems they were causing. And judging by the files that remain it was an issue that the running department had raised with Gresley himself before that. He, according to Thompson:

Had come to realise that an improvement was needed, but in the end simply admitted that he could not make any better of it. I remember that on the

By 1942, the external condition of most locomotives was at its worst, making it almost impossible to identify one engine from another. This begrimed, anonymous A4 is a perfect example of the way once glamorous engines quickly slipped into this appalling condition. (BS)

cover of one report about the performance of the 600 odd locomotives fitted with this type of motion Gresley had written 'the performance of these engines is shown to be inferior'!

With Gresley in charge, these concerns were probably only whispered, but with Thompson's arrival the debate became more heated. This was hardly surprising when considering the power to wield a big stick vested in the Divisional Managers, with the all-powerful Newton in the background. They could, if they so wished, demand urgent action from Thompson on any issue over which they felt strongly and the deteriorating state of the Gresley three-cylinder engines proved to be just such a case.

The first signs of this increasing disquiet were probably picked up by Cyril Elwell in his role as Assistant Mechanical Engineer (Outdoors). He had been appointed to this position by Thompson to sort out production delays and he did much to increase efficiency and flow rates throughout all the LNER's workshops. It was he, supported by Bert Spencer, Gresley's one-time assistant at King's Cross and now Elwells's deputy, who soon began to collect evidence from shed and workshop staff about the deteriorating state of these locomotives, the availability of the P2s in particular and many other related issues. More demanding words soon flowed from the General Managers and the Works Managers as the size and severity of the problem became even more

apparent. All of this material was collated, analysed and compared, resulting in a summary that would have made difficult reading for a CME struggling to make sure the railway had sufficient working engines to meet so many pressing needs.

In confirming this Bert Spencer later wrote:

All the LNER's workshops had to work flat out to meet demand, at the same time as absorb and train many new staff as skilled men left to join the forces. Most of the replacements were women, who soon impressed us with their enthusiasm, hard work and desire to learn. But it still took time to train them to anywhere near the standard of those who had departed, many of whom never returned.

The main crisis did not occur until late 1941 when lower maintenance standards and heavy workloads had taken their toll of locomotives and rolling stock and their overall condition had slipped badly. Also by this time the workshops had taken on many additional tasks not related to the railways, such as weapon production and repairs to damaged aeroplanes. All these tasks had to be co-ordinated and production rates monitored, with progress chasing a key part of the daily routine. All this had to be recorded and reported to the CME, who regularly faced grilling's by the General Manager and various wartime committees ever eager to increase production rates.

Although our workload was extremely heavy and the hours very long we all felt that our contribution was important and greatly valued by Thompson, who often expressed satisfaction with our work.

In his 1947 presentation to the Institution of Locomotive Engineers, which was an appreciation of all Gresley's locomotive work, Spencer expanded on this issue. By then, many in the audience were fully aware of the ever increasing concerns expressed during the war about the effectiveness of three-cylinders when matched to Gresley's conjugated valve gear. Sensing that this would be given a critical airing by members, he decided to strike first. So, in his summary he offered a partial defence of his greatly admired CME's work, perhaps playing down his own reservations, but revealing much in the process:

Gresley maintained that the clearly defined advantages of such an engine over a two-cylinder engine outweighed the complication introduced by a third cylinder. Fundamentally the more nearly the crank effort of a reciprocating engine can be made to approach uniformity the greater the advantage derived from a given adhesive weight. In this connection the superiority of the three-cylinder is apparent when the crank efforts of two, three and four-cylinder engines are compared.

As maximum hauling power is one of the primary requirements of a locomotive, the fact that a three-cylinder engine is capable of exerting a considerably higher mean tractive effort than that of a two-cylinder engine with the same adhesive weight is of the greatest importance … Whilst it can be urged that three independent sets of valve gear ensure a more accurate valve setting for the inside cylinder, the conjugated gear has the merit of simplicity and is not without advantages if due consideration is given to its inherent limitations.

He then went on to describe the conditions that had to met if these advantages were to be realised:

It is essential that the outside gears should be of sufficiently rigid construction and provided with adequate bearing surfaces for the additional duty they have to perform. Furthermore, it is of the utmost importance that the fit of all pins should be to close limits. With the conjugated gear the effect of the clearance on each of the six pins is cumulative and any clearance in the fixed fulcrum of the 2 to 1 lever and the floating fulcrum of the equal lever is multiplied by three and two respectively at the centre valve. Unit clearance at each of these eight points would consequently be multiplied by eleven at the centre valve … It will be clear, therefore, that on both the primary and the conjugated valve gears, bearings of ample proportions manufactured to close tolerances are essential to successful performance.

Towards the end of his life, he summed his thoughts on the Gresley three-cylinder engines very succinctly when he wrote that 'they did their job well and proved economical in practice. Three cylinders had many advantages over two'. Here he doesn't add 'until the war came and the standard of servicing required to maintain such close tolerances simply fell away causing significant availability problems', but the reservation is implied nonetheless.

His audience were quick to latch on to the weaknesses in his argument and the extent of problems the 2 to 1 gear appeared to have caused, in war or peace. Tellingly, in the question-

When pressed during his 1947 presentation to the Institution of Locomotive Engineers about the performance of Gresley's Pacifics, and the A4s in particular, Bert Spencer felt moved to produce this set of indicator drawings in their support. The criticism focussed on the performance of these three cylinder engines, most specifically on Gresley's conjugated valve gear and the effect this had on the centre cylinder caused by over-running. In the absence of any indicator diagrams for the A4s he plumped instead for a set taken from trials with A3 No. 2751 and suggested there was a natural read across to the streamliners. (BS)

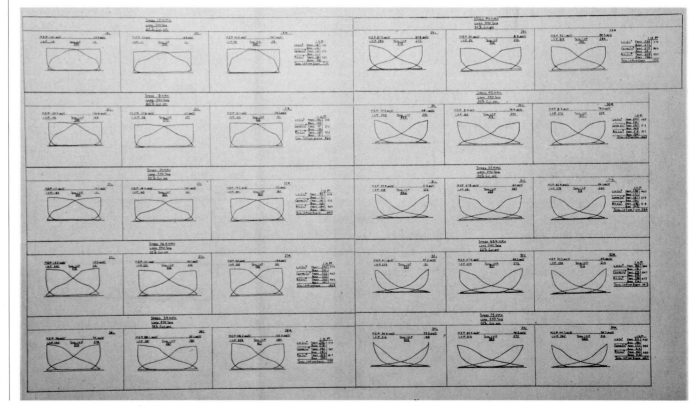

and-answer session that followed his presentation, the debate quickly turned to the apparent lack of evidence that Gresley had produced in support of his three-cylinder engines. They then moved on to the specific question of over-running of the centre cylinder in the LNER's fast-running Pacifics, particularly the A4s. To some, this appeared to be the crux of the matter and the cause of the problems. Spencer chose not to respond to the first issue and only partially to the second. However, he did when pressed produce a series of indicator diagrams taken during tests with A3 No. 2751 in support of Gresley's claims, adding that:

No indicator diagrams were taken on the A4s as the streamlined casing made it impracticable to find accommodation for an operator and direct reading instruments were not available. [However] diagrams had been taken on the A3s. From these it will be noted that the area of the centre cylinder diagram is not affected to any material extent until speeds of 60mph and over are reached at early cut-offs. Above this speed there is some difference in the power developed between the inside and outside cylinders, but the fact remains that engines fitted with this form of conjugated valve gear ran successfully and economically, in the pre-war period, some of the fastest trains in this country and one of them attained, and still holds, the world's record speed for steam rail traction.

Few it seems were convinced by his arguments and it was impossible

to deny that in the years following Gresley's death, the LNER had dropped the conjugated valve gear in favour of more traditional arrangements, as Spencer confirmed when pressed. 'The standard classes built since 1941 were evolved on the principle that two-cylinders should be adopted unless the required service called for more power than a two-cylinder engine could satisfactorily provide. The three-cylinder were provided with three independent valve gears.'

Left and below: **It became** quite common for A4s to be given the names of distinguished members of the LNER's hierarchy. In August 1942 No.4901 *Capercaillie* became *Charles H. Newton* after the Chief General Manager, who succeeded Ralph Wedgwood in 1939. Newton attended this muted ceremony and is photographed here on the footplate of the now black locomotive with NE marked on the tender. Newton would remain in post until 1947 by which time he had been knighted with the engine having 'Sir' added to the nameplate. (THG)

In 1947, all this was much clearer to the assembled crowd, but in 1941/42 evidence of poor performance was still being gathered, as Thompson and his team sought to improve the availability of Gresley's three-cylinder engines. One simple remedy quickly introduced saw more spares being held at the sheds so that fitters there could replace the conjugated valve gear when problems arose. Doing this meant that engines did not have to face the time-consuming business of returning to the main workshops for repairs following breakdown. In part it worked, but as time went on, wear and tear continued to take their toll and replacement of the valve gear took place with ever increasing frequency. At this point, Thompson decided that a third-party assessment was needed and recruited the help of his old friend William Stanier in undertaking this task. Spencer described what this entailed, having studied the problem in some detail himself before the review began:

A consensus had formed in the running department and workshops that they were not lasting well and were causing many unnecessary problems. By this stage [in early 1942] the CME had sought Stanier's advice on the issue and had an independent report, conducted by Ernest Cox, on the subject to consider. His report, which Stanier counter-signed, reached some unpleasant conclusions.

Cox's findings made sorry reading:

The '2 to 1' valve gear although theoretically correct is, in practice, incapable of being made into a sound mechanical job, and rapid wear of the pins, and incorrect steam distribution, are the inevitable results of its use. In view of its inherent defects and the discontinuance of its use throughout the world, a good case can be made for not perpetuating it in any future design.

It is certain that with this arrangement of valve gear it will be necessary to give the engines a frequent overhaul in the Shops and even then it is not possible to eliminate the effect of lost motion due to running clearance required in the pin joints and the effect of expansion of the outside valve spindle on the inside valve.

It is a matter of consideration, therefore, as to whether certain of the classes should not be fitted with an independent inside valve gear.

The excessive inside big end trouble experienced is, in my opinion, due mainly to the design of the big end. The alternative designs already developed by the LNER should alone bring about considerable improvements. The use of higher grade white metal and the elimination of the brass strip across the bearing are also, in my view, worthy of consideration in view of extensive experience with three-cylinder engines on the LMS.

Later on, having given the matter more thought, Cox added an even more telling note:

It was an unassailable fact that unit play at each of the eight pin joints was multiplied by eleven by the time it reached the middle valve, and in fully rundown condition the lost motion could amount to 3/8th. This resulted in reduced power at low speeds due to insufficient port opening, while at high speeds the combined effect of over travel of the valve, plus whip in the combining levers, could produce up to 50% more power in the middle cylinder than in either of the outside. There was also a spate of hot inside big-ends, ten times as many in the inside position as at the outside, six times as many as the LM experienced with the inside big-ends on a comparable number of its own three-cylinder engines. The high speed engines of the 4-6-2 class suffered the highest proportion of failures, the 2-6-2 and 2-8-2 types also being high. A certain lack of stiffness in the marine big-end arrangement also appeared to contribute to this result.

Spencer, having carefully considered this report, recorded that, 'these conclusions came as no surprise to our team, where day to day we had been dealing with problems developing with the Pacifics and the P2s in particular. All of this soon began to attract the ire of the Regional Managers to whom these engines were assigned'. Armed with such clear evidence of declining performance, Thompson had to do something if he wished to avoid censure or, worse still, insufficient locomotives available to do the work. Increased maintenance could only keep the problem in

The changing face of the P2s. In response to promptings from the Divisional General Manager, worried by the problems being experienced with his six 2-8-2s Thompson proposed rebuilding them as Pacifics. As a result, No. 2005 *Thane of Fife*, was the first to be converted. These two photographs show her before and after the work was completed. Some later condemned his actions as a form of cultural vandalism, even a desecration of Gresley's work sponsored by malice. These fantasies apart, Thompson seems to have chosen a practical, well-intentioned route that gave the Divisional Manager what he wanted. (THG)

check for so long, but at a cost the organisation could ill-afford. Something more was needed.

Spencer, with his usual clarity of thought, hit the nail on the head when he wrote 'the best long term solution was to rebuild the worst offenders, which would be costly and absorb precious resources, and replace the 2 in 1 gear in the others with a third set of Walschaerts gear. It was an issue I frequently discussed with the CME who seemed to agree with my summary'. As Gresley's long term assistant and confidant he might have been expected to take a different line, but he was a very talented, level-headed engineer who, first and foremost, saw issues and solutions with great clarity. And so, despite a strong attachment to Gresley's engines, he confirmed the problem and offered the most practical solution possible.

Although he would probably have liked to take action sooner in fitting these engines with a third, independent set of valve gear and implementing other changes suggested by Cox and Spencer, Thompson's hands were tied by circumstances beyond his control. With so many other

pressing demands being made on the locomotive fleet and workshop, staff time did not allow these proposals to be implemented. However, he took careful note of the conclusions reached, added them to what they already knew and planned for a future when some normality might return. The one exception to this was the P2s where problems were simply not all related to the valve gear, as Thompson recalled:

This conversion was instigated chiefly by troubles with the

conjugated gear, although tyre wear and performance were also contributory factors. The availability of the engines for the 12 months prior to rebuilding had been no more than 47% and on one occasion, three of the six were under repair at Doncaster [engine Numbers 2003, 2005 and 2006 all between September and October 1941].

With so much downtime, and under increasing pressure from the Divisional General Manager for Scotland, R.J. Inglis, had to do something. Thompson contemplated rebuilding one of them to Pacific configuration as a means of eradicating the problems, rather than simply modify the P2s as they were. But he also believed that this would have the added benefit of 'extending their range of operations in Scotland by making the engines less wasteful of coal'. Having reached this conclusion, he submitted a scheme to the company's Locomotive Committee in late-1942 seeking permission to modify the P2s. He later reported that his 'original proposal was at first opposed by Andrew McCosh, the Chairman, who eventually said 'Well, rebuild one'. A few months later, having received favourable reports from every driver he had spoken to, insisted on all six examples being rebuilt.'

The first member of the class to be converted, No. 2005 *Thane of Fife*, soon became the first of the new Class A2/2 Pacifics and appeared in its new form during January 1943, but the other five did not follow until 1944. They may have been accepted as an improvement over the P2s at the time but controversy over the need to rebuild them has dogged Thompson's reputation ever since. In truth, he took a series of well-considered, practical steps to overcome the problems highlighted by Inglis and others. Their concerns were genuine and could not be ignored. In response, Thompson presented Windle with his proposals and allowed the Chief Draughtsman and his team to produce a solution that best suited the need, with the A2/2 being the result.

It also helped that in 1942/43, Thompson was tasked by Newton

with producing a standardisation plan for the locomotive fleet, to be implemented when peace eventually returned. New Pacifics, that built on the work begun by Gresley with his A1s, A3s and A4s, were a key part of this emerging plan and the P2 to A2/2 programme, allowed the CME to experiment with some alternative arrangements, including three independent sets of valve gear.

As the war came to an end, Thompson advanced this work a step further by taking the last four V2s in the LNER's locomotive programme and building them as Pacifics as well, resulting in the A2/1s. This was shortly followed by another experiment when the CME obtained permission to rebuild an A1 to a new A1/1 standard, as opposed to making it an A3, the traditional path set for the A1s. Gresley's prototype Pacific, No. 4470 *Great Northern*, was selected for this purpose, an act that reinforced the views of those who thought that Thompson was deliberately vandalising his predecessor's work for some malevolent purpose.

In reality, the CME seems to have played little or no part in the selection of this locomotive, though would undoubtedly have been aware that it had been chosen, being so closely involved in the project. More likely is the view that it was the engine next in line for a General Repair and upgrading to A3 standard, with final selection falling to the Running Superintendent, George Musgrave, who nominated then released the engine to Thompson's workshops.

The performance of this 'new' Pacific came in for much criticism

later with some airing the view that it was inferior to the original. However, this was not an opinion shared by many in the LNER at the time, including Spencer who simply wrote that:

The rebuilding of Great Northern was a valuable experiment and gave an old and tired engine a new lease of life. Would it have been better as an A3 with conjugated valve gear? Undoubtedly not. The A1/1 was a much superior engine until A3s were fitted with double blast pipes, but it would have been too expensive to rebuild others into this new form, so the A1 to A3 programme continued when the war came to an end. However, Thompson and Windle did take forward all that they had learnt from Great Northern and this helped considerably in the development of the first post war Pacifics.

In support of this assessment a report produced by the RCTS in 1973 adds some weight. After sifting much evidence, it concluded that the A1/1s performance was superior to the average A3 or A4, suggesting that the conversion was justified, but the choice of engine might have been handled more sensitively. But with so much on his plate simply keeping trains running, with the increasing dilapidation of locomotives, rolling stock and workshop equipment, not to mention staff shortages and a significant skills gap, such an indulgence would have been a peacetime luxury few could afford to enjoy.

Towards the end of the war Gresley's prototype Pacific No. 1470/4470, described by Richard Hardy, then a draughtsman at Doncaster, as not being 'one of the best', was selected for rebuilding to test out developing ideas on a standardisation. The choice of this engine is held by some as evidence of Thompson's malice towards Gresley. The reality seems to be that the CME played little or no part in the selection. It was probably a case of taking the engine next in line for a General Repair and upgrading to A3 standard with the Running Superintendent, George Musgrave, nominating and then releasing the engine. In 1973, a report in the influential RCTS journal judged that the A1/1s performance was superior to the average A3 or A4, suggesting that the conversion was a justifiable experiment. (Top left) 1470/4470 as built in 1922. (Top right) As rebuilt by Thompson and team in 1945 in wartime livery. (Bottom) Before Nationalisation, the engine, now numbered 113, was fitted with very distinctive smoke deflectors plates. (BS)

Right and below: **A class** of thirty-five reduced by war to thirty-four. During a raid on York on 29 April 1942, 4469 *Sir Ralph Wedgwood*, which had been stabled overnight at North Shed, was blasted by a German bomb. It left a deep crater and threw the engine upwards and sideways shattering its casing and fracturing its frames in the process. Although rescued and re-railed it quickly became apparent that the loco was beyond economic repair and it was condemned in June. The tender, which as the lower photo demonstrates was soon covered in anti-Nazi, pro-USSR graffiti, proved to be repairable, though it would take until December 1945 for it to re-appear and then be attached to Thompson's 1944 built Class 2/1 Pacific No. 3696 *Highland Chieftain*. In January 1944, the Wedgwood name would pass to No. 4466 *Herring Gull*. (BS)

In a final flourish before his retirement in 1946, Thompson took the Pacific project a step further with the first of his fifteen A2/3s. It was a programme that Peppercorn would, in turn, develop and modify, under Windle's guiding hand until British Railways took over the 'Big Four' and brought these experiments to an end. Remarkably, or so it seems to me, with so much attention being focussed on the future of the LNER Pacifics by Thompson, any proposals to rebuild Gresley's ultimate steam locomotives, the A4s, were kept very low key or were simply not thought necessary. If the CME was indeed trying to eradicate Gresley's legacy they, one assumes, would have been at the top of his list. History would show that they were not.

When war began all this was still far in the future, with invasion and subjugation by Hitler's messianic hordes the most likely outcome. In the panic of September 1939 there were many knee-jerk reactions, including taking many Pacifics out of service and placing them in store. The naïve belief that such glamorous engines had no part to play in such a conflict seems ridiculous now. But in a country where pre-war propaganda had conditioned people to believe that German bombers would be overhead within hours or days, laying waste to vast areas of the country, killing hundreds of thousands of men, women and children in the process, such knee jerk reactions were perhaps understandable. Yet as the days passed, and the predicted mass bombing did not materialize, an expectant calm descended while people waited to see what would happen next, a pause that allowed wiser minds to slowly prevail.

So began the 'Phoney War', as Germany drew breath, consolidated her gains in the east and prepared for a war of conquest in the west. For Britain's political, military and industrial leaders there was now a short breathing space in which to try to correct the deficiencies of years of appeasement and marshall whatever resources they could to meet an onslaught that was unlikely to be long delayed.

Soon all available locomotives, including the A4s, were pressed into service and their loads and the mileages increased exponentially. For most of the 'streaks' this meant that they would travel anything up to 20,000 miles extra a year. While this was happening, the workshops were losing many trained engineers to the services, so reducing the quality of the maintenance work carried out. So, it is little wonder that this created a perfect storm of circumstances where engines quickly deteriorated and problems arose, with Gresley's three-cylinder engines appearing to be particularly vulnerable.

Quite independently of Thompson and his team, Cecil Allen, the noted railway writer, LNER employee and avid recorder of locomotive performances, confirmed all this when he wrote that:

Things went from bad to worse. In the early days of the

war the Pacifics were flogged unmercifully in handling trains of 700 and 800 tons gross weight, and sometimes even more, and with the shortage of staff and materials the standard of maintenance fell steadily. For example, the grease lubrication of the 2 to 1 motion, until then invariably carried out by a fitter rather than the driver, went by default, as did various other kinds of skilled attention to their motion that engines had been accustomed to receive. Wear in all the pins increased as a result of inadequate lubrication and the failure to keep the derived gear clear of ash during smokebox cleaning; excessive mileage between overhauls took its toll; the quality of lubricating

oil declined steadily. Thus the number of middle big-end failures went up by leaps and bounds.

Despite wartime conditions and restrictions, Allen continued to record train movements, their timings and performance, later publishing the results. In so doing he left us an invaluable archive of material that confirms how well or badly all of the LNER Pacifics performed, but particularly the A4s. Many of these he sent to Bert Spencer, with whom he seems to have established a fairly close relationship. Although not providing a complete picture they were, as Spencer, recalled, an 'invaluable supplement to all we were learning from footplate crew, workshop staff, maintenance

With little time to keep an engine clean the crew of No. 4463 *Sparrow Hawk* have made do with a quick wipe around her numbers on cab sides and nose. But even though covered with grime, the engine still makes an impressive sight at an unrecorded time and place. However, the date can be narrowed down a bit because the engine does not appear to have been painted black yet (a task competed in August 1943) and has had her side valances removed (November 1941). (BS)

records and the Flaman rolls that were produced when drivers remembered to operate the recorders'.

Perhaps Allen's most revealing report was produced in late 1942 and eventually found its way into the *Railway Magazine*, though by this stage Spencer and Co had received a copy and undoubtedly analysed the results and worked them into material being collected from other sources. Allen begins with a general summary before describing the performances he witnessed, including some pre-war runs for comparison's sake, where he thought these might be representative of peacetime running. To Spencer he wrote that:

Since the war began reference has been made to the abnormal trainloads hauled over the LNER main line. Now has come the time to present a detailed review of the work of the Pacifics in these conditions. Since the record size trains of the first Summer of the war, when 26 coach formations of 750 tons or more, with 1,300 passengers – giving 850 tons gross weight behind the tender – were not uncommon, the loads have settled down to a tare limit of 700 tons. However, as is clear from my report, the weight of the trains varies a great deal according to the number of articulated coaches that may be included (many of the twin coaches built for excursion are now incorporated in train formations).

In the runs recorded between King's Cross and Grantham, the trains ranged from 16 to 21 vehicles, with a tare weight from 520 to 695 tons and a gross weight of, as nearly as can be estimated, 560 to 760 tons.

On the first down run, streamlined A4 Pacific No. 4485 *Kestrel*, had been badly delayed as far as Hatfield by enemy action, but after passing Woolmer Green at 50mph got away well with this 560 ton train, covering the 50 miles from Knebworth to Fletton in 44 mins 10 secs, at an average speed of 67.9mph. The speed rose to 76mph at Arlesey and Holme and 62 at Fletton Junction before shutting of steam. The schedule for the train concerned – the then 1.15 pm from King's Cross to Leeds – was 93 minutes, and almost exactly 10 minutes was picked up by *Kestrel* from Hitchen to Peterborough; net time for the run was about 83 minutes.

In the second run recorded the double-chimney Pacific No.4902 *Seagull* made a good start with 590 tons until there were a number of signal checks and stops passed Wood Green which cost us 12 minutes. Driver Burfoot then covered the 43.1 miles from Hitchen to Fletton in 38 minutes and 58 seconds with speeds of 71½mph at Three Counties and then 73 at Holme. But we were stopped again at Crescent Junction which delayed us further. A magnificent effort followed, despite passing Peterborough at only 5mph, and signals against us outside Grantham. Despite these delays the 29.1 miles to Grantham were run in 31 minutes and 56 seconds. Thus we arrived on time and the engine had

Her record run of July 1938 now a distant memory 4468 Mallard continues to ply her trade but now her duties, although valuable, could be far less glamourous. Here she is making light of a very modest 'fast parcels' train near Marshmoor in Hertfordshire, having been painted black (June 1942) and having lost her valances at the same time. She would not be restored to garter blue glory until March 1948. (PR/RH)

No. 4464 Bittern must have recently left the works judging by the relatively clean state of her black paint, which was applied during a period of General Repair at Doncaster that ended in November 1941. She still carry's LNER markings on her tender. This will be shortened to NE in May 1943 when given another coat of black (BS).

32 seconds. By the time Empire of India reached Newcastle the train was 4 minutes less than schedule. Net running time for the entire 268.3 miles, which includes accelerations from three starts, slowing down to three stops and severe slowings through Peterborough, Selby and Durnham, was thus 277½ minutes, which means slightly more than a mile-a-minute running averaged throughout."

Allen then described eight more wartime runs where all the loads for the A4s were in the range 660 to 740 tons and so considerably heavier. By this stage, the engines were not only having to cope with the results of enemy action, but also declining maintenance standards and lack of attention. In a letter to Spencer, he made his concerns plain:

recovered 16 minutes caused by the delays on route.

The third run has been included for comparison purposes and describes a run made in peacetime, but under the shadow of war, for the occasion was an exceptional exodus from London on the down Flying Scotsman pulled by A4 No. 4490. The extremely heavy formation of the train introduced in 1937 had three more coaches added making 593 tons tare. But with four vehicles used for restaurant and buffet purposes, the crowded seating space did not make more than 635 tons. Nevertheless, this was an enormous train to work over

the 105.5 miles to Grantham on a schedule of 110 minutes.

The engine was not pressed in the early stages and lost time, and the start was not as good as Seagull. From Hatfield onwards the work was amazing. With speeds of 76mph beyond Hatfield, 65 minimum at Woolmers Green, no less than 91 at Three Counties … and 85 at Connington, 4490 covered the 44 miles from Stevenage to Yaxley in 34 minutes and 29 seconds at an average speed of 76.5mph. Driver Dalrymple of Gateshead then opened out the engine sufficiently to recover the two minute arrears of time, running from Peterborough to Grantham in 32 minutes and

There is no doubting that the Pacifics' condition is worsening. This is only too apparent when riding behind them in the first or second coaches or simply standing beside them immediately prior to departure. It is not simply a matter of cleanliness, but runs much deeper. Things are not helped by the greater loads they are obliged to pull, but also more broad operating issues. For example, and as pointed out to me by footplate crew on several occasions, with the relatively few departures of heavily-loaded expresses from King's Cross in the down direction, would it not be possible to clear the fast road to Finsbury

Right, below and opposite: A number of record cards, covering the lives of the A4s, have survived in public and private hands. Even though the information they contain seems rather slight they do offer us a brief glimpse of the work the engines did and their maintenance needs, albeit at the main workshops and not the running sheds. In the three cards, for No's 4489 *Sea Eagle*, 4484 *Falcon* and 4485 *Kestrel*, the increased mileages and the lack of evidence regarding any major problems are only too apparent. This suggests that any difficulties with the conjugated valve gear were dealt with at the sheds, as Thompson intended, or were not deemed sufficiently serious to be recorded. Sadly, the maintenance files for each locomotive, which would have contained much additional information, don't appear to have survived. If they had a more critical picture may have emerged. In the absence of this material, we are left with broad statements of those who were there who asserted there were increasing problems with the Gresley engines.

Park before departure and bank the trains as far as Holloway with the engines that have brought the empty coaches into the terminus? Starts might be improved in this way and drivers saved a good deal of effort and anxiety with the heavier loads, especially when the rails are greasy.

Before completing his report, Allen decided to compare the A4s performances with two Gresley A1s (No. 2545 *Diamond Jubilee* and No. 2557 *Blair Athol*) and a single A3 (No. 4479 *Robert the Devil*) over the same route. His purpose was a simple one – to see how the non-streamlined engines 'stood up against the streamlined engines when pulling the heaviest, twenty carriage trains and to take into account the different capacity of the boilers'. When recalling the debate that had raged over streamlining since the concept became a 'fashion', as some thought it in the 1930s, this was hardly surprising. Putting aside the insensitivity of pursuing such a discussion in print when war was raging and thousands dying on a daily basis, it is still interesting to note the results of Allen's work. And here two runs from Grantham to King's Cross – involving A4 No. 4466 *Herring Gull* and A1 No. 2557 – are particularly revealing. Both engines were not long out of General Repair so were probably in as good a condition as possible, with *Herring Gull* losing her side valances during this maintenance period, but not gaining a double blastpipe (eventually fitted in 1957). Allen recorded that:

Runs 14 (4466) and 15 (2557) are of interest, both as regards the magnitude of the loads – 668 and 695 tons tare and 740 and 750 tons gross respectively – and also because the performance of the A1 was in this case distinctly superior to that of the A4.

Herring Gull made a fine start, with 34mph attained up the 1 in 200 to Stoke, as

Part of Cecil Allen's report on the wartime performance of the A4s when running between King's Cross and Grantham with ever increasing loads. A second page compares the much older A1s with the A4s when operating under difficult wartime conditions and found them as good and on one occasion slightly superior. Bert Spencer, to whom Allen submitted his report before it was published in the *Railway Magazine*, simply wrote on the front sheet 'interesting, but the A4s are not operating under the conditions for which they were designed so these simple comparisons are of limited value'. Nevertheless, Allen's report does provide us with an interesting snapshot of lives of Gresley's Pacifics in war.
(BS)

L.N.E.R. KINGS CROSS—GRANTHAM

Distance	Run No. Engine, 4-6-2, No. (Class "A4") „ Name Load (vehicles) „ (tons tare) „ (tons gross)	1 4485 Kestrel 16 520 560	2 †4902 Seagull 17 546 590	‡ 3 4490 Empire of India 17 593 635	4 †4902 Seagull 19 608 660	5 2510 Quicksilver 20 620 675	6 2510 Quicksilver 20 623 680	7 4485 Kestrel 20 642 700
miles		m. s.	m. s.	m. s.	m. s.	m. s.	m. s.	m. s.
0.0	KINGS CROSS	0 00	0 00	0 00	0 00	0 00	0 00	0 00
		Sigs.						
2.5	FINSBURY PARK	8 27	7 20	7 33	13 45	8 50	7 33	8 10
5.0	Wood Green	13 08	10 43	10 58	18 13	12 30	10 54	p.w.s.
9.2	New Barnet	20 07	15 45	16 55	25 10	18 18	17 05	19 29
			sig. stop					
12.7	Potters Bar	sigs.	26 05	22 17	31 10	23 54	23 09	27 40
			sigs.					
17.7	HATFIELD	38 48	37 50	27 22	37 10	29 24	28 45	34 23
23.5	Woolmer Green	45 58	44 46	32 17	42 53	35 23	34 30	41 18
			sigs.					
25.0	Knebworth	47 38	46 31	33 35	44 37	37 15	36 15	43 16
28.6	Stevenage	51 07	50 11	36 36	48 12	41 00	39 51	47 19
31.9	HITCHIN	54 08	53 38	39 07	51 20	44 00	43 00	50 38
37.0	Arlesey	58 23	57 47	42 33	55 52	48 24	47 39	54 57
44.1	Sandy	64 15	64 18	47 46	62 32	55 21	54 24	61 04
					sig. stop			
51.7	St. Neots	70 51	71 15	53 55	76 35	63 15	62 12	67 48
58.9	HUNTINGDON	77 02	77 46	59 48	85 45	70 45	69 12	73 50
62.0	Milepost 62	80 13	80 59	62 49	89 05	74 24	72 39	77 05
69.4	Holme	86 52	87 37	68 30	96 00	81 54	79 48	83 38
								sigs.
72.6	Yaxley	89 35	90 23	71 05	98 56	85 06	82 54	88 15
75.0	Fletton Junction	91 48	92 36	73 17	101 36	87 54	85 27	sig. stop
			sig. stop					
76.4	PETERBOROUGH*	94 15	97 50	75 23	104 00	90 00	87 39	100 20
79.5	Werrington Junction		102 55	80 09	109 13	94 54	92 24	
84.8	Tallington		107 48	85 18	114 22	100 42	98 12	
88.6	ESSENDINE		111 03	88 50	117 45	104 48	102 21	
92.2	Little Bytham		114 20	92 17	121 10	109 00	106 27	
97.1	Corby		119 28	97 35	126 20	115 48	112 57	
100.1	Stoke		123 12	101 07	130 00	120 06	117 03	
					sigs.	sigs.		
105.5	GRANTHAM		129 46	107 55	137 10	127 00	123 39	
105.5	Net times (min.)	83	114	108	128	126½	123¾	91

* Service slack, severe. †With Kylchap exhaust and double chimney. ‡ Pre-war run

compared with *Blair Athol's* 30½mph; in Stoke tunnel these speeds fell back to 32¾ and 28½mph respectively. No. 4466's maximum at Essendine was 72mph; No. 2557 reached 74 at Little Bytham, eased to 68 through Essendine, and was doing 71½ by Tallington. After Peterborough slack the A4 was doing 62½mph at Holme and the A1 60; up past Ripton the minima were 41 and 42 ½; the maxima reached at Offord were 61½ and 67mph. From here onwards *Herring Gull* was doing moderately, and *Blair Athol* was gradually overhauling the streamliner, the difference in time being whittled down from 110 seconds at Abbots Ripton to 15 seconds at Arlesey.

Then the A1 had the misfortune to be checked by signal to 40mph and perhaps the finest work of the whole journey was the way in which this engine settled down to a steady 37½mph to the top of the long 1 in 200 climb past

Hitchin; the A4 dropping to 33½ by Stevenage. The latter then got a clear road to King's Cross and gained 2½ minutes on the schedule, but. *Blair Athol* suffered two more signal checks. Despite this the A1, with allowance being made for the checks, achieved a net time of no more than 124½ so a (theoretical) gain of 5½ minutes on the schedule."

When turning these findings into an article for the *Railway Magazine,* Allen chose to add an interesting footnote, perhaps suggesting where his thoughts on streamlining might lie:

When the late Sir Nigel Gresley designed his first A1 Pacific he claimed that it would be capable of handling 600 tons

tare loads on the then 122 minute booking of the Flying Scotsman between King's Cross and Grantham, at a time when 400 tons was considered heavy. Here was an engine of precisely the same type, unaltered except for its valve setting, tackling 695 tare tons and requiring only 2½ minutes to the 122 minutes of 1922, and this with maximum speeds well below those of peacetime, and with wartime maintenance and fuel conditions in place."

While the A1s' performance was undoubtedly impressive, it is probably true to say that a fairer comparison between the A1/A3s and the A4s would have required much more evidence for clear conclusions to be drawn. And the danger with on the road testing is

that there were too many variables in play, making the end results imprecise and less reliable. Spencer wrote little about Allen's report, but on his copy did scribble 'interesting, but the A4s are not operating under the conditions for which they were designed so these simple comparisons are of limited value. To take this matter further we need many more measured runs and the Test Centre at Rugby to be up and running'.

Despite his findings Allen was not slow to praise the A4s and ended his report, when it appeared in the *Railway Magazine,* with an account of exceptional work done by 4468 *Mallard*, in which he seems to have picked up the point made by Spencer:

One final run is worth mentioning; it was made by

A1 Pacific No. 2557 *Blair Athol*, which according to Cecil Allen, had the measure of the A4s when running under wartime conditions with an exceptionally heavy 750 ton load between Grantham and King's Cross in 1942. (BS)

No. 4482 *Golden Eagle* in reasonably clean condition suggesting that the war is nearing an end and workloads are reducing, allowing a little more time for good house-keeping. 4482 retained her black livery until September 1946, returning then to garter blue. (BS)

Mallard and is a tribute to the way in which a class designed in this first instance for continuous high speed work with streamlined train has proved itself equally adaptable to the haulage of extremely heavy loads.

On this occasion No. 4468 was coming down from Leeds with a train which at Wakefield was made up of 19 coaches, of 599 tons tare and 650 tons gross. The short falling start of 1.7 miles to Sandal produced a maximum of 47mph, and the 4 miles mostly at 1 in 150 to the summit just beyond Nostell were surmounted at 38½mph minimum – in itself a notable feat. The falling grades past South Elmsall and Hampole were then run in great style, with a top speed of 75½mph, and 72mph continued along the level to within 2½ miles of Doncaster. So Nostell, 5.5 miles, was passed in 8 minutes 56 seconds, South Elmsall, 11.2 miles, in 14 minutes 49 seconds, and Castle Hills, 17.1 miles, in 19 minutes 31 seconds, and with a very slow stop,

19.8 miles, was reached in 23 minutes 29 seconds, a gain of 2½ minutes on schedule and a very smart performance.

For Spencer, now sitting with Elwell on the periphery of locomotive design issues, and perhaps champing at the bit to return to the work he knew best, reports such as this were thought provoking, but in his current duties there was little he could do with the information collected. But a change was in the air. With the tide of war appearing to turn, the Allies achieving victories in North Africa, Sicily and now Italy, a future beyond the war could be glimpsed. And so, planning for peacetime needs began in earnest. Thompson, ever aware of the role played so successfully by Spencer as Gresley's trusted assistant, wished to re-engage him in this sort of work again and, in so doing, help him prepare a locomotive development strategy, a statement of requirement and a construction programme with standardisation at its core. Windle would be directly responsible for the final designs and overseeing the construction programmes, but it would be Spencer's primary responsibility to guide Thompson through all the issues involved, agree a policy and the requirement by class and type, then prepare a case to be submitted to the Chairman and the Board for approval to proceed.

This change of role may have been in Thompson's mind in 1941 when posting Spencer from London to Doncaster, and only awaited the right moment to implement. Alternatively, the CME may simply

have reviewed the resources he had available at this critical moment and acted accordingly. The only clue that remains comes from Spencer himself. Many years later he recalled that:

(When transferring to Doncaster and when time allowed) Mr Thompson suggested that I maintain Sir Nigel's papers and continue working on the ideas he had pursued regarding steam locomotives, but with an emphasis on alternative cylinder arrangements. Later on, I was called to the CME's office and it was agreed that I would work full time on

standardisation proposals. Over the next four years I did much personal work for the CME and sat near him in his office at Doncaster.

In 1941/42 Spencer little knew what the future held. So in his spare time, whether in the Works at Doncaster or sitting at a drawing board in his makeshift office at home, he considered the future of locomotive design. And with all his and Gresley's papers scattered around there was plenty to think over and experiment with, not least of all the A4s and streamlining, which both continued to fascinate him. In the last years of Gresley's

life he and the CME had toyed with idea of a 'super-A4' and even 4-8-4 and 4-8-2 type express engines. The last two of these Spencer thought might have been built if Gresley had lived and the war had come to a successful end sooner. But this was not to be, although a new A4 remained a distinct possibility, in Spencer's mind at least:

It would have been a simple step to take and would have followed the pattern set by Gresley when upgrading the A1 and producing the 'Super Pacific/A3s'. Thompson, who was a fan of the A4s, often discussed this possibility when

Before the war and acting under Gresley's instructions Spencer worked on a number of proposals for new express engines – a 4-8-4, a 4-8-2 and a new super A4. None of these came to fruition and few of the drawings appear to have survived, but in his archive this diagram, showing some of Gresley's assistant's rough workings for the new A9 Pacific were found. Although some of the writing is barely legible, Spencer's initials and a date of 6/46 can just be seen showing how long he toyed with these ideas, presumably with Thompson's agreement. (BS)

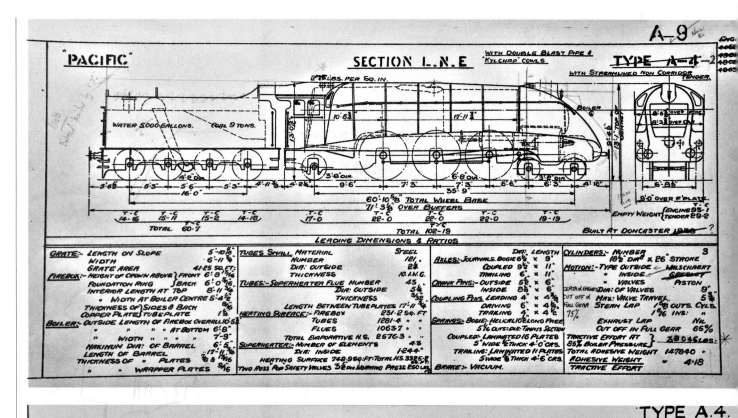

Windle's view of the future for the A4s – de-streamlined and built to a more traditional design. It was a move that Thompson apparently thought unnecessary, could not support and so it was quickly dropped. (PA)

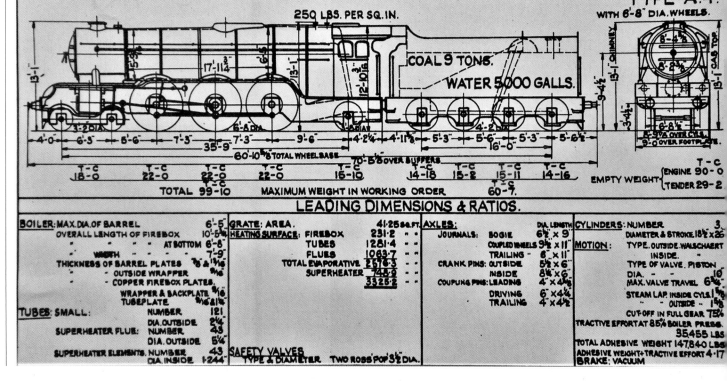

considering his plans for the future, but found in Windle a less than enthusiastic supporter. [In fact], Windle was keen to de-streamline them when removing Gresley's conjugated valve gear. Thompson was not prepared to sanction these changes and preferred to keep them as they were. Statistically they had performed well during the war, this, despite the very difficult working conditions. In fact, the valve gear had held up well, far better than on other engines. This convinced the CME that all they needed was remedial work to help overcome the detrimental effects of poor maintenance in the war and nothing else. This may simply have been a business decision, but I was left with the impression that he regarded the A4s as being too good to touch. He even made reference to them in the standardisation plan as worthy members of the new fleet.

To support his view, Windle had a diagram produced demonstrating how the A4s would look in a new, de-streamlined form. Thompson was apparently unmoved by Windle's proposal and it remained a concept only and went no further, but neither did the idea of a 'Super A4', though Spencer continued to toy with the scheme until the end of the war. By then it was clear in which direction Thompson wished to go with regard to the Pacifics and so there was little more to be done. However, as Spencer recorded:

Streamlining was not forgotten in plans for the new Pacifics –

the A1/1, A2/1s, A2/2s and A2/3s. Thompson was very keen on this, Peppercorn and Windle much less so, seeing it as an 'unnecessary extravagance', as the Chief Draughtsman put it. However, when considering a bigger A4 I did discard the three cylinder/conjugated valve arrangement and prepared sketches showing three independent sets of Walschaerts valve gear instead and other changes. I showed these to the CME, shortly after becoming his assistant, when he was considering his new Pacifics and these then went to Windle, who, at the time, was not wholly convinced that the Gresley solution should be dropped.

At this point the CME, armed with Stanier and Cox's report, and a substantial bank of evidence Elwell and I had been collecting, and under pressure from Newton, took the decision to discard the 2 to 1 gear and go for the three independent sets of valve gear instead in the rebuild of the P2s and the new Pacifics. But at the same time he still wished to continue exploring any benefits that might accrue from streamlining, despite Windle's reservations. This led to some modelling and wind tunnel testing to see if it could be included in the new designs. But all this was quietly dropped when Peppercorn became CME.

And so the concept of streamlining steam locomotives in the UK died. The LNER kept the experiment going longer than the LMS, which soon stripped its Coronations

Two of the streamlining schemes considered by Thompson and Windle for the new classes of Pacific. Wind tunnel testing of these models took place towards the end of the war, but any reports highlighting the results of this work do not appear to have survived. Thompson was keen to pursue this research, according to Spencer, but by the time of his retirement in 1946 little progress had been made and Peppercorn, when becoming CME, quietly let the matter drop. (ET/DN)

of their casing, returning them to a more conventional form. Meanwhile, Bulleid's 'air-smoothed' Pacifics, which he always declared were not streamlined, continued to be constructed at Eastleigh and Brighton until 1950, seemingly extending the research a bit further, but with no serious intent beyond smoke lifting. But that was all and when British Railways brought in their standardisation plan there was no attempt made to give it new life.

Spencer believed that it had been a worthy experiment to which Gresley's support had given much weight, but his going removed its greatest advocate and others felt unable to take up this particular baton. For the fast Pacifics capable of sustaining high speeds over prolonged periods, it had benefits in terms of fuel economy. However, as a Public Relations exercise it probably had even more and continued to do so until the A4s were withdrawn from service in the 1960s, so justifying Thompson's decision to let them be.

Even though streamlining of steam locomotives had runs its course in Britain, some companies or nationalised networks overseas still persisted in their endeavours. But with diesel and electric locomotives gaining ground as these technologies rapidly advanced, it was to be a last hurrah, most notably in the USA where streamlined designs seemed to grow increasingly more flamboyant. In many cases, form undoubtedly seems to have triumphed over function, giving the PR departments a field day with many glamorous, extravagant images handed to them to be exploited. As the war came to an end, Stateside railways

needed these icons to help draw the fare-paying public's attention and their money. In a country made wealthy by war and in thrall to consumerism, the companies had to fight to hang on to passenger traffic now seriously challenged by the ever-growing number of cars, buses and aeroplanes. And so several railroads chose to update existing engines with streamlined casings whilst others built from new.

These two approaches can best be observed in the Chesapeake and Ohio's Pacifics and the Pennsylvania Railroads T1s. In the former, Olive Dennis, one of the company's research engineers, was tasked in 1946 with modernising four old Pacific engines and carriages for employment on a 12 hour 30 minute service between Baltimore and Cincinnati. Publicity material produced at the time used the word 'styling' to describe this transition, so immediately placing great emphasis on the look and not the scientific function of streamlining.

The T1 sought to combine both, beginning with two prototypes that appeared in 1942, having been ordered two years earlier at a combined cost of $600,000. Their design built on experience gained with the PRR's prototype air-smoothed S1, with duplex drive, that had appeared before the war. Ralph P. Johnson, Baldwin's chief designer, seems to have taken the lead in producing the S1s and now the T1s, with Raymond Loewy being made responsible for streamlining both classes. In service, both prototypes developed many teething problems and were prone to wheelslip if not handled by skilled drivers. Nevertheless,

favourable test reports resulted in a production order for fifty T1s in December 1944, split between the PRR's own Altoona Works and Baldwins, at a staggering cost of a $14,125,000 ($282,500 each).

Although streamlining caught the eye, it was really the duplex system used that was more interesting. In principle, it worked by dividing the driving force on its wheels by using two pairs of cylinders rigidly mounted on a single locomotive frame. But it proved to be a very expensive experiment and one not destined to last long, with members of the class all withdrawn by 1952, having been downgraded to secondary routes and replaced by diesels. And with that, American designers' love affair with streamlined steam locomotives seems to have come to an end.

In France, external streamlining had all but disappeared from engineers' vocabularies by 1945. Their work on air-smoothing had probably reached its peak when eight very elegant Class 232s 4-6-4s were authorised in 1939 for use on high speed services in the Nord region of the SNCF. In the hands of the Office Central d'Etudes de Material's (OCEM) Marc de Caso, the 46-year-old Italian born designer, three 232R 3-cylinder and four 232S 4-cylinder compound engines were built and delivered in 1940. But with German occupation of France changing all priorities, these impressive engines were soon ignominiously pressed into Nazi service. The eighth engine, which had not been completed, was to be a fourth compound, but a proposal to build it with turbine drive was injected into the programme

For a time after the war, some US railroad companies persisted in producing streamlined engines, even though diesels were quickly taking over. (Left) In 1946, Olive Dennis upgraded four old Pacifics and carriage sets for use on the Baltimore to Cincinnati long distance service. At the time, the new, sleeker outline was thought to be a case of form triumphing over function with the public relations people being the most likely winners. (Below) At about the same time, the Pennsylvania Railroad decided to build fifty T1 streamlined duplex engines at a cost of more than $14 million. Ralph Johnson produced the designs and Raymond Loewy the air smoothed casing for these impressive engines. But even when entering service, they had already become dinosaurs and all were withdrawn by 1952. (THG)

instead. Due to the pressing needs of war any forward movement was impossible and in 1949, after a long delay, it finally appeared as a 4-cylinder compound with piston not poppet valves, as fitted to the other members of the class. In this form it was designated 232 U1 and became the last of the SNCF streamliners.

In 1945, long before the single Class 232U1 engine entered service, Andre Chapelon tried to revive interest in streamlining, but to no avail. With the end of hostilities, he identified a need for a motive power strategy for steam. Even though there were many voices raised in support of diesel and electric locomotives, he believed that there was still a role for the old technology to play. A backward view perhaps, but a realistic one

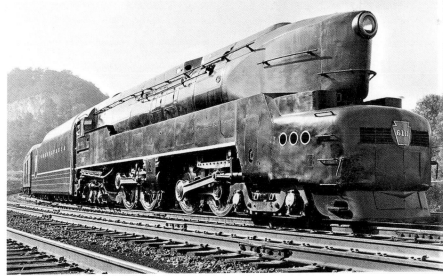

nonetheless, bearing in mind the state of the railways in France. The network had been badly knocked about during the war and needed

massive investment to restore it to its pre-war condition at a time when France, like Britain, faced bankruptcy.

The last of the Class 232 French streamliners appeared in 1949, but only because its construction programme was delayed by the war – seven of the class all appearing in 1940. The final engine was designated 232 U1 and after its service ended in 1961 it went into preservation. A sister engine, 232S, is shown here. (THG)

Sticking with steam was a pragmatic response in the circumstances and so, in 1945, Chapelon, after much thought, presented a paper to the influential Association Français des Amis des Chemin de Fer (AFAC) outlining his thoughts and plans for steam engines. Standardisation of locomotives was one of his key solutions and he produced a list of classes of engines that should be included in the plan. Amongst them a streamlined 4-6-4 was prominent; clearly he hadn't lost sight of the benefits to be gained by tackling the problem of air resistance in this way. But as the plan moved from drawing board to workshops, with work beginning on 2-10-4 type 152 and 4-6-4 tank engines, politicians in Paris took the decision to phase out steam in favour of electrification and diesel railcars. As a result,

Chapelon's programme was wound up and funds transferred to these new projects. And so the sole 232U1 brought these endeavours to a fitting end.

In many ways, the course of action taken by Chapelon mirrored that adopted by Thompson at Doncaster. They were both pragmatic men, conscious of the limitations placed on them by circumstances beyond their control but determined to take their respective organisations forward in a practical way, using the technology available to best effect. The only real difference between them was that Chapelon was operating in a state owned business and Thompson a private company. One had to look to a government department for approval and funds, the other to a Chairman and General Manager answerable to

shareholders, who were likely to be more cost conscious and driven by a need to produce an annual premium to appease investors. As a result, and boosted by a massive injection of cash from the US driven Marshall Aid programme, the French decided to leap ahead with a more ambitious modernisation programme, sounding the death knell for steam as they did so.

The LNER, without the same level of funding, had to take a more restrained approach in which existing assets had to be exploited for much longer while its modest plans for electrification slowly expanded. The start they had made before the war with the Sheffield to Manchester and Liverpool Street Station to Shenfield lines, though noble and ambitious in scope, had barely scratched the surface of what was required. In the event, the LNER's Board were left with no option but to let steam continue to be its mainstay until the economy perked up or the government took action centrally. And in 1948 they did so with nationalisation. To some it was a saving grace, to others a regressive step that would swamp free enterprise in a sea of bureaucracy.

If some believed that this would give true modernisation a spur and a release of cash to help realise these dreams, they would soon be divested of this belief. In a country still desperately short of money and in the grip of rationing – until 1953 as it turned out – but with vast reserves of coal and many hundreds of thousands employed in that industry, steam power was the only realistic option. However, there would be a nod to diesel and electric power in Whitehall's plans,

ROLLING STOCK

Here in summary form is our programme :—
THE L·N·E·R FIVE~YEAR PLAN FOR ROLLING STOCK

	To be built by L.N.E.R.	To be built by Contractors.	Total
Locomotives	500	500	1,000
Carriages	2,100	3,400	5,500
Wagons	50,000	20,000	70,000

L.N.E.R. "A.I" 4-6-2 PACIFIC "GREAT NORTHERN" No. 113

LOCOMOTIVES
Immense war-time traffics meant that the scrapping of locomotives had to be postponed, since very few new ones could be built. The fleet of 6,400 engines is to be overhauled and 1,000 old locomotives will be replaced by new machines during the next five years.

STANDARDISATION POLICY
Types are to be simplified ; whilst the engines to be scrapped are of 49 different classes, those to be built will comprise only ten different designs.

L.N.E.R. "A.2" 4-6-2 "PACIFIC" No. 500 "EDWARD THOMPSON"
BUILT 1946 AT DONCASTER WORKS, THE 2,000th ENGINE CONSTRUCTED THERE

The term "standardised" does not mean that design is going to be fettered, or that hard-and-fast rules will be laid down from which there may be no departure. The aim is that a limited number of engine classes shall be able to handle the great bulk of the traffic, and that important components shall be interchangeable within the classes. On the other hand, continuous study and testing will be undertaken to see whether improvements or modifications are required from time to time. Thereby we shall realise the advantages of standardisation without stagnation.

The new standard types include, first of all, two classes of "Pacifics." One will be streamlined for use on the fastest expresses, and will be a modification of the class that already holds the world's speed record for steam traction—126 miles an hour ; the second, such as "Edward Thompson" illustrated on the opposite page, will have rather smaller driving wheels, and will be used for fast passenger work and also fast and heavy freight trains.

HOLDER OF WORLD SPEED RECORD FOR STEAM TRACTION—126 M.P.H.
L.N.E.R. "A.4" 4-6-2 PACIFIC No. 22 "MALLARD"

The next type is a general purpose 4-6-0 locomotive, known as the "Antelope" class, suitable for either passenger or fast freight trains ; no fewer than 400 are included in the programme.

L.N.E.R. "B.1" 4-6-0 No. 1003 "ANTELOPE" CLASS

The first entirely post-war design to appear was the L.I. class mixed-traffic locomotive. One of the class is illustrated on the next page. This engine will undertake passenger and goods services at present handled by a large number of different types of locomotives.

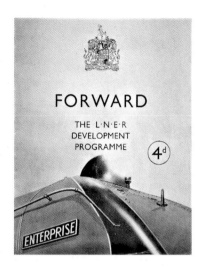

FORWARD

THE L·N·E·R
DEVELOPMENT
PROGRAMME

4d

ENTERPRISE

(Left and below) Thompson's plans for the future of locomotion on the LNER came together in 1945 with the publication of the booklet above with its bold title *Forward* and a streamliner suitably emblazoned with the name *Enterprise* (a name that was, at one time, considered for Gresley's W1). Interestingly, the A4s featured large in his plan as it did the publicity produced from the occasion. If he had been truly determined to eradicate Gresley's legacy, as some believe, they would undoubtedly have been quietly forgotten, scrapped or rebuilt. In truth he was a great admirer of the class and a believer in streamlining as his papers on standardisation reveal. (Left below) A page from Thompson's plan which summarizes his, Spencer and Windle's developing views on the range of standard engines to be employed. (ET/THG)

TYPE A-2, DIAGRAM No I.

TYPE A-4, DIAGRAM No 2.

TYPE B-1, DIAGRAM No 3

TYPE O-1, DIAGRAM No 4.

TYPE J-11, DIAGRAM No 5.

TYPE L, DIAGRAM No 6.

TYPE Q-1, DIAGRAM No 7

TYPE J-50, DIAGRAM No 8.

The war is over and some semblance of order returns to the lives of the A4s, albeit in a cash strapped country on a railway system in serious need of a huge injection of funds. Post the conflict, the A4s soon began to pass through the workshops to be restored to something near pre-war condition. The side valances would not be restored, but wartime black was discarded in favour of garter blue again. The first engine so completed was No. 4496 in 1945, with eleven more following in 1946, twenty in 1947 and the final two in 1948. The single streamlined W1 would follow suit in 1947. During 1946, the LNER introduced a new numbering system for their engines and in this guise the engines shown above soon appeared. Post 1948 they would, of course, be re-numbered again and receive BR logos. (Top left) No. 3 (ex-4494 *Andrew K. McCosh*, which remained a King's Cross engine until 1957. (Top right) No12 (ex-4491) *Commonwealth of Australia* at Newcastle Central. (Middle) No. 21 (ex-4467) *Wild Swan*. (Lower left) No. 15 (ex-2510) *Quicksilver*. (Bottom right) No. 32 (ex-4900) *Gannet*, although restored to glory in garter blue, finds the habit acquired during the war of pulling heavy freight trains continued. Possibly a waste of their talents, but as Gresley affirmed in 1939, when objecting to the A4s being mothballed, they 'were just locomotives and capable of pulling huge loads of any type'. So mixed traffic engines they became. (THG)

but there would be little more than this until the economy picked up. The phrase 'make do and mend' although not a stated Government policy adequately described its nature, though 'wait and see' perhaps defined it better.

So, in France, a government faced with a badly bombed and ruined network invested heavily in new forms of motive power and kept steam going until this work was complete. In Britain, the Ministry of Transport decided to keep and develop steam, with little attention being paid to genuine modernisation, with the stated hope that it would last into the 1970s and '80s, perhaps longer.

In 1945, before nationalisation became government policy, Thompson, while he waited to see what would happen, pressed ahead with his standardisation plans for steam and some limited diesel development work. At the same time, his counterpart Henry Richards, the LNER's Chief Electrical Engineer, did what he could on electrification and revived pre-war plans and projects in the hope that they might be realised. In France, Chapelon was simply divested of his plans for steam and gradually side lined by the modernisers, who, with government, support, took over. As his distance from the centre of future activity grew, so he found himself working on steam locomotives for export to Brazil until his retirement from the SNCF in 1953. To be associated in this way with an aging and soon to disappear technology can be a damning business.

By comparison, Thompson, who was happy to embrace electrification and dieselisation, found steam forced on him by a post war recession. When he went in 1946, his successor, Arthur Peppercorn, would fare little better, though in his case both hands were tied, in 1948, by a Ministry of Transport and British Transport Commission lacking ambition, funds and overwhelmed by a degree of political meddling.

Before this happened, Thompson and Spencer's standardisation plan attempted to produce a document which highlighted the problems the company faced and outlined a balanced solution, knowing full well it was all based on the shifting sands of uncertainty over the future. And in their thinking, both the A4s and streamlining continued to play a part, something they made clear in a report they submitted to Newton in March 1945, and through him to the Chairman of the Locomotive Committee. In terms of the general policy to be followed, and the 'streaks' and streamlining in particular, they wrote:

The term standardisation should not be misunderstood. It is not intended to lay down hard and fast rules from which there may be no departure, but to see whether the bulk of the traffic can be met by a limited number of locomotive classes, keeping in mind the necessity for continuous study and testing to see whether improvements or modification are required from time to time. By this means the advantages of standardisation would be secured without involving stagnation so far as research and development are concerned.

From this starting point the LNER proceeded to consider a more comprehensive policy of standardisation. The first step was to divide its locomotive types into three groups.

The first group represents the new standard types, of which there are ten, nine of which have already been constructed … It will be observed that the suggested A1 type Pacific [the Gresley A1s having become A10s in the meantime] is not shown in its streamlined form. This is because the existing engine, [4470 *Great Northern*] which is 24 years old was converted to produce this type, but it is understood that if this conversion is satisfactory the new A1 Pacifics built on this principle will have a streamlined covering [The new A2 is not listed for a similar makeover though].

The second group includes existing locomotive types (including the A4s) which it is considered worth maintaining until the end of their useful lives – that is to say that, new boilers will be built for them as required, and they will not finally be broken up until they are obsolete.

The third group includes all the remaining locomotives, nearly all considerably older types which are no longer satisfactory…When spares are used up these engines will be scrapped and replaced by one of the standard types.

It may be noted that after a considerable amount of investigation, the principle of abandoning the conjugated valve gear operating the middle cylinder has been decided. By dividing the drive as in the new standard Pacific engines, separate valve gear is given to each cylinder and the very

The avuncular and talented Arthur Peppercorn in 1946 when succeeding Edward Thompson as CME. As Thompson's deputy, he was closely involved in all production tasks but also the design policy initiated by the company during the war. To him would fall responsibility for enacting the LNER's 1945 Standardisation Plan and carry on with the production of new Pacifics and other classes of engine. The most important of these was to continue with construction of the B1 4-6-0 mixed traffic locomotives which began in 1942 and would continue on until 1952, by which time 410 had been built. (BS)

large stresses are divided in proportion to 1/3 on the cranked axle and 2/3 on the straight axle instead of all three being put to one cranked axle.

So the A4s were safe, while Thompson remained CME, and streamlining, whether to further scientific research or simply as a PR exercise, was given a brief afterlife. However, the paper carefully sidesteps the more important question of removing Gresley's conjugated valve gear and fitting a third set of Walscherts. Bearing in mind the reported deterioration of the locomotives with three-cylinders and the 2 to 1 gear, and the problem of maintaining them in good condition, this is interesting. Perhaps it was, as Spencer later recorded:

… a matter of cost, it being much more expensive to rebuild the engines than meet the expense of the increased servicing involved. In any case, after the war when proper maintenance routines were restored and many trained men returned to do the work, the engines were kept in much better shape and the problems decreased slightly. In this position the Chairman felt that the cost of rebuilding so many engines could not be justified. It was a view that was restated when Peppercorn took over and sought to take action.

Although not Thompson's final act as CME, forging a path for the LNER to follow was probably one of his most important contributions to the future life of the company. It was this chalice, poisoned or

otherwise, that Arthur Peppercorn inherited in July 1946. But in the background, hidden from most in the industry, were the government's slowly evolving nationalisation plans which exploded a year later with publication of a Transport Act, with a Whitehall take over scheduled for the following January. All the CME, and his opposite numbers in the other companies, could do was carry on as before until a new directive came from BR's headquarters at Marylebone. In truth very few people, even the politicians who dreamt up these huge changes, seemed to have fully understood what they were taking on and the difficulties they would face in trying to make a dilapidated system work let alone modernise it.

During the two world wars, central government had assumed a dictatorial role in running the railways, so may have come to believe that they had the measure of the task. But running an organisation during a war, where everything and everybody is committed to the fight, no voice is likely to be raised in opposition and normal performance and maintenance standards do not apply, is a simpler task than running the same organisation in peacetime. Profit and loss and commercial necessity, let alone trying to undo the attritional effects of conflict, are things that cannot be swept to one side by the exigencies of war. In these circumstances a noble intention or a political doctrine can quickly, if not handled competently, unravel and be exposed for what it is.

While all this was happening, Peppercorn had to manage a fleet of locomotives depleted by war

(Left) A gleaming
No. 24 (ex-4483)
Kingfisher just out of
the works awaiting
restoration of
nameplates before
entering service again.
(Below) The same engine
back in service based at
Haymarket where she
will remain until 1963,
ending her career at
Aberdeen in 1966 when
withdrawn and scrapped.
(THG)

and made the LNER's plans for standardisation a reality as best he could, all the while trying to second guess where the newly formed BTC might take them. In the circumstances, he carried on with Thompson's Pacific programme, completed the A1 (now A10) conversion project and began the arduous process of restoring engines to their pre-war condition. In addition, he pursued the construction of other engines already in the LNER's programme, the most notable being the 410 mixed traffic B1 4-6-0s. All the while the A4s, having survived the war, continued to do sterling service, soon picking up where they had left off in 1939 with high speed expresses. Only time would tell if they would survive the machinations of British Railways and their team of designers.

The BR influence takes effect and the A4s acquire new nationalised insignia on their tenders. In these cases it is (Above) No.21 (ex-4467) *Wild Swan* which was restored to garter blue in April 1947 and (Right) No. 4 (ex-4462) ex-*Great Snipe* now *William Whitelaw* which was repainted blue in November 1946. No.21 would be based at Grantham during 1948, then at King's Cross in 1950. No. 4 was assigned to Haymarket. (THG)

Chapter 2
AN UNCERTAIN FUTURE

After the big build up to nationalisation and celebrations surrounding the event had died away, the reality of what the BTC and BR's Railway Executive, chaired by Sir Eustace Missenden, late General Manager of the Southern Railway, had inherited soon sank in. For those who had lobbied hard for this day, all along trumpeting this panacea for the railway's ills, the truth of their situation could no longer be ignored. The task they faced, even if they simply maintained the status quo, was an enormous one. But their new political masters wanted much more than this if state ownership were to be justified.

The problems the railways faced were only too apparent to those in the Big Four companies – limited funds, a dilapidated network and tired fleets of locomotives and rolling stock. Worse still, they were losing an increasing amount of traffic to the roads and employees were beginning to see the railways as a poor place to work as other new, cleaner industries were established. And those who did choose to join or remain with the railways insisted on better pay and conditions of service. When employers were tardy in meeting these demands, as they were bound to be in such straitened

circumstances, industrial disputes became more commonplace. After the sacrifices of the Great War, change had been demanded and strongly resisted by the government and employers more used to subservience than equality, now a second sacrifice had been made and voices were far less likely to be stilled so easily.

So British Railways faced a perfect storm of problems that individually might have been resolved, but together created

a huge and unwieldy block to progress. To say that politicians and BR's new management had their fingers crossed hoping that all would be well was, perhaps, an understatement. It would take much more than that to turn the railways into a modern going concern able to meet the growing aspirations of a people weary of war and the inevitable recessions that followed. Luckily for Whitehall, the clamour for change was still a whisper, but growing

In late 1947, news of the railway's impending nationalisation was made public, setting off feelings of uncertainty across the industry. The public, on the other hand, if newspapers of the time are to be believed, saw the change as a positive step and hoped to see restoration and modernisation of a very jaded, steam orientated system quickly implemented. (RH)

Members of the newly constituted British Transport Commission pose for the press, possibly in late 1947. In very short order, Sir William Hurcomb will be elected Chairman and choose, with the Minister of Transport, Sir Eustace Missenden as Chairman of the Railway Executive. (RH)

Left to right : MR. JOHN BENSTEAD, General Secretary of the N.U.R., Member of the T.U.C. General Council and President of the International Transport Workers' Federation, THE RT. HON. LORD ASHFIELD, Chairman of the L.P.T.B., Chairman of the Northmet Power Co., Director of the Midland Bank and of I.C.I., SIR CYRIL HURCOMB, Secretary to the Ministry of Transport, and Chairman of the Electricity Commission. During the war SIR CYRIL was Director General M.W.T., SIR WILLIAM V. WOOD, President of the L.M.S. is an authority on Railway Finance and was one of the original members of the Railway Executive Committee, LORD RUSHOLME, General Secretary of the Co-operative Union. Has travelled widely in Europe on Co-operative business.

louder each day and yet more of the old was hardly a recipe for success.

Sadly, in Missenden they did not seem to have been given a leader suited to such a challenging task.

This despite the fact that as the SR's 1941 appointed General Manager, he had acquired first-hand knowledge of running a company that had been committed to

electrification for decades and had advanced more in its modernisation plans than the GWR, LNER and LMS. He also understood the problems of operating a large fleet of steam locomotives, including Bulleid's unique Pacifics, in difficult circumstances. Perhaps more tellingly, he also knew how seriously the war had exhausted the railway's ability to perform effectively, a fact only too apparent to him in the south-east where the bombing campaign, doodlebug and then the V2 rocket attacks had been more intense and prolonged than in any other part of Britain.

So, on paper he seemed to be a good choice for the post, but in reality this was not the case. Although described as a 'competent railwayman and manager' with wide experience of railway operations, he lacked the intellectual and management

Thompson's experimental A1/1 Great Northern, which had taken Gresley's prototype Pacific and modified it, is soon to embrace state ownership with a new number and new logo on her tender. She was supposed to herald a new range of streamlined A1s, but this proposal was quietly dropped after Thompson departed the scene. The engine is photographed here at Hadley Wood in, according to Bert Spencer's notes, 1948. (BS)

a blow to them might well be an understatement. And added to this they would have seen how Riddles filled his team with LMS men and so feared losing any influence they might have had in the new organisation; all except Ivatt, perhaps, who had already forged close links with these men.

It would not have helped if they could have read H.C.B. Rogers' 1970 biography of Robert Riddles, which the BR man approved. In assessing the work each of the Big Four's CMEs were doing when nationalised, he concluded that:

The erstwhile CMEs at this time were variously engaged. Ivatt was busily occupied with his diesel locomotives and the troubles that arose with them;

Apart from the thirty-four A4s the streamlined B17s and W1 survived to serve BR in this guise, but the two 4-6-0s (Nos. 2859/61659 and 2870/61670) only for a while. In 1951 they returned to their original form whilst undergoing General Repair at Gorton, perhaps confirming for some that the 1937 streamlining programme had been primarily a publicity exercise to help promote the East Anglian service from Norwich to Liverpool Street Station. In the picture to the right, taken in 1948 at King's Cross, B17 No. 61659 *East Anglian* is departing with a Down service to Cambridge, while the A4 (possibly No. 60029 *Woodcock* which was turned out that year in 'BR trial purple' having been painted garter blue in June 1947 after nearly five years in black) though carrying no headboards is recorded in pencil on the back of the print as pulling the Flying Scotsman. (BS)

Bulleid was trying to make a success of his controversial 'Leader' class of steam engine and was busy as well with his double-deck carriage and other imaginative projects; the amiable Peppercorn was happily turning out lots of the last LNER Pacifics; and Hawksworth watched approaching events in the comfortable knowledge of the Great Western superiority.

If true, this is hardly a ringing endorsement of their work or their attitude towards the creation of BR. More a case of 'we are carrying on with what we are doing until told otherwise', perhaps. Something had to give and within two years of nationalisation, Peppercorn, Bulleid and Hawksworth would be gone, replaced by men probably closer to the model Riddles and BR wished to see operating. Ivatt hung on until 1951 then retired to be a consultant, then became General Manager of Brush Bagnall. In this role he took the lead in developing the Type 2 diesel for BR. So his former employers continued to benefit from his skills, though it might have been better if they had harnessed his knowledge of diesels when he was still employed by the nationalised company.

Riddles' method of working and the management structures he wished to see in place were soon made clear to the teams he had inherited. In many ways, it built upon principles long established by the Big Four. There would be a CME in overall charge, but now with four regional heads under him – the four ex-CMEs in due course being given the title of Mechanical and Electrical

22 April, hauled by GWR King Class 6018 *King Henry VI* in the Down direction.

23 April, hauled by GWR King Class 6018 *King Henry VI* in the Up direction.

27 April, hauled by SR Merchant Navy Class 35019 *French Line C.G.T* in the Down direction.

28 April, hauled by SR Merchant Navy Class 35019 *French Line C.G.T* in the Up direction.

29 April, hauled by SR Merchant Navy Class 35019 *French Line C.G.T* in the Down direction.

30 April, hauled by SR Merchant Navy Class 35019 *French Line C.G.T* in the Up direction.

4 May, hauled by LNER Class A4 60033 *Seagull* in the Down direction.

5 May, hauled by LNER Class A4 60033 *Seagull* in the Up direction.

6 May, hauled by LNER Class A4 60033 *Seagull* in the Down direction.

A stranger from the Southern gathers a crowd at Paddington at the end of a run from Plymouth in late April 1948. In comparison to the GWR's locomotives, with their tapered boilers and elegant looks, the air-smoothed Pacific, in this case 35019 *French Line C.G.T*, had a functional, even box like look worthy of the nickname' 'Spamcan'. (BS)

(Right) No. 22 *Mallard* was first choice for trials on the Western Region, but on a preliminary run from Plymouth to Paddington on 28 April her middle big-end overheated and she was taken off the train at Savernake in Wiltshire where she was photographed awaiting rescue. (Below) A little later the engine appeared at Reading Shed where, presumably efforts were made to get her working again, but to no avail and she was returned to the Eastern Region for closer inspection and repair. (BS)

7 May, hauled by LNER Class A4 60033 *Seagull* in the Up direction.

18 May, hauled by LMS Coronation Class 46236 *City of Bradford* in the Down direction.

19 May, hauled by LMS Coronation Class 46236 *City of Bradford* in the Up direction.

20 May, hauled by LMS Coronation Class 46236 *City of Bradford* in the Down direction.

21 May, hauled by LMS Coronation Class 46236 *City of Bradford* in the Up direction.

25 May, hauled by LMS Rebuilt Royal Scot Class 46162 *Queens Westminster Rifleman* in the Down direction.

26 May, hauled by LMS Rebuilt Royal Scot Class 46162 *Queens Westminster Rifleman* in the Up direction.

27 May, hauled by LMS Rebuilt Royal Scot Class 46162 *Queens Westminster Rifleman* in the Down direction.

28 May, hauled by LMS Rebuilt Royal Scot Class 46162 *Queens Westminster Rifleman* in the Up direction.

After a series of preliminary runs to allow the foreign footplate crew a chance to familiarise themselves with the features of the Western Region, the visiting engines began their measured trails on 27 April. First up, after *King Henry VI* had set the standard by completing two

return trips to Plymouth four days earlier, was the Merchant Navy, then A4 *Seagull*, which was a late entry, as Bert Spencer recalled:

Peppercorn wanted No. 22 *Mallard* to run to Plymouth and back. With the 1925 trials still in living memory, and the way Gresley's Pacifics had been bested by GWR Castles still raising hackles, choosing the world record holder to restore LNER prestige seemed a natural thing to do, despite my advice to the contrary. Sadly, the powers that be ignored the fact that by then the engine was not thought to be one of the best performers, despite a recent General Repair. Unfortunately, this proved to be the case and she then embarrassed herself by failing on a return familiarisation run on April 28th when her middle big-end overheated and she failed in Wiltshire and was then ignominiously towed to Doncaster for repair having been replaced by a Hall from Swindon.

My recommendation that No. 22 should be withdrawn from the trials completely, having been with her when she failed, with immediate effect, and be replaced by 60005 *Sir Charles Newton*, which had a much better reputation, did not carry the day. The end result was that she failed again in a later test. Instead of 60005, 60033 was substituted, with Driver Burgess in charge, although there were mild signs of overheating with her too on each of her four runs, though not sufficient to pull her up. Nevertheless, the engine required gentle handling and could not be flogged unduly.

As things turned out the engine failed to sparkle and did not run to time once, but neither did the Coronation, the Royal Scot or the Merchant

***Right, below and opposite:* A4 No. 60033**
Seagull was pressed into service on the Western Region over four days in May, accompanied on two occasions by Bert Spencer, the second of these journeys on the footplate. He wrote later that 'I wanted to see how the best of Gresley's engines would perform in the world of Brunel, Gooch and Churchward. As things turned out the engine failed to sparkle and did not run to time once, neither did the Coronation, the Royal Scot or the Merchant Navy except on 28 April when she came in 2.3 minutes early. In contrast the King did best on its home turf running ahead of schedule on two occasions and only a 1.9 and .8 minutes late on the other two'. These four photos capture the A4 at 'various stages of her adventures in the West Country' as Spencer noted on the back of these prints, though did not give times or dates. The top photo is of particular interest because it shows 60033 running into Paddington alongside a GWR Hall, so providing a thought-provoking comparison of style and look. (BS)

Paddington-Plymouth route.
DOWN: 4th and 6th May.
UP: 5th and 7th May.

Date	Location	Miles from Padding-ton.	Mile Post	Gradient 1 in	Speed m.p.h.	Recorded		Equivalent		Cut-off. %	Boiler Press. Lbs/ sq.in.	Steam Chest Press. Lbs/ sq.in.
						Pull Tons	DBHP.	Pull Tons	DBHP.			
May.												
4	Rattery Bank	203.25	223.1/2	71R	44	4.6	1211	6.2	1630	40	222	200
4	Rattery Bank	205.75	226	90R	35.8	5.75	1230	8.1	1728	35	250	235
5	Hemerdon Bank	220.25	240.1/2	41R	20.2	12.6	1050	12.6	1522	53	248	235
5	Burlescombe	156.00	176.1/4	115R	51.4	3.83	1178	4.9	1498	25	230	220
5	Bruton Bank	110.75	125	93-140R	46.1	4.01	1102	5.0	1361	25	240	220
5	Lavington	86.00	86	222R	58.8	3.35	1180	3.9	1356	20	250	235
6	Whiteball	152.00	172.1/4	80R	31.1	5.8	1180	7.5	1390	39	240	225
6	Dainton Bank	196.25	216.1/2	57R	35.2	4.72	994	7.1	1481	35	213	200
6	Rattery Bank	205.00	225.1/4	60R	24.6	7.15	1051	10.0	1457	42	245	230
7	Hemerdon Bank	220.25	240.1/2	42R	21.0	8.75	1111	12.75	1598	53	245	235
7	Bruton Bank	111.00	125.1/4	140R	46.0	4.35	1195	5.2	1422	25	243	230
7	Pewsey	74.50	74.1/2	264R	60.8	3.05	1108	3.9	1418	22½	237	205

Driver Brooker fought to bring his 456.05-ton train home on time, despite being delayed by eleven signal and permanent way checks on the way. His sterling service brought the following praise from Cecil Allen:

Of all the amazing feats that Driver Brooker achieved with his Royal Scot this one must stand in the very front rank. He had to retrieve the loss of 14 ½ minutes from Taunton, due to signals and slack, and then a delay caused by stopping at Reading for three minutes. But for this there is little question that he would have reached Paddington on time [as it was the train arrived only 3.2 minutes late, according to dynamometer car readings, having made up fourteen plus minutes from Westbury. During this run she maintained an average speed of 46.7mph overall, and in doing so compared very favourably with all the other engines involved].

The start out from Westbury was another of these well-nigh incredible exhibitions that one may not see repeated over many years. The amazing time of 27 min 27 sec was made up over the 25.5 miles from dead stop at Westbury to Savernake. I know of no precise Great Western parallel to this feat.

And so the Western Region element of the programme drew to a close, perhaps not adding a great deal to BR's collective knowledge, but proving interesting none the less. Spencer's only comment was that:

The King's performed pretty much as expected and did not suffer from firing with Yorkshire coal, though we did tease Sam Ells that Swindon may have surreptitiously swopped it for South Wales coke when no one was looking. The Pacifics did not give of their best, possibly because the conductors did not allow drivers sufficient freedom of action and they may have been too cautious on unfamiliar routes. The big surprise, for this and the other regional trials, were the performances of the two rebuilt Royal Scots. In this much credit must go to my old friend Tom Coleman at Derby under whose guiding hand the Fowler engines were very successfully modified.

The last trial run on the Western Region by 46162 coincided with the final day of operations on the West Coast main line with A4 No. 60034 hauling a 498 ton train from Carlisle to Euston. However, without a Great Western representative able

No. 60033's performance summary from the Western Region phase of the trials. It seems to be agreed that she did not perform as well as she could. One reason cited for this was restrictions placed on the driver by the conductor, but this level of constraint was likely to have been applied to all five sets of crew. Equally so the number of permanent way checks seem to have been similar for all the classes involved. In the circumstances one can only assume that Driver Burgess was possibly being very cautious, not wishing to push an engine where a suspicion of an overheating middle big-end existed. (BS)

35017 photographed passing through Harrow and Wealdstone Station on the up express to Euston in May (information on the back of the print does not indicate the day). During her four runs she suffered two mechanical problems. On 11 May, her tender water pick-up was damaged and this necessitated a water stop at Lancaster. Two days later four stays were found to be leaking in the firebox with two blowing badly. A repair had to be effected at Carlisle Shed. (BS)

to participate, 'the programme seemed incomplete' to Spencer. And if the crews involved thought the number of permanent way checks and other unscheduled stops on Eastern and Western Regions had been excessive, this was nothing compared to the delays they faced while running to and from Euston.

In her four runs, No. 60034, for example, faced fifteen delays twice and fourteen on the other two occasions. The other three fared just as badly if not worse, with 35017 topping the list with nineteen on 13 May and twenty a day later. These challenges, as O.S. Nock commented, made these runs the 'least satisfactory during the entire series'. But as the seasoned Spencer, who was not slow to see beyond timings and speeds achieved, pointed out:

There were undoubted problems in running smoothly and to time even with some very generous allowances being made by the planners, but this was only part of the picture. More important was the way they performed despite all the stopping and starting and the way they responded to such difficult working conditions. However, for the most part this information simply confirmed what we already knew or suspected.

The programme followed the Royal Scot schedule, using the old L&YR Dynamometer Car, with a departure time from Euston of 10.00 am and Carlisle at 12.55 pm on successive days:

20 April, hauled by LMS Coronation Class 46236 *City of Bradford* in the Down direction.

21 April, hauled by LMS Coronation Class 46236 *City of Bradford* in the Up direction.

22 April, hauled by LMS Coronation Class 46236 *City of Bradford* in the Down direction.

23 April, hauled by LMS Coronation Class 46236 *City of Bradford* in the Up direction.

25 May, hauled by LMS Rebuilt Royal Scot Class 46162 *Queens Westminster Rifleman* in the Down direction.

26 May, hauled by LMS Rebuilt Royal Scot Class 46162 *Queens Westminster Rifleman* in the Up direction.

4 May, hauled by LMS Rebuilt Royal Scot Class 46162 *Queens Westminster Rifleman* in the Down direction.

5 May, hauled by LMS Rebuilt Royal Scot Class 46162 *Queens Westminster Rifleman* in the Up direction.

6 May, hauled by SR Merchant Navy Class 35017 *Belgian Marine* in the Down direction.

7 May, hauled by SR Merchant Navy Class 35017 *Belgian Marine* in the Up direction.

13 May, hauled by SR Merchant Navy Class 35017 *Belgian Marine* in the Down direction.

14 May, hauled by SR Merchant Navy Class 35017 *Belgian Marine* in the Up direction.

25 May, hauled by LNER Class A4 60034 *Lord Faringdon* in the Down direction.

26 May, hauled by LNER Class A4 60034 *Lord Faringdon* in the Up direction.

27 May, hauled by LNER Class A4 60034 *Lord Faringdon* in the Down direction.

28 May, hauled by LNER Class A4 60034 *Lord Faringdon* in the Up direction.

Despite the many signal and permanent way checks along the West Coast route the time lost by each engine over the near 300 mile journey was in most cases understandable. In the case of the Royal Scot, the engine actually arrived 5½ minutes early on 4 May, though did not repeat this feat.

The best the Merchant Navy could do was 8½ minutes late, the A4 10 minutes behind schedule and the Coronation 3 minutes late on 23 April. Perhaps because the LMS crew knew the line so well their other late times were respectable ones – 3.3 min, 4.8 min and 13 minutes.

Cecil Allen caught a flavour of the problems this caused when describing *Lord Faringdon*'s run on 27 May:

With 504 tons tare and 540 tons gross – the train having a considerably heavier passenger complement (than 35017 on another run he recorded) – we were slowed for permanent way or bridge repairs to 19mph

at Willesden, 27 at Watford, 26 at Cheddington and 22 after Bletchley, reaching Rugby 7½ minutes late. Here again the driver (Moore of King's Cross) accelerated to 52½mph at Hatch End and 53mph beyond Berkhampstead, although the A4 was, on the whole, putting less energy into the running than the Merchant Navy.

Leaving Rugby 5¾ minutes late, the train arrived in Crewe 1½ minutes behind schedule with slacks at Atherstone and Lichfield only and an easing up to 58mph through Trent Valley Junction at Stafford. The best effort here was the run from Stafford to Crewe in 26 min 33 sec, with a speed of 56½mph

A4 No. 60034 *Lord Faringdon* appears to be coasting when passing an LMR track maintenance team standing back to let her slide by. The West Coast trials were severely hampered by many permanent way checks and delays, far more than on any other Region. The reason for this was given as the poor state of the track and infrastructure after the long very cold and damaging winter the year before, plus damage done by overuse during the war. (BS)

Lord Faringdon passes Bulkington, south east of Nuneaton in Warwickshire apparently at speed. This was something that proved difficult to achieve or sustain during her four trial runs on the West Coast main line. (BS)

60034 runs through Dillicar troughs near Tebay whilst running from Euston to Carlisle on either 25 or 27 May. Whichever date it is, the engine's performance was severely hindered by the many delays caused by track or bridge maintenance. On the 25th she arrived at Carlisle 12.5 minutes late and 20.3 on the 27th. As Spencer later wrote, 'the engine performed well and no overheating in the middle big-end was apparent. But in the conditions that prevailed she struggled to make up lost time and had a driver who was probably over cautious in not wishing to extend his engine unnecessarily'. (BS)

Euston-Carlisle route.
DOWN: 25th and 27th May.
UP: 26th and 28th May.

Date	Location	Miles From Euston	Miles From Carlisle	Gradient 1 in	Speed m.p.h.	Recorded Pull Tons	Recorded DBHP.	Equivalent Pull Tons	Equivalent DBHP.	Cut-off. %	Boiler Press. Lbs/ sq.in.	Steam Chest Press. Lbs/ sq.in.
May.												
25	Carnforth-Oxenholme	237.4		134R	64.1	3.1	1172	3.6	1393	20	233	215
25	Carnforth-Oxenholme	248.1		111R	44.6	3.4	907	4.1	1090	20	225	207
25	Tebay-Shap Summit	265.0		75R	33.4	4.8	949	5.9	1167	25	225	205
25	Tebay-Shap Summit	267.0		75R	17.0	7.5	760	9.6	975	40	239	223
26	Carlisle-Plumpton		1.17	131R	35.0	6.7	1395	8.1	1696	38	233	215
26	Penrith-Shap Summit		22.4	125R	39.2	5.5	1278	6.6	1539	29	230	180
26	Penrith-Shap Summit		18.0	616R	19.3	7.5	865	9.2	1060	42	230	160
26	Crewe-Whitmore		143.5	269R	44.0	4.8	1267	5.8	1528	30	224	200
26	Crewe-Whitmore		141.7	330R	29.5	5.6	988	7.1	1250	35	212	187
27	Norton Bridge-Whitmore	146.9		398R	56.2	3.2	1080	3.7	1245	20	227	208
28	Preston-Euxton Jct.		92.1	106R,314R	40.5	4.4	1053	5.5	1330	23	237	217
28	Bletchley-Tring		254.9	660R,1683R	59.2	2.8	981	3.1	1084	18	215	195

The official summary of 60034's performances between 25 and 28 May. (BS)

Nine Elms based Merchant Navy No.35018 *British India Line* was the third member of the class to be used during the Interchange Trials and then only on her home metals. The photo below captures the engine on Devon Belle duty shortly before these trials began. (BS)

sustained from Standon Bridge to Whitmore, and 74mph at Betley Road.

Lord Faringdon left Crewe on time but started with such unaccountable lethargy as to lose 3 minutes to Warrington – then the trouble began. We were stopped by signal for 2 minutes at Winwick Junction, and after the Wigan slowings there came permanent way or bridge slacks to 22mph at Euxton Junction, 19 for something like 2 miles past Barton, 22 before Lancaster and 25 at Low Gill, followed by the crowning infamy of a signal check almost to a dead stand just before Tebay! After this, I fancy that Driver Moore lost any further interest in proceedings, for he achieved the somewhat unusual feat of running from Shap down to Carlisle barely exceeding 60mph at any point. So we arrived 20 minutes late [or 20.3 minutes in the official log] on the only day on which we left Crewe on time

The final phase of the trials was soon underway with the Spencer led committee hoping that the problems that had plagued the engines running to and from Euston would not be repeated on the Southern Region. In this case, the four locomotives would be hauling the *Atlantic Coast Express,* with the GWR Dynamometer Car again attached, all set to leave Waterloo for Exeter at 10.50 am, returning a day later with the 12.37 pm from Devon. The order of service saw the SR's Merchant Navy No. 35018 British India Line first to run, following the pattern set in other Regions where the 'home' engines set the running:

1 June, hauled by SR Merchant Navy Class 35018 *British India Line* in the Down direction.

2 June, hauled by SR Merchant Navy Class 35018 *British India Line* in the Up direction.

3 June, hauled by SR Merchant Navy Class 35018 *British India Line* in the Down direction

4 June, hauled by SR Merchant Navy Class 35018 *British India Line* in the Up direction.

8 June, hauled by LNER Class A4 No. 22 *Mallard* in the Down direction (loco declared a failure at Exeter).

Mallard's appearance at Waterloo, as a replacement for Seagull, attracted much press attention. Sadly she failed near Salisbury and had to be substituted by 60033 by then repaired. Here this iconic locomotive is photographed passing in front of Waterloo's easily identifiable signal box. (BS)

Mallard being made ready at Nine Elms on 8 June for her first run to Exeter. As in all the Interchange Trials, the coal is being carefully measured to ensure that comparative usage is carefully assessed. This corridor tender (number 5323) was fitted to No. 22 immediately before the trials began having been taken from A4 No. 4/60004 *William Whitelaw* which was undergoing a General Repair at Doncaster at the time. (BS)

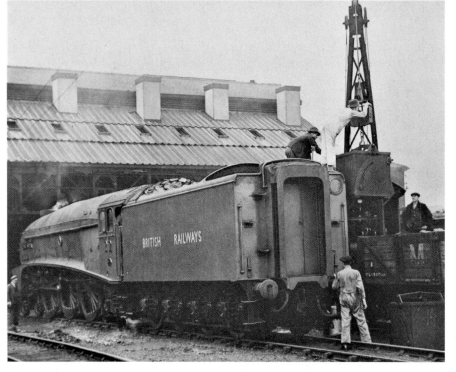

9 June, hauled by LNER Class A4 No. 22 Mallard in the Up direction (test terminated at Salisbury due to engine failure).

10 June, hauled by LNER Class A4 60033 *Seagull* in the Down direction

11 June, hauled by LNER Class A4 60033 *Seagull* in the Up direction.

15 June, hauled by LMS Rebuilt Royal Scot Class 46154 *The Hussar* in the Down direction.

16 June, hauled by LMS Rebuilt Royal Scot Class 46154 *The Hussar* in the Up direction.

17 June, hauled by LMS Rebuilt Royal Scot Class

46154 *The Hussar* in the Down direction.

18 June, hauled by LMS Rebuilt Royal Scot Class 46154 *The Hussar* in the Up direction.

22 June, hauled by LMS Coronation Class 46236 *City of Bradford* in the Down direction

23 June, hauled by LMS Coronation Class 46236 *City of Bradford* in the Up direction.

24 June, hauled by LMS Coronation Class 46236 *City of Bradford* in the Down direction.

25 June, hauled by LMS Coronation Class 46236 *City of Bradford* in the Up direction.

By the time the trials on the Southern Region began there was a sense, as Spencer put it, 'that the programme had run its course and there was little more to learn. Many of the footplate crew were eager to get back to their normal

duties having grown tired of these extra onerous responsibilities. At the beginning there had been some novelty value but by June this had all but disappeared.'

In some ways, this final phase of the trials was enlivened by the return of *Mallard* to the fray. Having failed on 28 April on the Plymouth

to Paddington express she was returned to Doncaster to be stripped down and repaired. The work was completed by 13 May and the engine was returned to traffic at King's Cross shortly afterwards. But after a couple of days, she was back at Doncaster for some 'non-classified repair' work, which kept her in the

No. 22 backs down with the dynamometer car onto her train on 8 June. There appears to be no record of Oliver Bulleid being at Waterloo to witness first-hand the Interchange engines get underway. But seeing an A4 and one of his Merchant Navys side by side would have undoubtedly interested him, reflecting, as they did, two distinct phases of his career. On this occasion, the Southern Pacific is also running the Atlantic Coast Express but the engine's identity is not recorded. (Below) Rebuilt Royal Scot No. 46154 The Hussar makes ready for departure, During the Southern trials this engine performed surprisingly well. (BS)

City of Bradford comes to rest at Waterloo looking rather odd with an ex-War Department tender attached. With no water troughs to fill her tank while moving, the engine had to rely on what she could carry herself and the Coronation's own tender had only a 4,000 gallon capacity, which was insufficient. The ex-WD, eight-wheeled tender could carry 5,000 gallons so gave a greater margin for safety. (BS)

workshops until 21 May. Another period of normal running followed and when *Seagull* failed during a preliminary run from Waterloo on 1 June, *Mallard* took her place in the programme, despite the fact that 60033 was quickly repaired in London and was ready for duty before the first formal test began. Perhaps the high profile nature of the world record holder came into play, as it had done during the Western Region trials. Sadly, history would be repeated and *Mallard* again failed when hauling the Atlantic Coast Express from Exeter on the 9th.

However, before that No. 22 had one day of fairly good running to her credit. After the timing problems caused by permanent way checks on the West Coast main

line, the Southern presented no such problems for the A4s or the other engines for that matter, except 35018 which had six on 4 June when running up from Exeter and arrived 9 minutes late. So, on the 8th *Mallard* set out, with Driver Bob Marrable at the controls, in fine dry conditions, with only a slight breeze from the south, and met only two unpredicted checks, but one of these was for nine minutes at Hook, which slowed progress considerably until Salisbury. So it was, perhaps, surprising that the engine reached Exeter, according to the official report, well ahead of time. But, as Spencer who was on board later wrote:

Marrable was keen to demonstrate what No. 22 could

do and gave her the 'full whip' when he could. There was an appreciative crowd at Waterloo as we departed, and cheers from the signal box too, so this may have encouraged him to give them something to watch. Unfortunately, our progress westwards did not live up to expectations and we reached Salisbury nearly six minutes late. But things picked up after that and Marrable took us onwards to Exeter very smartly.

Cecil Allen described the remainder of the journey:

Because of the Hook delay there was a late start from Salisbury, and this seemed

A4 No. 22 *Mallard* passing through Vauxhall Station heading westwards from Waterloo on 8 June. All seems to have gone well on this journey to Exeter and the engine completed her run under time by nearly 12 minutes in fine and dry conditions (a booked running time of 209 minutes and a recorded running time of 197.1, according to the official report). However, things went badly wrong the following day when returning to London. (BS)

entirely to Marrable's liking. A very fine start was made up the 1 in 115 to milepost 85, and excellent work continued to Semley summit; the only restraint was from Semley down to Gillingham and up the 2¾ miles of 1 in 80-100 past Templecombe, on which speed fell to 42½mph. But from there onwards all went well. The minimum of 36mph up 2¾ miles at 1 in 80 past Crewkerne to Hewish summit was good, but excelled by the 33½mph on entering Honiton tunnel, after 1½ miles at 1 – 100 and 4½ miles at 1 – 80 up the formidable Seaton Bank.

There had been some good travelling past Axminster, with a top speed of 82mph, and the impetus obtained was helpful, as is obvious by the speed of 73½mph past Seaton Junction, and of 47½mph as high up the bank as milepost 150½. By milepost 149½ the engine was within an ace of even time from the start with a 510 ton train [according to the official report 480.25 tons] over this difficult road. Some slight slipping in Honiton tunnel brought the speed down to 30mph, but was soon grappled with, and with a gentle ascent past Honiton, Mallard reached Sidmouth Junction in 79 min 24 sec, 10½ minutes inside schedule.

Allen then recorded that two minutes were lost between Sidmouth and Exeter due to a permanent way check with the train then arriving 8½ minutes early. Here these figures do not correspond with those taken in the dynamometer car which gave the 'actual' time as 197.1 minutes, 11.1 min ahead of schedule. But having done so well, *Mallard* failed on the 9th on the return journey and was taken off at Salisbury, much to Spencer's irritation. He wrote that this was 'a great disappointment, especially as the engine had so publicly failed once already. But it was the old overheating problem and allowed critics, once again, to condemn Gresley's three cylinder engines and their 2 in 1 valve gear'.

However, newly repaired 60033 was available and swiftly replaced

Although repaired after her failure on 1 June there were continuing concerns about Seagull's condition, but she was passed fit for use and to Waterloo she went, with Spencer keeping his 'fingers crossed that all would be well'. This photo records her departure from Waterloo on 10 June. (BS)

Mallard for the final two test runs. And on the 10th nearly equalled No. 22's time by bringing her train into Exeter 6.7 minutes early, then only 1.3 minutes late on the return journey to Waterloo on the 11th. Allen commented briefly on the down test by simply writing that

'my run with *Seagull* was of less note. Certain maximum speeds were higher, but the minima were lower'. But to this understated response he did add a pleasing footnote that Spencer copied and kept in his personal records. 'An impression along this length

[between Sidmouth and Exeter] that sticks with me was the sight of the entire shed staff at Exmouth Junction – or so it seemed to me – lined up to see us pass.'

Such was the impact of the A4s.

Of the other three engines involved, Allen saved most praise for the Royal Scot. 46154 *The Hussar*, which, like her sister engine earlier in the trials, kept good time on her first three trips, but on the fourth turned in a performance that drew only praise. He began with the effusive words, 'I was there to see the "baby" of the series beat every Pacific competitor with a demonstration of running little short of miraculous for an engine of such dimensions'. He then added more praise in describing individual elements of the journey, paying particular attention to the final phase from Salisbury to Waterloo

The date with this print is indistinct but the subject is clear. *Mallard* has arrived in Devon and is being serviced by local shed staff at Exmouth Junction. The photo is most likely to have been taken on either the 8 or 9 June. She is flanked on this occasion by a local Merchant Navy, No. 21C1 *Channel Packet*, soon to be renumbered 35001, on her left with light Pacific, No. 34003 *Plymouth*, up from Plymouth Friary where she was based from April that year, on her right. (BS)

where Driver Brooker gave 'another outstanding demonstration of the power of the Royal Scot'. In so doing, he brought the train in 5.9 minutes early easily beating the other three engines – 46236 1.2 minutes early, 60033 and 35018 1.3 and 9.3 minutes late respectively.

Allen's final words on 46154's performance drew attention to the key issue of coal consumption, which he reported as only 3¼lb per mile and so much lower than the Pacifics, with the Merchant Navy being highest at 6½lb per mile. It was, as he made clear, 'another feather in the cap of this remarkable engine and her crew'.

With all the trials completed, it fell to Spencer, and a small team working directly under him, to gather all the information and try to make some sense of the findings and all the variables that came into play when comparing performances. There was also the thorny issue of politics to consider. When judging BR's legacy from each of the Big Four's locomotive programmes, scrupulous impartiality might not be enough for the conclusions

reached to gain acceptance. If one was shown any favour over the others, no matter how justified this might be, there were likely to be accusations of favouritism, especially with so many LMS managers being placed in senior positions in the Railway Executive. In 1948, Regional teams were still imbued with a sense of their own rightness and retained a strong

desire to remain independent. So, to avoid confrontation and achieve something positive from the exercise the report had to be scrupulously fair, and, more importantly, must not throw fuel on the fire of attitudes already inflamed. In the circumstances, it is hardly surprising that Spencer, when writing the report, chose to let the facts and figures speak for

11 June and the A4s' participation in the Interchange Trials comes to an end with 60033 barely drawing a glance from the few people on the platform at Waterloo. It is interesting to note the West Country Class engine, No.34005 *Barnstable* in the background with an LMS tender. This engine will participate in the mixed traffic group beginning on 22 June running between London St Pancras and Manchester pulling 300 tons successfully – on one occasion ahead of schedule with three other runs virtually to time. (BS)

The official report's summary of performance for the two A4s involved in the Southern Region trials. (BS)

```
Waterloo-Exeter route.
DOWN: 8th and 10th June.
UP:   9th and 11th June.
```

Date	Location	Miles from Waterloo	Gradient 1 in	Speed m.p.h.	Recorded		Equivalent		Cut-off %	Boiler Press. Lbs/sq.in.	Steam Chest Press. Lbs/sq.in.
					Pull Tons	DBHP.	Pull Tons	DBHP.			
June.											
8	Semley	100.50	145R	49.5	3.45	1020	4.61	1360	21	230	225
8	Crewkerne	132.00	80R	44.5	4.0	1064	5.24	1390	22	235	230
8	Honiton	152.00	80R	35	5.6	1172	7.32	1530	30	235	230
9	Chard Jct.	139.50	120R	47	4.4	1236	5.42	1520	25	225	220
9	Sherborne	120.00	448R	53.5	4.3	1378	4.97	1590	25	230	225
9	Milborne	114.00	170R	46	4.8	1318	5.79	1590	30	210	205
10	Seaton Jct.	149.25	80R	52.5	4.4	1380	5.35	1680	26	230	215
11	Chard Jct.	141.00	140R	45	4.4	1182	5.6	1505	30	215	205
11	Sherborne	116.50	80R	27.5	7.0	1150	9.3	1550	42	212	200

themselves and kept conclusions as broad as possible.

In early 1949, the final report was being considered by all those involved, with Spencer still fulfilling his co-ordinating role and trying to reach some sort of consensus and agreement on future policy. For those who doubted the validity of the exercise, and there appear to have been many, they would have found ample ammunition to support this view. When finally issued the tone of the report was probably summed up in

TEST RESULTS.

EXPRESS PASSENGER ENGINES - Eastern Region 'A.4' Class.

	60033				60034				60034				22	60033	22	60033
ENGINE NO. / TRAIN AND ROUTE	DOWN:1.30pm Paddington-Plymouth N.Rd. UP:8.15am Plymouth M.B.-Paddington				DOWN: 1.10pm King's Cross-Leeds UP: 7.50am Leeds - King's Cross.				DOWN: 10.0am Euston-Carlisle UP: 12.55pm Carlisle-Euston				DOWN:10.50am Waterloo-Exeter Central UP:12.37pm Exeter Central-Waterloo			
	Down	Down	Up	Up	Down	Down	Up	Up	Down	Down	Up	Up	Down	Down	Up	Up
DATE	4.5.48	6.5.48	5.5.48	7.5.48	20.4.48	22.4.48	21.4.48	23.4.48	25.5.48	27.5.48	26.5.48	28.5.48	8.6.48	10.6.48	9.6.48	11.6.48
WT.OF ENG.(In W.O.) TONS	167.9	167.9	167.9	167.9	167.9	167.9	167.9	167.9	167.9	167.9	167.9	167.9	167.9	167.9	167.9	167.9
WEIGHT OF TRAIN BEHIND DRAWBAR. TARE. TONS. (Inc.Dynamometer Car)	Paddington 482.0 Newton Abbot 324.5	Paddington 482.0 Newton Abbot 324.5	Plymouth Mill Bay 328.30 Newton Abbot 489.95 Reading 454.80	Plymouth Mill Bay 330.15 Newton Abbot 491.80 Reading 454.80	K.X. 500.5 Wakefield 372.75	K.X. 499.25 Wakefield 371.5	Leeds 298.5 Wakefield 425.25 Doncaster 457.00 Grantham 493.50	Leeds 298.5 Wakefield 428.75 Doncaster 460.50 Grantham 497.00	Euston 504	Euston 503	Carlisle 503 Crewe 477	Carlisle 498 Crewe 465	Waterloo 481.25	Waterloo 480.9	Exeter Central 480.25	Exeter Central 477.9
TRAIN MILES (Actual)	225.1	225.1	225.8	225.8	185.7	185.7	185.8	185.8	299.5	299.5	299.6	299.6	171.5	171.5	88.0	171.6
TON MILES EXC.WT.OF ENG.	103480	103480	104120	104470	91760	91520	86570	87190	150948	150649	146583	143977	82540	82470	42270	82000
" " INC.WT.OF ENG.	141270	141270	142020	142370	122940	122699	117766	118386	201234	200935	196884	194278	111330	111260	57050	110800
TIME. BOOKED RUNNING MINS.	287	287	287	287	236	236	241	241	366	366	373	373	209	209	123	218
" ACTUAL " "	296.3	295.5	287.3	288.1	239.5	236.0	238.3	243.4	378.5	386.3	383.7	388.8	197.1	202.3	126.2	219.3
" OVERALL (Inc.stops)	326.7	326.5	328.7	331.5	260.0	259.1	265.7	272.6	388.2	398.3	402.7	410.0	219.6	216.6	141.0	241.1
SPEED M.P.H. AVERAGE	45.6	45.7	47.2	47.0	46.5	47.2	46.7	45.8	47.5	46.5	46.9	46.3	52.2	50.9	41.8	47.0
WORK DONE. H.P. HOURS	3000	2930	2919	3174	2513	2469	2557	2420	4106	4520	4009	3810	2243	1946	1596	2501
H.P.MINS/TON MILE (Train)	1.740	1.699	1.682	1.824	1.654	1.618	1.772	1.665	1.630	1.801	1.640	1.587	1.630	1.416	2.266	1.830
COAL. TOTAL WT.LBS.	8950	9494	9710	10132	7453	7023	7500	7060	11997	13111	12248	11968	7130	6570	5102	7622
" LBS/MILE	39.76	42.18	43.00	44.87	40.12	37.3	40.35	38.0	40.05	43.74	40.89	39.92	41.57	38.31	57.98	44.42
" LBS/TON MILE (Exc.Engine)	0.087	0.092	0.093	0.097	0.081	0.077	0.087	0.081	0.080	0.087	0.084	0.083	0.086	0.080	0.121	0.093
" LBS/TON MILE (Inc.Engine)	0.063	0.067	0.068	0.071	0.061	0.057	0.064	0.060	0.060	0.065	0.062	0.062	0.064	0.059	0.089	0.069
" LBS/DBHP.HOUR	2.98	3.24	3.33	3.19	2.97	2.84	2.93	2.92	2.92	2.90	3.06	3.14	3.18	3.38	3.20	3.05
" LBS/SQ.FT.GRATE/HR. (Running Time)	43.9	46.8	49.2	51.2	45.2	43.3	45.7	42.2	46.1	49.3	46.4	44.8	52.6	47.3	58.8	50.6
WATER. TOTAL GALLONS	7409	7406	7145	7562	5217	5139	6150	6031	9995	10972	9794	9610	5548	5302	4039	6234
" GALLONS/MILE	32.9	32.9	31.6	33.5	28.1	27.6	33.1	32.5	33.4	36.6	32.7	32.1	32.3	30.9	45.9	36.7
" LBS/TON MILE (Inc.Engine)	0.524	0.524	0.503	0.531	0.424	0.419	0.522	0.509	0.497	0.546	0.497	0.494	0.493	0.477	0.708	0.566
" LBS/DBHP/HOUR	24.70	25.27	24.47	23.82	20.82	20.5	24.1	24.92	24.35	24.27	24.42	25.22	24.74	27.26	25.31	25.18
" LBS WATER/LBS COAL (Actual)	8.28	7.80	7.36	7.46	7.00	7.32	8.20	8.56	8.33	8.37	7.99	8.03	7.76	8.07	7.92	8.26
GROSS CALORIFIC)AS VALUE OF COAL)REC'D	13570	13770	13730	13340	13847	13632	13782	13646	13450	13700	13800	13600	13540	13720	13730	13570
B.T.U'S/DBHP.HOUR	40500	44600	45700	42600	41100	38800	40400	39800	39300	39800	42200	42700	43400	46300	43900	41400

* Test terminated at Salisbury due to engine failure.

Above and opposite: The Interchange Trials Report was published in early 1949 after many months of preparation and debate. For the most part its conclusions were couched in generalised terms, Spencer, in particular, not wishing to be drawn into any long protracted debate about which company had produced the best locomotives. But the devil was in the detail and it was left to the reader to consider the mass of fine detail the report contained and reach appropriate conclusions. Each class of locomotive used during the trials was covered in some detail, as demonstrated by these two summary sheets for the A4s taken from Bert Spencer's annotated copy of the report. (BS)

TEST RESULTS.

EXPRESS PASSENGER LOCOMOTIVES - Eastern Region 'A.4' Class (Contd.)

ENGINE NO.	60033				60034				60034				22	60033	22	60033
TRAIN AND ROUTE	DOWN:1.30pm Paddington-Plymouth N.Rd UP:8.15am Plymouth M.B-Paddington.				DOWN:1.10pm King's Cross-Leeds UP: 7.50am Leeds-King's Cross				DOWN: 10.00am Euston-Carlisle UP: 12.55pm Carlisle-Euston				DOWN:10.50am Waterloo-Exeter Central. UP:12.57pm Exeter Central-Waterloo.			
	Down	Down	Up	Up	Down	Down	Up	Up	Down	Down	Up	Up	Down	Down	Up	Up
DATE	4.5.48	6.5.48	5.5.48	7.5.48	20.4.48	22.4.48	21.4.48	23.4.48	25.5.48	27.5.48	26.5.48	28.5.48	8.6.48	10.6.48	9.6.48	11.6.48
TRAIN MILES (Under Power)	182.7	184.1	169.2	174.6	159.1	162.8	162.4	157.1	231.7	235.2	230.6	220.6	151.2	151.1	73.2	150.1
TIME (Under Power) MINS	236.1	233.8	210.2	213.5	201.1	201.0	202.0	199.5	295.3	305.7	276.3	284.7	170.6	175.5	104.4	190.0
NO. OF SIGNAL & TEMPORARY P.W. CHECKS	5	9	8	11	9	5	6	5	14	14	14	13	1	1	2	3
NO. OF UNBOOKED STOPS	-	-	-	-	-	-	1	1	-	1	-	2	1	-	-	-
AVERAGE D.B.H.P. (Under Power)	763	752	832	892	750	737	759	728	833	886	867	800	789	664	917	790
AVERAGE D.B.PULL. TONS. (Under Power)	2.75	2.66	2.89	3.04	2.64	2.54	2.64	2.58	2.96	3.22	2.90	2.88	2.48	2.16	3.65	2.79
COAL. LBS/HOUR. (Running Time)	1812	1929	2028	2110	1866	1785	1887	1741	1902	2036	1917	1848	2171	1949	2426	2085
" LBS/HOUR. (Under Power)	2275	2436	2772	2847	2222	2097	2228	2123	2438	2571	2658	2521	2508	2243	2933	2407
" LBS/SQ.FT.GRATE/HR. (Under Power)	55.1	59.1	67.2	69.0	53.9	50.8	54.0	51.5	59.1	62.4	64.4	61.1	60.8	54.4	71.1	58.4
WATER. LBS/HOUR (Running Time)	15010	15040	14920	15750	13070	13070	15470	14870	15350	17030	15310	14810	16890	15730	19210	17230
" LBS/HOUR (Under Power)	18820	19010	20400	21250	15560	15330	18260	18120	20310	21520	21270	20250	19520	18100	23210	19880
GENERAL WEATHER CONDITIONS	Showery	Fine & Dry.	Fine & Dry.	Fine & Dry.	Fine. Dry Rail.	Fine. Dry Rail.	Fine. Dry Rail.	Fair. Dry Rail.	Fine	Fine throughout.	Showery.	Fine throughout.	Fine & Dry.	Fine start. Rain later.	Fine start Rain later.	Fine & Dry.
WIND	South Moderate breeze.	N.W. Light breeze.	West. Light breeze.	N.E. Light air.	S.W. Light.	Nil.	S.W. Light.	Nil	Slight	Slight to Fresh.	Slight.	Fresh to Slight.	South. Light air.	N.E. Light air.	N.E. Light breeze.	North. Light wind.

• Test was terminated at Salisbury due to engine failure.

the opening pages, which recorded that the trials 'provided valuable and interesting information'. Yet the nine conclusions reached were, with few exceptions, nebulous, to say the least.

Spencer probably caught the general feeling of the time when he wrote:

The trials were useful up to a point. Each class had its own strengths, but the variables involved in such trials made such a broad comparison most difficult and speculative in nature. By this stage the new Test Centre at Rugby was finally opening and it was hoped that this facility would soon provide more information. But it was not until January 1950 that serious testing of any of the Interchange engines took place, by which time standardisation plans had been formulated by Cox and his design team, which included Windle.

From the point of view of the A4s, the report provided a lot of information for the team at Doncaster to mull over. With Peppercorn still in charge until December 1949 there was still a feeling that LNER working practices and principles might still prevail. But with John Harrison in his new role growing daily

COAL CONSUMPTION - SUMMARIES.

Express Passenger Engines.

	Engine	Route	Lbs/ train mile	Lbs/ train ton mile.	Lbs/ DBHP. Hour.	Lbs/sq.ft. grate/hr. (Running time)
W.R.	'King'	Western Region	48.82	0.082	3.74	67.5
		Eastern Region	47.25	0.091	3.39	64.9
					3.05	
E.R.	'A.4'	Western Region	42.45	0.067	3.19	47.8
		Eastern Region	39.08	0.081	2.92	44.1
		L.Midland Region	41.25	0.083	3.00	46.7
		Southern Region	45.57	0.070	3.20	52.3
L.M.R.	'Duchess'	Western Region	41.67	0.067	3.24	38.5
		Eastern Region	44.05	0.091	3.04	41.6
		L.Midland Region	44.09	0.088	3.07	42.7
		Southern Region	42.74	0.067	3.17	42.0
L.M.R.	'6P'	Western Region	42.76	0.076	3.64	62.6
		Eastern Region	46.66	0.097	3.26	67.4
		L.Midland Region	41.42	0.099	3.37	62.0
		Southern Region	44.39	0.071	3.24	68.3
S.R.	'Merchant Navy'	Western Region	48.02	0.080	3.61	45.9
		Eastern Region	49.41	0.102	3.73	47.9
		L.Midland Region	50.66	0.103	3.57	48.0
		Southern Region	50.85	0.081	3.52	50.8

WATER CONSUMPTION - SUMMARIES.

Express Passenger Engines.

	Engine	Route	Galls/ train mile.	Lbs/ train ton mile.	Lbs/ DBHP. Hour.	Evaporation Lbs. water/ Lb.coal.
W.R.	'King'	Western Region	36.2	0.606	27.71	7.41
		Eastern Region	41.2	0.866	29.60	8.73
	Castle	W.R.			26.74	
E.R.	'A.4'	Western Region	32.7	0.521	24.57	7.73
		Eastern Region	30.3	0.631	22.63	7.76
		L.Midland Region	33.7	0.509	24.55	8.18
		Southern Region	36.5	0.563	25.62	8.01
L.M.R.	'Duchess'	Western Region	37.6	0.601	29.27	9.03
		Eastern Region	37.2	0.769	25.71	8.45
		L.Midland Region	37.9	0.572	26.41	8.59
		Southern Region	36.8	0.574	27.26	8.61
L.M.R.	'6P'	Western Region	32.2	0.574	27.53	7.60
		Eastern Region	35.2	0.731	24.62	7.55
		L.Midland Region	30.7	0.555	25.02	7.42
		Southern Region	36.2	0.572	26.56	8.24
S.R.	'Merchant Navy'	Western Region	41.4	0.685	31.17	8.67
		Eastern Region	39.5	0.812	29.82	7.99
		L.Midland Region	43.1	0.670	30.28	8.49
		Southern Region	43.9	0.701	30.45	8.65

Fuel and water consumption were two key issues considered by the committee and given much prominence in their report. This was probably because they were scientifically based and carefully recorded. As a result, conjecture could not sully or distort the picture that emerged, although the Western Region might still decry the enforced use of unfamiliar Yorkshire coal. The two summaries here, once again annotated by Spencer, give clear evidence of the A4s ability to run economically. He has also added a brief reference to a trial carried out later in the year with a GWR Castle Class locomotive. (BS)

more influential, at Doncaster and Marylebone, a new corporate way of doing things was steadily spreading and with it an end to the independence of thought and action they had long enjoyed. So they scrutinised the report and considered how its findings might inform their work without knowing if anything they attempted would ever see the light of day, whether it be new locomotives or modifications to the old, such as the A4s. This role had now passed to Riddles and with it the power to implement the report's findings if he and his team saw fit.

When back at Doncaster and compiling the trials report Spencer discussed his findings with Peppercorn at some length, recording that:

The CME was eager to learn all he could about the way the A4s performed. He and I believed that they still had an important role to play in day to day service but also in deciding a future standard locomotive policy, which Riddles was keen to pursue. However, he was not imbued with any great desire to modify them by removing the streamlined casing or replacing Gresley's 2 in 1 gear with a third set of independent Walshaerts valve gear. If anything he preferred to see them remain largely untouched, if this was possible. Windle and I, on the other hand wished to see some of this work carried out, especially the valve gear modifications, especially when the later Pacifics had shown how these changes might be accommodated in the design successfully. Windle also thought de-streamlining would be beneficial. I did not share this conclusion.

When Riddles came to consider the report, by which time his standardisations plans were well advanced, he thought any modification to existing locomotives should be driven by hard evidence of poor performance, genuine concerns over safety or ever increasing and unjustifiably high cost of running and maintaining them, not because it would be nice to do so. It was an argument he later employed against Bulleid's Pacifics and led to their rebuilding, encouraged in part by several incidents of fractured crank axles – a problem that also afflicted the P2s as built, which Thompson also corrected by rebuilding.

It seems to me that he, Bond and Cox saw the strengths of the A4s, did not see them as an expensive luxury and probably appreciated their continuing PR value at a time when BR needed some good headlines. Of course, during the Interchange Trials they failed on three occasions, which was a poor record by any standards especially when considering that they only ran about 20 measured or familiarisation runs. But this seems only to have confirmed them in the belief that three cylinders, with or without

No. 60034 Lord Faringdon (according to notes that came with the print) passing over the Royal Border Bridge at Berwick on Tweed in the late 1940s (BS).

Gresley's valve gear, were not their preferred option for the new standard engines – or four for that matter. So when it came to the A4s they remained quite sanguine in their views about their future and were prepared, as Thompson before them, to let them run on without modification until the end of their economic lives, because they met a specific need very well. Of course, this meant accepting that there would be a continuing need for shed staff to inspect them more frequently, and probably undertake more maintenance and repair work at sheds and workshops, than other engines. If they did deteriorate, even with such a regime in place, rebuilding could be considered then.

And so the A4 came through the Interchange Trials, and the political fall-out, with some success, and then appeared to find favour amongst BR's new managers – for the time being anyway – despite any regional prejudices that might exist. But the same could be said for the other engines involved in the trials, accept, of course, Bulleid's Southern Pacifics.

In summing up the Locomotive Testing Committee's findings, Spencer added five more conclusions to the four described earlier in this chapter. As before, his words were those of an experienced engineer, imbued with great common sense. So they were deliberately presented as observations, hinting at areas where further research might prove beneficial and avoided any suggestion of criticism or any

sense of triumphalism over the conclusions reached:

The importance of correct firing technique in relation to the type of coal used and the necessity for adjusting details of design, such as spacing of firebars, to suit the type of coal used were especially evident in connection with the higher power output.

Steam temperatures were not recorded but there were indications that an increase in the degree of superheat effected an improvement in efficiency in the case of Express Passenger and Mixed Traffic locomotives. In the case of Freight locomotives, the improvement was much less marked.

With regard to slipping, the performance of the different locomotives was variable and further investigation is desirable.

In view of the irregular drawbar pulls recorded in certain cases, it is considered that further investigation should be made into the effects of balancing, valve settings and other relevant factors on the smoothness of drawbar pull.

The Express Passenger and Mixed Traffic locomotives with the smaller diameter coupled wheels experienced no difficulty in attaining the speeds necessary to maintain the schedules.

With the trials out of the way Spencer wrote:

[I was] pleased to get back to my normal duties at Doncaster

and allow the findings to sink in. There were a number of meetings at Marylebone to consider the lessons we had learnt, but it was soon apparent that the exercise was deemed of limited value in terms of determining future locomotive policy. Peppercorn, for one, thought that the programme had simply been a means of appeasing the CMEs of the old companies and giving the Railway Executive time to 'get their feet under the table' and decide what to do next. There was much talk of electrification and dieselisation, but it seemed to me that the Labour Government lacked the ambition and the funds to pursue these options, preferring instead to invest heavily in the National Health Service. There was also the question of fuel to consider. With so much cheap coal available and mining being one of Britain's biggest industries and employers, the Government would inevitably wish to exploit this valuable resource as much as possible and not import more oil than they needed to.

With Peppercorn, Hawksworth, Bulleid and Ivatt retiring in fairly short order it made it easier for Riddles to select replacements who would be keener to implement his plans and do his bidding. This proved to be the case with Harrison at Doncaster.

Roland Bond, being at the centre of all that happened during these challenging months, probably best described the outcome and

No. 28 *Walter K. Whigham*, soon to become 60028 in June 1948, was painted garter blue in October 1947. She was one of four A4s chosen to receive a purple finish in June the following year. She carried this colour until 1950 when painted dark blue and then in February 1952 became a green engine. (RH)

influence of the Interchange Trials with remarkable candour when he wrote:

Thus the facts were established. The results of the tests could certainly have been used to support a case for adopting the existing LMS locomotives as they stood as the new standards if Riddles had wished to follow this course. But equally, nothing which emerged from the tests required us to hesitate in the resolve to produce a new series of locomotives combining in them the best of contemporary practice. While all this was happening Cox

had been busy formulating proposals for the new standard engines, 999 of which were ultimately built ... The whole trend would be towards simplification, good accessibility of all parts requiring attention and reduction in time required for repairs and servicing. But new designs should not be undertaken for their own sake and when an existing design offers all that is available from the present state of the art, it should be continued with only detailed modifications.

In the circumstances, this approach was probably all that could be

hoped for with so many restrictions in place and was clearly designed to see BR through some difficult times. It also allowed time to study and develop some viable diesel and electric alternatives and find the cash to pay for such a substantial modernisation programme.

In the meantime, BR's fleet of 20,000 plus steam locomotives would have to bear the brunt of the government's great expectations for the foreseeable future. Inevitably, this meant advertising and selling the services the railways had to offer and here adding a little glamour would not come amiss. Undoubtedly the best examples of this were the Pullman services

Perhaps one clear sign that the railways were returning to something near normal after the war was the return of glamour. The best example of this was probably the Pullman services. In austerity hit Britain they were an anachronism, but some still had money and were prepared to spend it on luxuries few others could afford. (Top) Here the Yorkshire Pullman plies its trade in the charge of a newly restored blue A4 (possibly No. 2 *Sir Murrough Wilson*). (Below) Garter blue and British Railways picked out in white on tenders were soon discarded in favour of new BR blue then green liveries, with four of the class briefly painted in an experimental purple in 1948. Green began to be applied in 1951 with BR's lion over a wheel crest on the tender. No. 60003 *Andrew K. McCosh*, pulling the Yorkshire Pullman, is captured here in her new green livery early in the 1950s. (BS)

and other high profile passenger trains, with their comfortable often regal fittings and their speed. In austerity hit Britain they were probably an anachronism, but some still had money and were prepared to spend it on luxuries few others could afford. But even though freight was a bigger money spinner than express passenger traffic, the glamorous trains were more likely to grab headlines and promote the business.

Some of these trains had been slowly restored to service in the aftermath of the conflict, when time and money could be found to reverse the effects of war time wear and tear. The most noteworthy of

these was the Yorkshire Pullman which first ran in 1935 on the Harrogate to King's Cross route and was suspended when war came. In late 1946 it was restored to service more often than not, or so it seems, pulled by an A4. But this proved to be a false dawn and within three months a national fuel crisis, coupled to an exceptionally cold winter, had caused it to be suspended again. Such was the parlous state of Britain at the time, and for that matter the LNER's finances, that the service wasn't restored for another eight months, just in time for Nationalisation. Aware of its potential in helping to sell BR, it was allowed to

continue and by 1950 had become so popular that it was formed of eleven carriages and could entertain more than 100 first class and 192 third class passengers. In this form it would survive until 1978, long outliving the A4s that had once been its mainstay.

In September 1948, this was followed by the Tees Tyne Pullman running between Newcastle and London which appears to have proved equally successful. Although the inaugural run was pulled by a brand new Peppercorn A1, No. 60115 *Meg Merrilies*, it seems that it was much more common to find an A4 heading the service. And as the market

The Tees-Tyne Pullman service was inaugurated in September 1948 and became a regular turn for the A4s, as shown here with No. 60003 *Andrew K. McCosh* again in charge. She was a King's Cross engine from 1941 to 1957. (BS)

The long distance, non-stop, high speed services so beloved of pre-war days were slow to be restored after the war. It is recorded that the most famous of these, the Flying Scotsman, only began again on 31 May 1948, perhaps encouraged by a Railway Executive eager to show that 'normal business had resumed'. This photo shows A4 No. 60012 *Commonwealth of Australia* passing through Newcastle in July that year. Two months earlier she had completed a period of general repair when her British Railways insignia had been applied having turned blue the previous August. Before the war she had been a Haymarket engine and would remain so until 1963. (RH)

for such things picked up, so BR quickly sought to publicise other fast express trains operating all over the UK. Perhaps the most famous of all these was the non-stop summer scheduled Flying Scotsman which began in June 1948 hauled by 60009 *Union of South Africa* and 60034 *Lord Faringdon*, fresh from the Interchange Trials.

However, it was not plain sailing that year because during August severe weather conditions caused much flooding particularly in North-East England and South-East Scotland severely damaging

the line North of Newcastle. This meant diversions were necessary, but due to the efforts of the crew and the strength of the A4s this service remained non-stop in both directions. By late September, repairs were complete and the usual service had been restored.

With the 1949 Summer season approaching, BR's managers began considering ways in which the service between King's Cross and Edinburgh might be improved. A faster schedule was one option and in May a test run, pulled by 60017 *Silver Fox*, was arranged.

One of the main concerns in doing this was the state of the track and its ability to withstand the higher speeds these services demanded. The damaging effects of over-use and reduced maintenance in wartime couldn't be ignored, so any added stresses imposed by the fast, heavy passenger services could not be ignored. So *Silver Fox* went through her paces and the ghosts of past glories were echoed when the engine ran down Stoke Bank hitting 102mph on the way. It was a feat that soon caught the attention of the Civil Engineers who, it seems, had advised caution. As a result, they quickly slapped a speed restriction on this and other services, which would only be raised as and when restoration work was completed. Such was the slow speed of progress that it would take until 1951 for the faster stretches to have the speed limit raised to 90mph.

As BR's managers slowly brought the four disparate companies together and tried to resolve many operating problems there was one event that all welcomed – the opening of the long planned Locomotive Test Centre at Rugby. It is probably true to say that no other major railway project

had taken quite so long to reach to fruition. Of course, the GWR under Churchward had realised the benefit of having such a facility early in the twentieth century and built their own at Swindon. And this the other companies had observed working with growing envy, noting the advantages it

On 19 October 1948, the Locomotive Testing Station at Rugby was finally opened by Alfred Barnes the Minister of Transport. It had been a long gestation reflecting the country's dire financial state for most of the 1929s and '30s and then the coming of war, but its supporters finally achieved their goal. Sadly, it probably came too late to be of real value, with steam's demise growing ever more likely each day. Despite this, the facility was gainfully employed for eleven years before being virtually mothballed in 1959 when steam locomotive testing drew to a close. This group of photos, from Bert Spencer's collection, captures the opening events on 19 October, with 60007 as centrepiece and being run up to 62mph on the rolling road. (Upper left on adjoining page) This picture is particularly interesting because it captures the various CMEs lined up behind and to the left of the Minister of Transport – Thompson, Riddles, Stanier, Peppercorn and Ivatt, but not Bulleid who was also there. (BS)

Even Gresley's rebuilt and streamlined W1, formerly No. 10000 now numbered 60700 but still unnamed, found a role in BR's fleet amongst the A4s and other Pacifics. Until withdrawn and scrapped in mid-1959 she was thought to be a good performer and worked many express passenger services, as shown here. (Above) at Potters Bar in the summer of 1947, according to Spencer's notes, having been painted garter blue late the previous year. (Opposite) Now painted in BR's Brunswick green. From 1942 until 1953 she was based at King's Cross but was then transferred to Doncaster for the last six years of her life. (BS)

gave Western engineers when creating or refining new or existing locomotives.

Gresley, in particular, had strongly advocated building such a facility to serve the LNER and enlisted the support of many, including Stanier, in this great endeavour. After years of campaigning, he finally achieved his aim and saw, in 1938, work begin on a facility to serve all companies should they need it. Unfortunately, the war intervened, and construction work did not get underway again until 1945/46, by which time Gresley was long dead and the need for such a

facility was growing less as plans for steam's demise were actively being pursued. Nevertheless, it was a moment to be celebrated and when it finally opened, A4 *Sir Nigel Gresley* was chosen for a demonstration run on the rolling road. To recognise Stanier's contribution to the project, his Coronation Pacific 46256 *Sir William A. Stanier FRS* was also present but was not test run on this or any other occasion, though sister engine No. 46225 *Duchess of Gloucester* would pass through the centre in 1955.

Many past and present CMEs were there – including Stanier, Thompson, Peppercorn, Bulleid, Ivatt and Riddles – and the event attracted wide press and newsreel coverage. And the A4 briefly went through her paces causing Bert Spencer to contemplate the past and consider the future. He later wrote:

It was a great shame Sir Nigel could not be present, but seeing his A4 go through its paces from close too was an experience that few who saw it would quickly forget. Thompson and I spoke at length during the day and reminisced about the past. A little later he asked Riddles if an A4 might soon undergo a prolonged period of testing to assess what it could really do. Riddles said he thought not, and when pressed about the other LNER Pacifics was similarly unresponsive. If anything he was more interested in the plans for standardisation that Thompson had been pursuing until retirement, in particular his express passenger and mixed traffic engines. They then debated the comparative merits of Thompson's A2/3s, the A4s and the other principal Pacific designs.

The Thompson B1s and Stanier Black Fives also came in for discussion, particularly the use of two cylinders, which Riddles clearly saw as a major bonus. So it did not surprise me that the classes of standard engines he later commended to the Railway Executive should all, with one exception (the 8P Pacific, which would have three) should be fitted with two-cylinders. I can't say I disagreed with this conclusion which, in the circumstances, seemed a reasonable one. It also fell in line with Windle's thoughts, having, as I did, seen how three worked, with or without Gresley's valve gear.

So, as the decade came to an end, BR continued its slow struggle for life, as senior managers tried to make some sense of all they had been bequeathed by the Big Four. The Railway Executive needed to develop a strategy that took account of a plethora of conflicting demands, but with money short, Riddles and Co settled on an unambitious plan that focussed on steam locomotives as motive power and little else. New standard engines would be built in great numbers allowing much of the inherited fleet to be discarded. But the best of the old, with considerable economic life left in it, would be allowed to continue until electric and diesel engines could take over at some unspecified time in the future. And so, as Spencer noted, 'Gresley's Pacifics carried on, their future certain for a time, though not their form. Windle, in particular still wished to make changes, though for a time he was deflected from doing so by the need to design and build the new standard engines in which he played a leading role'. In 1950, few probably believed that the A4s would survive the decade, let alone still be running express services into the mid-1960s. But the engines were exceptional and BR's ability to modernise hamstrung by circumstances often beyond their control.

THE A4s IN A CHANGING WORLD (1941–2022)

The changing face of the A4s is best summed up by the colour schemes that were introduced from 1941. Each reflected the nature of events or changing fashions (Top left) For wartime came a utilitarian black livery for all the A4s, here repeated on the recently restored *Sir Nigel Gresley*. (Top right) The same engine as she appeared when the A4s were restored to their former glory in the post war years. (Bottom left) BR brought with it a new numbering system and so *Sir Nigel Gresley* became No. 60007 and for a time ran in this striking blue livery with white and black lining. (Bottom right) Finally BR settled on a 'corporate' green as seen here on 60004 *William Whitelaw*. (THG)

Post-war, one of the clearest signs of a huge social change taking place was the rapid and irreversible rise of car ownership. Before the war, only a small percentage of the people could enjoy such a benefits. But this changed very quickly in the 1950s as a settled economy and higher wages provided the means and a burgeoning auto-industry provided the product to meet a growing consumer demand. The annual Motor Show at Earls Court was the car makers' show room and this stimulated sales even more. Aspiration turned to reality for many and so they began to choose road over rail in ever increasing numbers, aided by the growth in 'A' roads then motorways. (THG)

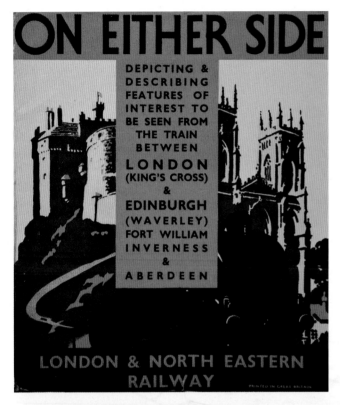

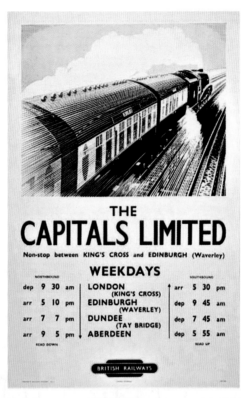

(**Top left** and top middle) For a short period after the war, before nationalisation, the A4s once again dominated the East Coast main line and featured large in advertising campaigns. When Hornby Dublo began production of their model trains, one of their best sellers was the *Sir Nigel Gresley* set. (Upper right and lower right) The big event of 1951 was the Festival of Britain on London's South Bank which, amongst other things, showcased many products of the country's industries. This included new steam locomotives and BR's plans for a range of standard classes, so providing an interesting juxtaposition with the modern world. (THG)

The 1950s were years of great change on the railways as BR's management sought to find long term solutions to many inherited problems. BR's Locomotive Standardisation Plan envisioned, amongst many things, new classes of Pacific, ostensibly building on the experience gained by the LNER, LMS and Southern Railway – a 6P, 7P and an 8P. With so many Pacifics already in service, and some diesel alternatives becoming available, this element of the Plan was possibly an unnecessary luxury. In the event, sixty-six of all three types were built (ten 6Ps, fifty-five 7Ps and one 8P), with fifteen more 6Ps later cancelled before construction could begin. Their impact was muted and there was little danger that they would replace any of the LNER's Pacifics and particularly the evergreen and, some would say, the greatly superior A4s. (Top) An artist's impression of the way the new Class 7P would look. (Below left)) BR Class 7P No. 70015 Apollo and (below right) the sole Class 8P 71000 *Duke of Gloucester*, provide an interesting illustration of the way Riddles and Co were moving with their standardisation plans. (THG)

THE
FLYING SCOTSMAN
1862 - 1962

While the Standardisation Plan was being enacted English Electric pressed on with their plans for diesels including its Deltic Co-Co prototype (top left the protototype Deltic - DP1- on display in the 1950s, bottom left the arrival of the Deltics was accompanied by extensive publocity as shown here). Following trials with the LMR, it found favour on the Eastern Region and twenty-two were ordered, with the first being delivered in 1961. With their arrival the death knell was sounded for the A4s. (Top right) A Class 55, now in BR blue, is captured passing through Doncaster, steam and the A4s now a distant memory. (Bottom right) 'Old and dirty steam locomotives' looked increasingly out of place in a modernising world as this scene, with A4 No. 60004 *William Whitelaw* at its centre, ably demonstrates. (BS/RH)

More often than not the fate of a locomotive had a random element to it. The survival of *Mallard* and *Sir Nigel Gresley* can easily be explained, but not so this group of four which seems to be more about being in the right place at the right time, though their condition would have undoubtedly been an issue. (Above left) 60004 *William Whitelaw* – cut up at the Motherwell Machinery and Scrap Co, Wishaw in 1966. (Above right) 60028 *Walter K. Whigham* cut up at Doncaster Works in 1963. (Below left) 60019 *Bittern* sold for preservation in September 1966. (Below right) 60009 *Union of South Africa* sold for preservation in June 1966. (RH/THG)

As diesels gradually took over their duties the remaining A4s found a sanctuary of sorts in Scotland where they would often be seen up to 1966, though towards the end mostly on 'Specials'. (Above left) 60034 *Lord Faringdon*, and (above right) 60006 Sir Ralph Wedgwood on duty in and around Edinburgh towards the end of their lives. 60034 will be scrapped in late 1966 and 60006 in late 1965. (Below left) 60024 *Kingfisher* involved with another Special this time for the Locomotive Club of Great Britain. (Below right) 60010 seemingly destined to be a pile of scrap metal will be restored externally and presented to the Canadian Railroad Historical Association for permanent display in Montreal during 1967. (THG)

Saved from the cutters torch and preserved for prosperity. For the enthusiast, there are six A4s still in existence to enjoy, four of which have been returned to steam. Sadly, the first of the class, *Silver Link*, is not one of them having been broken up at Doncaster in early 1963. The earliest surviving engine is 60007 (above left). Of course, the most famous A4, 60022/4468 *Mallard* (above right) was saved for the nation to become a key exhibit at York. (Lower left) 60019 *Bittern* photographed near Westbury when operating under the guise of 4492 *Dominion of New Zealand*, which itself had been scrapped in 1963 (Lower right) 60009 *Union of South Africa* near Westbury again. She remained a star performer until laid up in 2021, destined for static display, for the time being anyhow. (To the right) The never to be forgotten 'Great Gathering' of 2013 when all six survivors went on display to great public acclaim. (THG)

Chapter 3
AN INDIAN SUMMER

In 1950, after two years of hard work, BR's managers were beginning to bring some order to the running of the railways. But with political interference a daily occurrence, there was a danger that original thought might be stifled in favour of safe, quick fix solutions. Coal was still king as far as power generation, industry and domestic users were concerned, so Whitehall could do little else but promote its continued use. There was also the question of its extraction and movement to consider and the work it provided for huge numbers of men and women. This was an issue that could not be ignored or taken lightly, especially when the alternative, oil, still employed fairly few people in the UK. But things were slowly changing as the number of road vehicles increased feeding a demand for more and more oil. And so the requirement for coal began to decline, though it would take many decades for it to reach a state of obsolescence, aided by the need to reduce air pollution, to which the railways added considerably.

Here the 'Great Smog' of 1952, which descended on London with very serious health and safety consequences, played an active part. Although considered an inconvenience for many, the

periodic bouts of smog are thought to have exacerbated the health problems of those suffering from chronic heart and lung conditions. As a result, an additional 4,075 deaths were reported, though the number was considered by many in the medical profession to be nearer 10,000 or higher. In truth, air pollution had been a growing problem across many of Britain's towns and cities for many decades, but events in 1952 proved to be the trigger for change.

Extreme public pressure forced the government to take action, though their response was predictably tardy. Eventually, in the summer of 1953, a committee was set up under the chairmanship of Sir Hugh Beaver, the engineer and leading industrialist. Its remit was to investigate and consider any technical issues they could identify and recommend ways of improving air quality. Initial findings reported in December 1953 produced a list of quite

A sign of permanence – quickly applied hand painted 'British Railways' insignia on tenders gives way to a more identifiable BR branded emblem, backed up by a variety of new paint schemes applied to passenger engines. (THG)

Those who lived through the London smogs of the late Forties, Fifties and even into the Sixties, which frequently spread out over the Home Counties, will always remember them as very unpleasant 'pea soupers'. Unlike mists and fog, they were dense, choking and often impenetrable, making it difficult to breathe and making your eyes sting. Face masks, mostly of the self-help variety were essential, and buses could, on the worst days, be seen with their conductors walking in front with a torch or a lit flare so they didn't get lost or run into other vehicles and pedestrians. There were even stories of footplate crew on locomotives having to stop when they knew a signal was close by to climb up and see what it was registering. Such caution was necessary because fog was a contributory factor in a number of accidents, the Lewisham rail disaster of 1957 being the worst. The Great Smog of 1952 was the most serious, though, and its severity led to new anti-pollution legislation being introduced although it would take many years to have a real effect, during which one of the great polluters, steam locomotives, would face their demise. The photos above and the lower left, all taken in London in December 1952, clearly show the severity of the problems the Great Smog caused and its stagnating effect. Of particular note are barely visible factories in the East End of London and the problems faced by engines departing from King's Cross. The final photo shows the poor conditions faced by railway crew and the rescue services before and shortly after the Lewisham crash (RH).

simple interim measures which might lessen the impact of future smogs. These included warning the public, advising vulnerable citizens to wear masks and stay indoors and increasing the supply and encouraging the use of smokeless fuels. However, at this stage it fell far short of recommending meaningful and complex legislation to permanently eradicate the problem. If the government hoped for a quick fix by simply offering advice, they would be disappointed and pressure continued to grow for a more radical solution to be implemented. So the committee carried on working.

In November 1954, the committee finally completed work and issued a report that was for the time quite controversial. Its most important recommendation concerned the need for a 'Clean Air Act' which would provide clear and unambiguous anti-pollution legislation. This, it was hoped, would establish a framework for determining which fuels could be burnt in new 'Smoke Controlled Areas.' A critical feature of the Beaver Committee's work was that control in these areas should be applied equally to both industrial and domestic users. After two more years of deliberation and discussion, in which those supporting British produced fossil fuels actively campaigned for minimal change, the Clean Air Act was finally passed into law in July 1956. For a country so heavily reliant on coal this was a significant moment in time and heralded a huge transformation in the way the country was run and how people lived. Needless to say, such a huge programme would prove difficult

to implement politically, financially and culturally and take a long time to enact. But the die had been cast and with strong legislation at its core, with much more to follow, opposition would gradually fade away.

Smogs became a regular feature of everyday life for many years, increasingly irksome and invariably dangerous to live with. As a schoolboy living in London, I remember them well – the inability to breathe when they were at their worst, the constant griminess of your clothes and any skin or hair exposed to the sulphurous pollution. You got used to it, as you did the loss of bearings in familiar streets and roads, but it was a cloying, foul environment in which to live and you longed for it to lift so you could see the sky

again. So it isn't surprising that public pressure eventually forced the political hand and a slow, ponderous programme was set in motion. The consequences of this for industry as a whole and the railways in particular would be profound indeed.

While this happened, coal continued to dominate the railways and the government continued to baulk at anything but steam locomotion, lacking the money and political will to introduce cleaner forms of motive power. But they did find money to finance other matters of great public concern, ever aware of the problems that beset their forebears in parliament after the First World War when Lloyd George's emotive words 'a land fit for heroes' was exposed for what it was – jingoistic nonsense. And

The early years of nationalisation would see few visible signs of change on Britain's railways, as this picture of Peppercorn A1 Pacific No. 60119 *Patrick Stirling* and Grantham based A4 No. 60026 *Miles Beevor* reveals. Steam still dominated, as it did the design work of the old Big Four companies. For the LNER, this meant Gresley, Thompson and Peppercorn Pacifics continuing to dominate the Eastern Region network. The last of these, A1 No. 60161 *North British*, was completed at Doncaster in December 1949. (RH)

this was followed by two decades of recession and immense social upheaval as 'the heroes' fought for equal rights and better living and working conditions. Sadly, these hopes were often dashed by one financial crisis after another, though some progress was made. Needless to say, after nearly six years of another sacrifice and hardship much more was expected in 1945.

This time there would be no repeat of false promises only people being urged to work hard for the common good and, hopefully, a better future. But this time there would be the benefit of a safety net – growing health and welfare services to help people survive during some difficult years. And by 1950 many saw their lives improve with high employment rates in evidence and more money to spend as a result, although rationing would still exist for a few more years yet and only end in 1954.

Consumerism, although a long-understood concept by those with disposable incomes, was now growing more commonplace as the economy revived and wages gradually rose. So it was unsurprising when home ownership began increasing exponentially each year as did car ownership, with nearly three million privately owned vehicles on the roads by 1955. Another sign of increasing affluence could also be seen in the number of homes possessing a television which in 1953 was estimated to be over 2½ million, with the number continuing to rise rapidly. Shopping habits were also changing as luxury items and consumables became more freely available. And in 1948, the first supermarket opened setting

a trend that soon spread more widely feeding an ever-growing demand for products unseen for many years, if ever.

Here developments to meet wartime operational needs quickened the pace of progress with science and industry continuing this level of innovative research and development now fed by growing consumer demand. So buyers could now choose from a range of new and updated products and services, with state of the art cars, TVs, refrigerators and other kitchen gadgets and new medicines to speed the treatment of many illnesses amongst them.

The 1951 Festival of Britain on London's South Bank became synonymous with this period of reconstruction and modernisation. The festival provided a platform for architects, engineers and artists, amongst others, to show off their new products and hint at what might be waiting in the wings to tempt consumers eager for the latest products. For a people used to wartime austerity, it was a revelation and one that soon echoed widely, with particular emphasis on the use of new materials and the careful mix of art and science in these designs.

During the war, plastics had been essential in producing military equipment such as waterproof tents, goggles, parachutes, electric wiring and parts of weapons. As demand for these wartime items faded, factories making these synthetic products moved into the domestic market and during the 1950s the impact of these changed priorities began to be felt more widely. Materials such as PVC (polyvinyl chloride), fibreglass, melamine,

aluminium and vinyl were now used to produce a whole range of products including such things as kitchen utensils, plastic crockery, furniture and even polythene bags all of which transformed domestic life, feeding a need for more in the process.

In 1944, kitchen necessities had been listed as a sink, draining board, working surface, ventilated larder, and cupboards. Ten years later, in 1954, the most coveted kitchen goods were refrigerators, washing machines, electric cookers and stainless-steel sinks. By then, reliable electricity supplies reached most of the United Kingdom, giving a boost to the ever-growing demand for new electric products.

During the 1920s and '30s, radio, the cinema and an ever-increasing number of magazines had become central to the spread of news, but this media had also become a strong lifestyle influence. Businesses of all types offering all sorts of services could advertise their products in a more meaningful way and easily reach millions in the process. In the early 1950s this effect simply grew and grew, with television gradually adding an even stronger focus. And all this was greatly assisted by the launch of the Independent Television company (ITV) in 1955, with its very heavy emphasis on advertising and product placement. This meant that viewers could now be tempted into buying household goods and a variety of services from the comfort of their homes, drawn by an array of programmes deliberately designed to attract an audience from all walks of life. It was a model spawned in the USA that would soon embed itself in the psyche of British life.

The Festival of London in 1951 was to be a celebration of a new, post-war Britain, but it became a focus for people's aspirations after the suffering of two world wars and years of poor living conditions. By itself, it didn't raise expectations but did tap into a mood of dissatisfaction with the way things were and fed an ambition for much more. Although steam locomotives played a part in the exhibitions it was obvious that they were a symbol of the past and their going wasn't a matter of if, but when. This was made patently clear when seen beside more recently introduced diesel and electric locomotives. In this case, there was one of the first Standard Pacifics, No. 70004 *William Shakespeare*, sitting close to the Southern Region's 1950 built diesel-electric Co-Co locomotive No. 10201 and the Eastern Region's newly constructed Bo-Bo electric engine No. 26020 which was built to operate over the Sheffield-Manchester-Wath line. (THG)

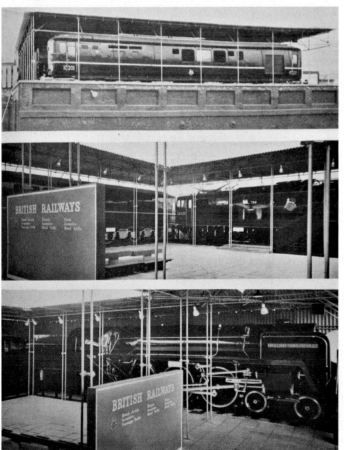

The modern world with some of its many attractions as seen through the eyes of advertisers eager to sell their products – cars, goods, modern locomotives and the growing allure of commercial aviation. In the 1950s, flying was a dream for most but quickly became a reality that would within two decades begin to strip the railways of many customers. (THG)

Once this Pandora's box of delights had been opened, expectations were quickly raised and people began to demand more than the regurgitation of an old way of living. And so, the consumer world that had begun to see the light of day before the war snuffed it out now grew more intense. There might be some nostalgia for what had gone, with rose-tinted spectacles colouring collective memories, but the demand for what could be was even stronger. Inevitably, many people looked with a deeply critical eye at their homes, their schools, their workplaces, the old, grimy transport systems that kept their lives moving and the environments in which they lived and wanted

and deserved better and when they could see bright, new, state of the art alternatives becoming available, they longed for cleaner, more modernistic lives.

It is probably true to say that Britain's crumbling and dilapidated steam locomotive-based system hardly met these expectations. Its many long-suffering users would probably have agreed with a report collected by the Weaver Commission:

The pollution created by the railways is not only a contributory factor to the very high level of pollution found in all areas of the country, but also makes the service most unpleasant for its customers. There is little doubt that its reliance on steam motive power, although understandable in the circumstances that prevail at this time, is undoubtedly something that must end if pollution is to be reduced to a manageable level and the service made more attractive to the travelling public. Complete electrification must be the goal as soon as possible, with diesel power being an interim measure only.

Despite all the problems they faced, trade on the railways continued to blossom. In part this was because industrial production was picking up and people had more money to spend but, just as importantly, Britain's road network could not handle the volume of traffic to provide a viable alternative. In effect, BR held the whip hand and would continue to be the main provider of the country's transport

needs no matter what powered its trains. When the government finally committed itself to a massive road building programme, particularly new motorways, things would change, but at the dawn of the 1950s this was a dream yet to be realised. However, an experimental section of motorway, called the Preston Bypass at the time, had opened in 1958, and its success led to an accelerated construction programme. A year later, the first 50 mile section of the M1 opened and by 1969 the network had expanded to 1,000 miles and continued to grow.

In trying to assess how popular these roads might become, the Ministry of Transport predicted in 1960 that the M1's annual usage would peak at 14,000 vehicles a day. The reality was very different. Fifty

years later usage had risen year by year to ten times that number, with the size and power of heavy goods vehicles also growing larger each year, supported by a booming motor industry. In 1950, loads in excess of 15 tons were unusual, whereas by 1970 this had risen to 30 tons and continued to climb. As this happened, so trade on the railways diminished, and to make matters worse, the growth of car ownership began to affect passenger traffic, even the lucrative commuter services – both long and short distant. In the fifties, this had become a staple part of BR's business, especially with a boom in holiday traffic and now all this was slipping away.

So, by the beginning of the 1950s, with their position in

Although fascinating to view from any angle, a typical steam locomotive shed was a dirty and dangerous place to work. As a result, during the 1950s BR began to have serious recruitment and retention problems as cleaner and better paid jobs grew in number. This was especially so in the big cities. This photo of King's Cross, captured here in the 1950s with A4 No. 60022 *Mallard* easily identifiable, with others lurking anonymously in the background, sums up the apparent industrial squalor but also the enthralling atmosphere of a main line engine shed for the casual visitor. (BS)

Britain's transport system secure, but still wholly reliant on steam locomotives, BR were able to drum up sufficient trade to turn in a small working profit. But in proposing to build more steam locomotives, rather than invest in newer technologies, Britain would fall further behind more forward-thinking countries in Europe, where dieselisation and electrification advanced more rapidly. This despite the equally parlous state of finances in France, Germany, Italy, amongst others and, in some cases, the availability of home produced coal in great quantities.

It is easy to see that there were political pressures in Britain that encouraged the Railway Executive to stick with an aging technology, but there also seems to have been something else in play – part emotional and part cultural. To some, there appeared an inability to

For the railway enthusiast, the creation of BR made for some interesting inter-regional bedfellows and allowed them to make a very direct comparison between designs of the Big Four engines. This is very apparent in this photograph of two A4s. 60005 *Sir Charles Newton* and possibly 60008 *Dwight D. Eisenhower*, and ex- LMS Jubilee Class engine No. 45597 *Barbados*. (BS)

let steam go. Bert Spencer, who was well placed to comment, probably came closest to describing this phenomenon when he wrote:

It was easy to see why the Labour Government of Clement Attlee did not want to reduce the demand for coal in favour of imported oil. Doing so might have affected the country's balance of payments deficit and potentially caused an increase in unemployment rates at a critical time. Yet the Minister of Transport was able to approve a massive investment in so many more standard steam locomotives, when the money might have been better spent on a number of diesel and electric projects.

By 1950, the technology for both was well established, as witnessed by the Southern with their growing network

of third rail electrics, the LMS with their diesel engines and the old LNER with mainline and goods electric locomotives as well as electric commuter trains in various locations. The existing fleet of locomotives could easily have coped whilst the changeover was taking place. There was also the issue of companies such as English Electric who had been working in the diesel field for some time and making huge advances in the engines they were producing. It was obvious to many that they were other companies in Britain who could have assisted BR in designing and building a new diesel, electric or even gas turbine powered motive power fleet. We could also have looked overseas, as Gresley did, and absorbed the lessons being learnt in France, Germany, Spain, the Netherlands and Italy. In each country giant steps were being taken which offered us many working examples to study in the years after the war. But all this appears to have been ignored in favour of more steam locomotives, which if allowed to have fulfilled expected economic lives of 33 to 35 years will still be running in 1980s.

Despite all this Riddles was doggedly determined to stay with steam and held firm to his belief that diesels would be too expensive to build and run, by comparison. But he also revealed another motive during a number of conversations with me and others, which for a man like myself, who was brought up with steam, is not hard to

understand. He felt that it still had much to offer and had not reached the full extent of its development and potential. This created a suspicion that Riddles and his senior managers were too attached to steam and simply did not wish to give a familiar and much liked technology up. They ceased to be impartial and so took BR down a path of stagnation not modernisation, backed by Government concerns over the economy.

Wherever the truth might lie, Riddles and the Railway Executive decided to continue ordering more

While BR struggled to make headway in modernising its motive power fleet, preferring to remain with steam for the foreseeable future, the French forged ahead with a massive electrification programme that began before the war. (Top) In 1949 this development programme resulted in this Co-Co CC 7001 electric locomotive for use on long distance fast express services along the main routes across France. In trials this engine was recorded reaching 105.6mph (and six years later CC 7107 and BB 9004 would top 205mph), a speed which it was designed to sustain (58 of these locomotives would be built by 1955). (Lower) By 1951 work on a number of main lines was well advanced and that year the Le Mistral service between Paris and Marseilles was inaugurated to great acclaim (in this case pulled by 2D2 9103, one of 35 built). (THG)

While the government controlled SNCF investing heavily in electrification after the war, building on development work begun in the 1930s, Britain's railways played safe by building more steam locomotives and stagnated as far as modernisation was concerned. While the magnificence of steam could not be denied, as A4 No. 60032 *Gannet* clearly demonstrates, BR's policy was deeply flawed and took no account of the way society was advancing and the growing impact of alternative forms of transport. (THG)

steam locomotives on a massive scale, instead of speculating on what they thought was still untried technology. So, between 1948 and 1953, they approved the construction of 1,487 new standard and inherited classes of locomotives, with the last of them rolling out of the works at Swindon in 1960. They did counterbalance this by withdrawing and scrapping a large number of the older, probably less efficient steam engines, but overall they missed an opportunity to begin modernising Britain's railways when their European neighbours were taking giant steps forward. And so it remained until the mid-1950s,

when it became crystal clear how short-sighted this policy had been. By then British Railways were in trouble as an ever-growing deficit in its finances quickly revealed. Traffic, particularly in freight haulage, was being lost to the roads and an increasing amount to a rapidly expanding commercial air fleet. As a result, the government ordered an urgent top to bottom review of the way the railways were run and how they might be brought into the modern age.

In December 1954, a report entitled *Modernisation and Re-Equipment of the British Railways* was published. By comparison to BR's earlier effort, it embraced new

technology more wholeheartedly and so its recommendations were genuinely more far seeing. Acceptance of its recommendations followed and in 1956 a government white paper set the seal on the plan which, it was hoped would help eliminate BR's financial deficit by 1962. The aim was to increase speed, reliability, safety and line capacity, through a series of measures that would make services more attractive to passengers and freight operators, thus recovering traffic that was being lost to the roads. The total cost of the plan was projected to be £1.24 billion (approximately £29 billion in 2020), with the key areas of development being:

- Electrification of principal main lines, in the Eastern Region, Kent, Birmingham and Central Scotland.
- Large-scale dieselisation to replace steam locomotives.
- New passenger and freight rolling stock.
- Resignalling and track renewal.
- Closure of small number of lines which were seen as unnecessary in a nationalised network, as they duplicated other lines.
- Building of large freight marshalling yards, with automated shunting to streamline freight handling.

The strengths and weaknesses of this report and the White Paper that followed have long been discussed and in some quarters condemned for lack of ambition. There were also mutterings that the authors failed to appreciate how the profoundly BR's market was changing – both passenger and freight. But at least it did begin a long-delayed move to a modernised rail network.

It also demanded a huge injection of cash to fund all proposals. For example, a total of 2,500 locomotives for mainline service were to be procured over ten years at a cost of £125 million, with more to follow as the steam fleet was run down. Then there was the replacement of large parts of pre-war passenger rolling stock, plus the addition of 5,000 diesel or electric multiple units at an estimated cost of £285 million. Beyond this it set out an ambitious plan to electrify all the major routes, important secondary lines and the remainder of the suburban network. This called for the purchase of 1,100 electric locomotives at £60 million, with £125 million added to cover the costs of upgrading the infrastructure to take these trains. With this element of the plan to be enacted at some time in the future, it was essential that there be an adequate stop-gap in place. The only way of doing this was to maintain the steam fleet until sufficient numbers of diesels were available allowing withdrawal to begin.

And so the death knell for steam was heard by many for the first time and the folly of Riddles' steam building plans were laid bare. Within twelve years all would be gone, with many new standard engines being scrapped when virtually new. Even the older engines such as the A4s would depart the scene with another twenty or so years of life left in them, such was the ineffectual way in which Britain's railways were managed after nationalisation.

The sage and ever present Spencer probably captured the essence of this issue best when he wrote that:

It is always best to remember that you can't hold back change. Even if you cannot embrace it fully for good practical reasons you can at least plan it sensibly and expose comparative costs and the risks involved in doing or not doing something. By this stage Cost–benefit analysis was a technique widely used within the LNER offices mostly because it made you stand back and consider the strengths and weaknesses of alternatives.

When considering the future it seems to me that Riddles simply took the line of least resistance and plumped for steam. It was a measure of political expediency, not sensible long term planning. He and those around him should have been bolder and demanded more from the Minister of Transport and the BTC than simply more of the same.

Later, having thought deeply about the way BR was run in its early years, he added a few telling sentences about the way Gresley

While plans for the future of BR slowly lurched forward the network continued to depend on a comparatively small number of drivers and fireman to keep the trains running safely and on time. The skills needed to do this, in an age before many safety and operational aids were in common use while working in the most difficult and dirty conditions, are rarely appreciated though truly astounding in their complexity. These anonymous heroes, one of whom is portrayed here with his mount, made sure that BR kept running despite its tardiness in embracing the future and lethargy in providing a cleaner, safer and less exhausting working environment. (THG)

would have managed in this situation:

I was lucky enough to see the CME's ideas on electrification finally come to fruition after the war and see his influence continue to spread. Whilst his steam locomotives clearly pleased him I have no doubt that he would have been proud to have witnessed the Shenfield line open and the electric locomotives he planned come in to service and move Britain's railways into the future.

I think Gresley would have been a far better man to have shaped BR when it was formed in 1948 if blessed with good health. Although in his early 70s by then he would have grasped the need to develop electric and diesel alternatives and not simply have built more and more steam locomotives as Riddles did. He was a practical man and a pragmatist who took change in his stride and would have fought for more efficient and effective solutions.

We shall never know if Britain's railways would have been better served by a man of his undoubted skill and vision. Like Riddles, Bond and Cox, during his life steam was the only practical option – coal was cheap and plentiful and fuelled the economy let alone locomotives. But unlike these men, he does not seem to have been wedded to this ageing technology, as his seminal work on electric alternatives had proven. True, he had inherited the basics of an electrification programme from Vincent Raven and the North Eastern Railway in 1923, only to see it shelved for lack of money following amalgamation. But when the political and financial climate changed in the 1930s, and the National Grid had grown strong enough to provide the

Although pursuing an active steam locomotive programme in the last decade of his life, Gresley increasingly focussed his efforts on electrification projects, seeing them as the way ahead. In this he was ably assisted by Henry Richards, a noted authority in this field, who he astutely recruited in the 1920s. Their work resulted in two major development projects, which, but for the war, would have begun the transformation of the LNER and set the pattern for future developments. Unfortunately, he died before either project was completed, with the war delaying the opening of the first of them, the electrification of the line from Liverpool Street to Shenfield, until 1949, as portrayed here. (THG)

The creation of the electrified line from Sheffield to Manchester was probably more important than the Liverpool Street to Shenfield project, because it experimented with engines that could be used more widely for express and freight services across the network. Two classes of locomotive were built – fifty-eight Bo-Bo EM1/BR Class 76s and seven Co-Co EM 2/ Class 77s. The long-delayed line was fully operational in 1955, a very long time after its inception by Gresley and the LNER, but in time to greet BR's re-worked Modernisation Plan that finally addressed life after steam. Four EM1s are captured at the Wath Motive Power Depot in 1952. The cleanliness and ease of working with electric engines is only too apparent; all a far cry from life in a steam shed. (BS)

energy needed, Gresley was quick to begin exploiting its potential with two new schemes and more undoubtedly planned.

The first of these involved the LNER's heavily graded Woodhead Line across the Pennines from Sheffield to Manchester and Wath, which had become a major route for carrying coal, with passenger numbers increasing each year. The second focussed on commuter routes from Liverpool Street to Shenfield in Essex.

The cost of developing the commuter line was estimated at £3.4m, with an outlay spread over a four or five years period. It was hoped that this would increase traffic by about 30-40 per cent and reduce running costs by a third. The Pennine link produced similar figures making both projects capable of a return on the investment in a 10 to 12 year period.

In forming his ideas on locomotives and carriages to populate both lines, Gresley sought advice and support from Metropolitan-Vickers, English Electric and Metropolitan-Cammell, amongst others. As a result of this joint effort, it was decided that three different types of engine would be needed for the Pennine route – mixed traffic, express passenger and banking locomotives, with sixty-nine, nine and ten being considered necessary for the three tasks. At the same time, a study to consider the commuter trains needed for service in Shenfield resulted in a plan for three car multiple units, a hundred of which were deemed necessary – ninety two for London and eight for use on the Manchester to Glossop section of the Woodhead Line.

The first batch of electric locomotives for the Pennine route were commissioned in 1937, but the coming of war and problems with the design contrived to delay the appearance of the first locomotive, No. 6701, until August 1940. However, war also put paid to the line's construction which was soon suspended 'for the duration', though this did not stop the testing of the new engine until October 1941. The project was resurrected after the war, but it would not be until 1955 that the entire line opened.

By September 1939 long planning delays had also affected progress on the Shenfield line. The reasons for this are unclear, though may have stemmed from checks and balances being applied by the Minister of Transport who was part-funding the work. The result was that LNER managers felt unable to sign the contract allowing construction to begin in 1939. With war only a few months away further delays were inevitable, and little had been completed before Germany invaded Poland. It would be ten more years before the project was completed, but work on developing the new multiple units had advanced quite a long way before this postponement became a reality. By this time, it is thought that six units were all but complete and these were subsequently placed in store, somewhere in the Midlands, painted in a blue and cream livery, awaiting the outcome of the conflict. They would remain there untried and untested until the war's end when the project was resurrected by the LNER.

Although these two electrification projects were only a small part of Gresley's work, their contribution to Britain's railway history was out of all proportion to their number. In their functionality and practicality, they embraced the future, seeing beyond the end of the steam and, for that matter, dieselisation as well. In the work he did in bringing electrification projects to the fore, Gresley set down a worthy example that BR could well have followed post-1948, rather than take the course they did.

So, perhaps Spencer was right in his assertion that Gresley, or someone with his skills and vision, would have been better placed to lead BR in 1948 than Riddles. But it was not to be and valuable time was lost in modernising motive power in Britain. This despite the examples the LNER had set in producing a modern electrified network and Ivatt and the LMS's work on diesels. Then there was the Southern Railway's not inconsiderable contribution to the future with their own third rail electrification projects, which Oliver Bullied added to with three experimental Co-Co electric locomotives during the war. During trials these engines produced a significantly higher Drawbar Horse

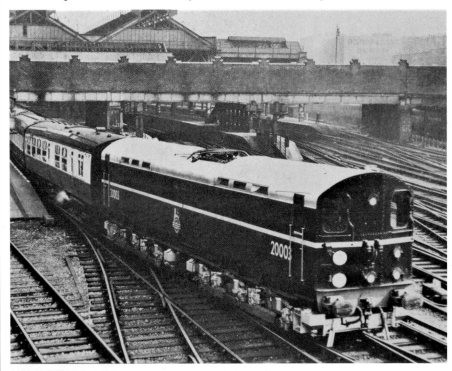

While Gresley experimented with electrification and Ivatt with diesels, Bulleid crossed both boundaries with two groups of new locomotives. One of these was a Co-Co electric design (Right) specifically for use on the Southern Region's third rail network and the other a diesel Co-Co (Below) for more general main line duties. Three of each type were built, but in BR's new world did not find favour despite the advanced nature of their designs. (JC)

Power than either his heavy or light Pacifics (2235 DBHP compared to 1755 and 1392 DBHP respectively). It was a worthy experiment, which Riddles also seems to have ignored, as he did Bulleid's work in designing three Co-Co diesels for mainline duties, two of which appeared in 1950/51 and the third in 1954.

With so much happening in the corridors of power and so much being promised, a visitor to King's Cross in the early 1950s, or any of the other major rail centres around Britain for that matter, might have expected that these machinations might have had some visible effect. But more of the same isn't modernisation, of course, and steam continued to dominate most services across the country. It worked as efficiently as it could, but the technology was labour intensive and expensive to operate, no matter how much coal was available and how low its price. It was also becoming a relic in a rapidly modernising world that demanded much more, especially from its creaking transport system. But with a modernisation plan that perpetuated steam, the old and well-established had to be exploited as best it could. And here the sleek and visually appealing A4s again found themselves in the forefront of BR's efforts to sell its services.

More often than not, it was simply a case of producing an eye-catching poster or publicity material for a particular service, with the Flying Scotsman top of the list. Then there were reports in the press describing their achievements and sparkling performances when these occurred – a leftover from

GIANTS REFRESHED

"PACIFICS" IN THE DONCASTER LOCOMOTIVE WORKS

their great days in the 1930s, but still capable of attracting press attention two decades later. And to top all this, an A4 service was chosen in 1953 to be the subject of a feature film made for general release in cinemas across Britain.

Produced by British Transport Films it was designed to advertise the newly created Coronation-related 'Elizabethan' service, but in such a way that everyone who contributed to the running of the railways was given credit for their work.

Faced with a sharp decline in their trade, as passengers and freight moved on to Britain's ever expanding road network, BR tried to boost business by a series of active advertising campaigns. With little modern to tap in to the PR department fell back on the glamorous locomotives of old, with the A4s again taking centre stage, as this advert of the 1950s reveals. Although its streamlined shape was very familiar, and their deeds well known, the class still had a modern, racy look which continued to appeal. With thity-four, plus W1, still in service there were sufficient numbers to provide a continuous presence along the East Coast Mainline on all the important services and much else besides. (BS)

The Coronation of Queen Elizabeth in 1953 was widely celebrated, none more so than on the railways. Here the Flying Scotsman pulled by A4 No. 60006 *Sir Ralph Wedgwood* has been suitably decorated for the occasion. (RH)

When released in 1954 the BTF film *Elizabethan* struck a familiar chord with those in the audience who remembered the pre-war Silver Link and Coronation services, plus *Mallard's* world record run of '38. After many years of war and austerity, it must have seemed that normality was returning, and good times were there to be enjoyed. This was a message the film heavily emphasized as did the presence of Gresley's A4 60017 *Silver Fox* at the head of the train. At a time when road traffic was eating away at the railways, it gave a timely reminder that the railways still provided a fast, comfortable and modern service for those wishing to travel long distances. To my mind, the most important part of the film is its focus on the people who made the railways work, not least of all the footplate crew and staff in sheds and workshops, whose working lives were hard, dirty and highly skilled. Bert Spencer kept a number of 'stills' from the movie which he inscribed with some of the names of those appearing in the film, particularly the footplate crew who are seen changing places using a corridor tender first introduced in the 1928. So we see Driver Marrable and Fireman Russell (or possibly Ruffel) manning the engine from King's Cross, then Driver McCleod and Fireman Scot taking over for the second phase of the journey to Edinburgh, and through them get a brief insight into their tough but honourable world. In many ways, this film tries to capture the spirit of *Night Mail* which appeared in 1934 and portrayed the work of the LMS on film. This time there would be no recitation of W H Auden's moving *Night Mail,* but a more jaunty, even comic, commentary in verse written by Paul le Saux. (BS)

It was an ambitious plan that might easily have missed the mark, but it succeeded in portraying the railways in a positive light and reflected the changing nature of society in the 1950s as Britain seems to have set the woes of the previous decades to one side. There is an optimistic feeling that things are getting better and will continue improving. So it is hardly surprising that Harold McMillan, who became Prime Minister in 1957, would utter the immortal words 'most people have never had it so good' when describing a growing affluence in many households across Britain at the time. True or not, and some have questioned McMillan's bold statement, there were changes in spending patterns with many

having disposable income for the first time, with railway passenger services being one beneficiary of this 'mini boom'.

Though deeply evocative in the way it captures a time very familiar to me but now long gone, I believe the true value of this film lies in its portrayal of life for employees of the railways at the time. In many ways, it hadn't changed a great deal in a hundred years or so and reflected the sheer physical effort required by footplate crew and maintenance staff to keep the railways running. The locomotives may have been more basic in the 1850s, with few creature comforts such as enclosed cabs to provide some protection against the elements, but the degree of effort required to keep them going had changed very little.

And for this level of commitment, they often paid a heavy price. Working long hours in extremely polluted, exhausting conditions did little for their health or safety, as accident reports and medical records bear stark witness. Theirs was a dangerous and largely unregulated business with as high a rate of industrial illnesses and accidents as any other industry in Britain, except, perhaps, mining. For example, during 1910, 30,000 work place deaths and injuries were recorded on Britain's railways, a number that did not include industrial illnesses. Although there was some improvement by 1950, the number had not reduced significantly, despite pressure from the Trades Unions and other groups to introduce safer working practices and the enactment of updated Factories Acts. The truth is that the dangers inherent in this heavy industry were difficult to reduce while steam dominated the railways.

A new standard 7P
Pacific, No. 70008
Black Prince, early in her
career. Inevitably these
engines were compared
unfavourably to the A4s,
and the later Pacifics
built by the LNER, when
operating in the Eastern
Region. This comparison
was not entirely a fair
one because the new
engines were registered
as fast mixed traffic
locomotives with wide
route availability. So a
fairer comparison would
have been the rebuilt
Royal Scots, Bulleid's
light Pacifics and the
GWR Castles which were
closer in power output to
the Britannia's. (BS)

By the time the Elizabethan was being filmed, many aspects of life on the old LNER had not changed a great deal, despite its loss of status as an independent company. The new corporate brand had been applied, but as Spencer later recorded:

[Most people] were waiting for something definite to happen and the way modernisation plans might affect their jobs. It seemed inevitable that the number of workshops would be cut and people be made redundant, but no one seemed to know when or if this might happen. It was a time of huge uncertainty made tolerable, to a certain extent, by the continuing construction

of new locomotives and the maintenance of the existing fleet. Harrison could offer the workforce no reassurance that all would be well and tried his best to keep morale as high as possible, but to no avail.

And so the months quickly passed, as did Harrison's time at Doncaster, with the first of the standard engines appearing in January 1951 to attract headlines and much interest and discussion in the industry.

As a Pacific, it would inevitably be scrutinised very closely and compared to similar types of engines already in service across the network, particularly the A4s, as Spencer recalled:

I accompanied engine No. 70000, *Britannia*, the first of the new Class of Pacifics, on a trip from Crewe and Carlisle in January 1951, when pulling slightly in excess of 440 tons. My first impression was that it was a good engine, even when still running in, but would struggle to compete with an A4 even one that was badly worn. Later on I witnessed one under test at Rugby and accompanied many others when working out of Liverpool Street Station into East Anglia, so was able to gain even wider experience of the type in different conditions. This included fuel economy, riding quality, maintaining a high average speed on steep gradients, ease of maintenance for crew, shed and workshop staff, pulling power and so on. This confirmed me in the belief that they were in many ways better than Bulleid's Pacifics heavy and light in their original condition, though not necessarily the rebuilds, a reasonable match for the Coronation Pacifics, but fell far short of the A4s in all categories except, perhaps, cost of maintenance.

Several drivers I spoke to, who had worked both types regularly used the analogy that the A4s were Rolls Royce's, while the Britannia's were good basic four door family Fords. From my own experience I think it a fair comparison.

With so many LNER Pacifics available to cover main line services to the North of England and Scotland, there was little need for BR's fifty-five new Pacifics to work these lines. So, a more direct

comparison between the types was never really necessary. In contrast, the LMS's Pacific fleet, of only fifty-one engines (fifty from 1952 when 46202 was written off following the Harrow and Wealdstone rail disaster) was considerably smaller so the new Crewe built 7Ps became a regular feature of life on the West Coast main lines until the end of steam on the network. Here, according to Brian Haresnape in his book *Ivatt and*

Riddles Locomotives they 'performed some of their best work'.

While production of the new standard fleet gradually advanced, the senior management of the various regional teams underwent change. Some of this was due to the departures of Bulleid in late 1949 and then George Ivatt in June 1951, but in other cases changes were initiated by Riddles, who was eager to break down some of the barriers

The summer of 1953 and the Up Elizabethan, hauled by A4 No. 60011 *Empire of India*, passes an express near Potters Bar with Peppercorn A1 No. 60117 *Bois Roussel* in charge. With so many Pacifics available, the running department was spoilt for choice which meant that the A4s were not automatically rostered to the premier services. (RH)

During the war years, the A4s found themselves undertaking all sorts of duties both passenger and freight – utilitarian locomotives in the truest sense. In the post-war years, they were restored to main line express work, but on occasions they could be found carrying out mixed-traffic turns. In this case, it appears to be No.60020 *Guillemot* working a fast freight in the early 1950s. (RH)

(Left) John 'Freddie' Harrison and (right) Kenneth John Cook who jointly led the Eastern Region's Mechanical and Electrical team from 1949 to 1959. Each man approached the tasks at hand in different ways, reflecting their different personalities, but both seemed to have been effective leaders. Spencer described them as being 'Jacks of all trades', a reference to their production engineering background. He then added that 'neither man had been exposed to design matters to any great extent during their careers and came to rely heavily on the Chief Draughtsman and his staff for guidance and advice. Where Cook excelled was in his ability to carefully analyse performance and, by using the techniques he had learnt at Swindon of applying precision engineering techniques, making engines work better and more reliably in the process.' *(RH)*

created by partisan attitudes in the regional teams he'd inherited. For staff in the old LNER this meant the departure of Harrison to Derby to replace Ivatt and the arrival of Kenneth Cook, for many years a major influence on the life of the GWR, as Mechanical and Electrical Engineer at Doncaster (a title altered to Chief M&EE on 1 January 1955). After a brief handover from Harrison, he took up his new post in July 1951. It proved to be an inspired move.

Since Peppercorn's retirement, Harrison had worked hard to bring his team into the new BR world. This had proved to be a difficult, time-consuming task which had severely tested his abilities at times. During these difficult months he completed the construction of the last LNER Pacifics and actively participated in the standardisation programme, overseeing some of the design work at Doncaster, then preparing the way for production

of some of these engines to begin in his region. But of rather more pressing concern was the state of the existing fleet of locomotives over which 'there was still cause for some concern, especially engines with Gresley's conjugated valve gear' as Spencer later related. It was a problem that would tax him and Cook for some time to come.

Cook was born in the Weston area of Bath in August 1896, the third of Walter, a wholesale clothing manufacturer, and Kate's four children. Coming from a relatively wealthy background, his parents chose to have him educated at King Edward VI School in the city. At 16, when his time there was drawing to a close, his developing interest in mechanical engineering convinced him that becoming a Premium Apprentice at the GWR's Swindon Works was the best way forward. Here he quickly came under influence of George Churchward, for whom he developed a deep

and lasting respect, but found his training temporarily halted by the coming of war. Although he could have claimed reserved status, he chose to volunteer for active service as a Private with the Royal Army Service Corps in 1915.

After basic training, he went to France later the same year and was attached to a Mechanical Transport Section for 'unspecified general duties'. Bearing in mind his engineering background, these most likely took advantage of his professional training. A rapidly expanding RASC were eager to recruit such men as it sought to operate a vast, complex transport system delivering ammunition, food and equipment to the front by any means at their disposal including railways, roads and waterways. Later in the war, he was posted to the British Salonika Force and remained in the Army until finally demobbed post war.

After this enforced six-year absence, he found Churchward ready to accept him back into the fold and continue his training. Initially this involved evening classes at Swindon Technical College, then attendance on a three-year course on a day release basis. Added together, these formed part of the prestigious GWR's Studentship Scheme. His performance was such that he was rated top of his class in all subjects each year and at the end of the course was awarded the coveted Chairman's Prize.

As his training came to an end, he was assigned to the CME's Drawing Office to study locomotive design for twelve months. And following this he was posted to the Experimental Section where

Swindon in war with Hawksworth as CME (the civilian in the centre of the front row) and Kenneth Cook, then Locomotive Works Manager (front row far right) playing host to a naval party from HMAS Australia. *King John*, No. 6021, provides the backdrop. This was probably the most demanding period of Cook's career as he sought to keep the GWR's loco fleet moving. It was also a time in which he began to introduce precision-based engineering methods to ensure the engines performed more reliably and effectively. These were techniques he then applied with great success at Doncaster, aided in no small measure by optical measuring devices developed by Taylor, Taylor and Hobson in the early 1950s. The chief beneficiaries of this work were the fleet of Pacifics Cook inherited (KC).

he could closely observe engines being run through their paces on the rolling road in the company's test facility. Having studied design and performance in such detail, and presumably proved himself an adept pupil in the process, Churchward appointed him Technical Inspector to the Locomotive Works. Further promotions followed as he moved, seemingly inexorably, to the top. Assistant to Works Manager, then Assistant Works Manager in 1932, Works Manager in 1937, Works Assistant to the CME in May 1947, Principal Assistant a year later and finally Mechanical and Electrical Engineer at Swindon in January 1950.

This was a moment that stirred his sense of history, as he later recalled:

On January 1st I occupied the Chair of Churchward in his old office at the east end of the main

office block looking towards the station and the main line to London. The great office and goal had been reached, but, of course, under nationalisation some of the prestige and trappings were reduced, nevertheless it was one of the pinnacles of my profession.

His time in charge of the Locomotive Workshops at Swindon covered the fraught years of the Second World War. It was a period that wrought many changes in production techniques as the shops were turned over to the manufacture, repair or maintenance of weapons and other high tech equipment, much of which was developmental or experimental in nature. As a result, locomotive construction took a back seat. However, when production resumed, the new more precise ways of working staff had learnt would be applied

to newly produced engines and the maintenance of the old. Cook became the past master at applying these techniques, later summing up their value in maintaining engines with the words, 'if and when the steam locomotive fades away in this country, it will not be on account of any decline in the excellence of its mechanism'.

Up to this time there were many in the scientific community who regarded railway workshops as a collection of antiquated facilities unable to work to the tolerances required in the production of high-tech weapons. So, in some quarters of industry it must have come as a surprise when they did so. When becoming President of the ILocoE in 1955, Cook described in great detail how he harnessed these skills at Swindon and then Doncaster to improve locomotive performances, most importantly with the high speed Pacifics.

In his 1955 address to the ILocoE, Kenneth Cook focussed on the improvements in efficiency and reliability that can be gained by the application of optical measuring equipment and precision engineering, these being techniques he had practised as Mechanical and Electrical Engineer at Swindon then Doncaster. It was a measure of improvement simply described by William Stanier with the words 'We used to think in thousandths and were proud of ourselves. Now we think in tens of a thousandth but do not boast about it'. By introducing these techniques in Eastern Region workshops, he ensured that all the high performance engines, particularly the A4s, ran more effectively. Cook illustrated his presentation with a series of diagrams and photos, some of which are reproduced here. (Above) Cook entitled this drawing 'The Essential Requirement of a Locomotive Alignment System'. (KC).

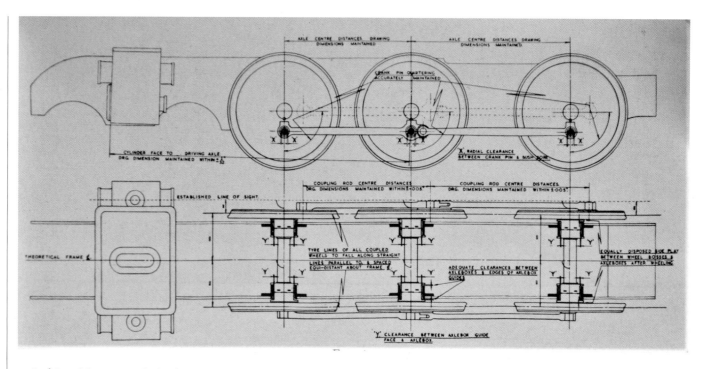

In his address entitled 'The Steam Locomotive – A Machine of Precision' he set out his thoughts on the subject and touched on some of the key issues involved – scientific, economic, social and political – and the benefits to be derived from these new techniques, all of which are important to the story of the A4s.

The technique of constructing and maintaining steam locomotives is now at the summit of accuracy.

A number of factors have combined to bring a point in the history of this country at which the steam locomotive must decline. In the decade which was closing in 1939, there is no doubt that the British steam locomotive was in its ascendancy and able to hold its own generally against other forms of prime movers on economic and mechanical grounds. There were plentiful supplies of coal, shed maintenance was at its best and continuity of railway employment was attractive. Now there are counter attractions in the form of a short regular working week in lighter industries, a dearth of coal and there is no longer a fear of shortage of oil in case of emergency. Nevertheless, the supersession of steam in Great Britain will take a number of years and in the meantime the steam locomotive will be called upon to meet many urgent calls.

The basic mechanism of an orthodox locomotive is unique in its power and is transmitted equally through two, three or four axes whose centres are partly fixed but are subject to considerable movement relative to their locations and to each other. Concentrated power is transmitted between the axles by rigid couplings subject to rotating and alternating tensional and compressive forces. These movements, caused from within the locomotive by its direct or induced forces and from without by irregularities of the track, have an effect upon the dimensions between axis centres and argument may develop as to whether extreme basic accuracy is necessary.

It is true that if there are errors in original setting, the movement of the axles during motion and power transmission may tend to cancel them out, but they may equally add to the error and also to the stresses set up. It is therefore fairly clear that the greater the original accuracy the lower will be the

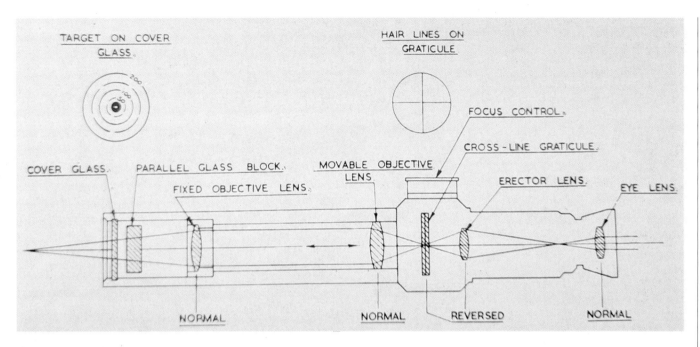

TARGET ON COVER GLASS.

HAIR LINES ON GRATICULE.

COVER GLASS.

PARALLEL GLASS BLOCK.

FIXED OBJECTIVE LENS.

MOVABLE OBJECTIVE LENS.

FOCUS CONTROL.

CROSS-LINE GRATICULE.

ERECTOR LENS.

EYE LENS.

NORMAL

NORMAL

REVERSED

NORMAL

The optics of the telescope used by Taylor, Taylor and Hobson. its accuracy was enhanced by an illumination system which provided light for projecting the image of circles - numbered to an appropriate scale and are concentric with the body diameter – forward from the end of the tube. (KC)

A diagram showing the application of optical measurement to a locomotive with an inside cylinder. (KC)

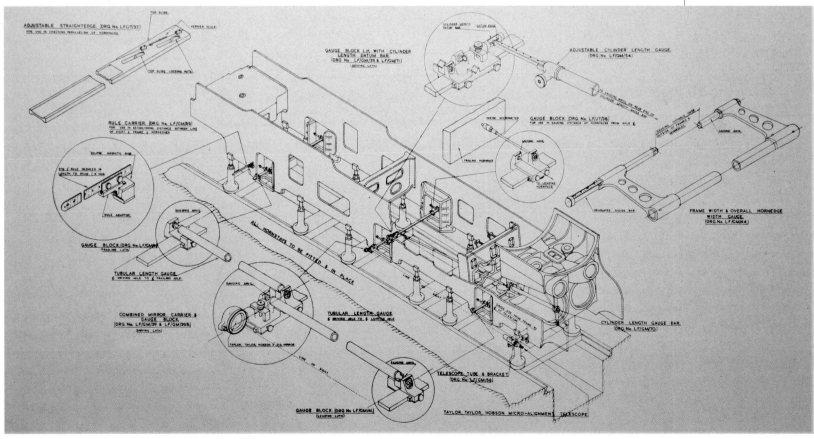

maximum stresses set up in components and it also enables initial tolerances of working parts to be reduced to a minimum, which itself reduces hammering effects in bearings and the rate at which wear and slackness develop.

I would like to emphasize that these remarks may only apply to certain parts of the locomotive and not necessarily to each and every part. In general, it is probably correct to say that the more accurately centres of holes are maintained the better, but there are some components in which very close tolerances are detrimental and therefore a proper balance is necessary. But on the other basic components of power transmission in a locomotive, and in many other parts, a high degree of accuracy is highly desirable and economical.

We should probably all agree that the economical criterion of

locomotive performance is cost per mile in similar conditions of operation and one of the greatest factors in producing low cost per mileage obtained between heavy repairs. In carrying out a heavy repair, the dismantling and erecting costs are fairly constant whatever the mileage and a higher mileage enables these to be spread and to produce a lower overall figure. High precision in basic details of a locomotive can make a big contribution to economy [and he might have added reliability, time keeping and overall performance which for the A4s and the other Pacifics was crucial, particularly when fitted with Gresley's conjugated valve gear].

There are two ingredients in the production of accuracy in a locomotive mechanism – measurement and working to measurement. Measurement has

to cater for three-dimensional requirements over an extensive area and many years have been needed to arrive at the present possibilities. Each Works has to cater for a number of combinations of these dimensions within the overall maxima and hence any system must be flexible enough to cater for these at reasonable cost and facility.

Cook then moved on to describe the 'subterfuge used in olden days' by workshop staff to make an engine 'appear to run true' by assuming that in the 'machining of components that wear or inaccuracies were equal on each side of the engine'. He accepted this as a natural consequence of the times in which they lived and worked, concluding that:

With good craftsmen working under favourable conditions fairly good results were still

(Below left) The cross tube and a collimator being applied to allow measuring to take place. In this position the telescope can also be sighted to scales fixed to each horn face or frame at any point. **(Below right)** The front view of an unidentified Eastern Region locomotive showing the telescope and length gauging rods in position. (KC)

obtainable and high-speed locomotives were repaired and maintained, although at the expense of slack initial fits of some wearing parts. But when things did not proceed according to schedule, poor light, blunt pops and a short-sighted erector, considerable inaccuracies did occur and many engineers spent much time endeavouring to develop better systems ['and', he added later, 'attempting to overcome the maintenance problems that arose from the additional wear created by these inaccuracies and slack fit'].

Overcoming these problems proved difficult and engineers spent much time trying to find a better way of working 'with little progress being made until optical methods became available and opened the way for advances in direct measurement,' which introduced the concept of frame alignment. This Cook succinctly described as the 'setting of axle centres relative to each other together with length of coupling rods and throw and angle of crank pins'. Following on this he concluded that 'a complete alignment throughout of wheels relative to framing is achieved'.

It was the development of these methods during the war that allowed Cook to introduce these new working principles at Swindon. All this was helped by significant advances made in optical measuring equipment and operating techniques first developed, rather ironically in Germany in the 1920s as Cook recalled:

The first major step was due to a well-known optical instrument maker [thought to be Moller-Wedel] who in the 1920s produced a telescope in conjunction with a collimator. The telescope enabled a line of sight to be taken free of all deflection and the function of the collimator was to pick this sight up in absolute parallelism. The cross lines of the infinite scale of the collimator will only register zero from the telescope if the former is correctly located parallel in the line of sight. Hence if this be suitably and accurately mounted at right angles to a straight edge or the tube supported horizontally in the driving horns, at the designed distance from the locating point on the cylinder, an axis has been set-up co-incident with the desired centre of the driving axle. By this means, an accurate survey of all guide faces relative to cylinders at the commencement of repair can be made and decisions taken as to the most economical directions for correction.

The optical instruments alluded to by Cook were first purchased from Moller-Wedel by the Deutsche Reichsbahn-Gesellschaft, after its creation in 1924 and gradually installed in twenty-five of its workshops across Germany. It was a project in which the company's General Manager Dr Julius Dorpmuller, and his Chief of

A Bert Spencer photo of an A4 undergoing a major overhaul at Doncaster – date and details of engine not recorded. However, he has added a note to the negative which reads 'an A4 stripped right back with re-assembly due to commence shortly. Engine generally in good nick despite high mileage between repairs. Optical measurement is the key to this'. (BS).

Design, Dr Richard Wagner, took leading roles. They are said to have been impressed by development work undertaken by scientists working for Moller-Wedel, a company formed by Johann Moller in 1864.

For a number of years, they had been working towards production of a telescope linked collimator driven by the need for greater precision when building or maintaining for then very advanced machines – cars, ships, locomotives and, later on, aero engines. In this they drew heavily on work undertaken in the early nineteenth century by Henry Kater FRS, the British scientist and inventor, who developed a floating collimator to aid astronomical research. He in turn was deeply influenced by conceptual work undertaken in this field by the Germans physicists and mathematicians Johann Carl Gauss and Freidrich Bessel.

As always in science there does not appear to have been a single eureka moment, but a series of often more modest steps in a gradual evolution of an idea where the eventual applications might not have been glimpsed clearly until late in the process. So, it fell to Moller, until his death in 1907, then to his son Hugo, to bring many scientific threads together and lead a team that would invent an apparatus that would play such an important role in engineering.

According to Spencer:

By the time the war started the effect of optical measurement and calibration was only too apparent in the performances of many German high-speed locomotives, most notably their Class 05 record breaker. I have no doubt that weapons then turned against Poland and the rest of Europe were made more effective and efficient by the clever application of Moller-Wedel's optical equipment. We in Britain were very slow to adopt these working principles or, for that matter, develop our own version.

In his paper, Cook alludes to one workshop in Britain acquiring this optical equipment from Germany in the 1930s but does not mention which company this was. However, when war broke out, other potential customers quickly lost this German supplier. Then after the armistice, specialist companies such as this were quickly absorbed by the Soviet occupation force and moved eastwards to produce advanced optical equipment for the Communist Bloc. It wasn't for some time that British scientists managed to produce a home-grown product as Cook related:

At the Machine Tool Exhibition in 1952, a British optical exhibit was noticed that appeared capable of development although at that time it had no reference to locomotives. The makers became very anxious to co-operate and quite quickly a method, utilising instead of a collimator a reflecting mirror fixed parallel to and in line with a straight edge method much simpler than the German, and capable of proceeding very much further in the quest for accuracy. It became known as the Auto-Reflexion

This apparatus proved fully usable in the construction of locomotives to ensure initial accuracy and during general repairs when it can ensure and maintain accuracy over a long working life.

And so, with such a product becoming available Cook obtained examples during 1953 which soon found gainful employment in the workshops at Doncaster and Darlington. However, it is not clear if these instruments found wider use across BR when dealing with steam locomotives. Nevertheless, their arrival was a godsend for the LNER's Pacifics, which soon showed the benefit of having such a tool to help improve performance and reliability.

For his part, Cook later made light of this contribution and even felt it necessary to pass a negative comment about his time at Doncaster, going so far as to suggest that it was a move he'd rather not have made. But first of all, he began by recalling the circumstances surrounding his appointment:

Towards the end of April 1951 Riddles came to Swindon and asked me if I wanted to move to Doncaster as M&EE of the Eastern and North Eastern Regions. After some discussion he asked me what I thought of that and I said 'frankly, not much!' He then left it for me to consider. Only after receiving satisfactory replies to a few questions did I agree to go.

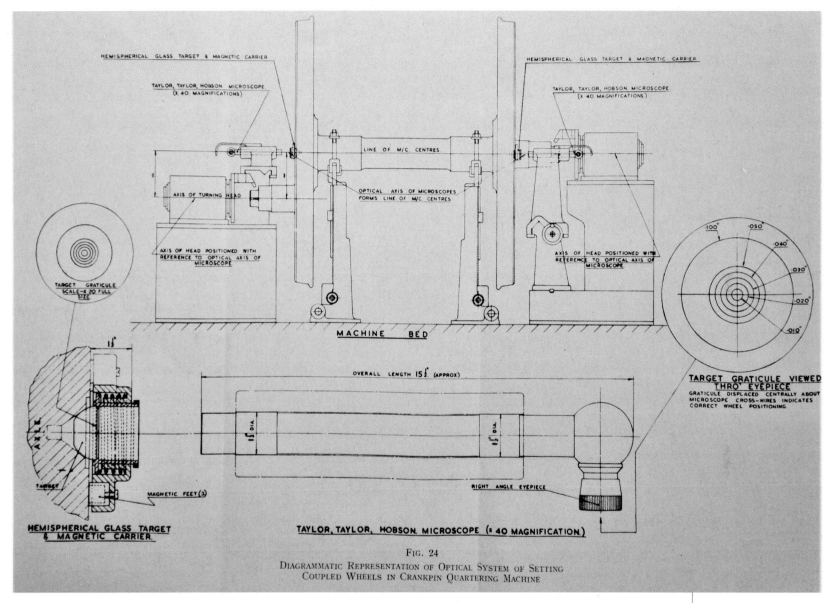

FIG. 24
DIAGRAMMATIC REPRESENTATION OF OPTICAL SYSTEM OF SETTING
COUPLED WHEELS IN CRANKPIN QUARTERING MACHINE

The key to the introduction of precision engineering through optical measurement in Britain may have been through the work of Moller-Wedel, but it did not become a reality until Taylor, Taylor and Hobson's developed a good working model in the post war years that British companies could purchase. They had, by this stage, a long history of producing high quality lenses which had helped develop the film industry in the early twentieth century. The reliability, accuracy and reputation of Taylor Hobson products was deemed second to none and led them into the world of component inspection and optical equipment to achieve the highest possible accuracy. Success in this field soon led to a wide range of metrology instruments becoming widely available. However, it was a link up with the J Arthur Rank Organisation in 1947 that broadened their research on lenses, precision photographic shutters and optical instruments. This included the Talyrond 1 – the world's first roundness measuring instrument – and two years later the Micro Alignment Telescope, which was given wide publicity during the 1952 Machine Tool Exhibition. It was this instrument that was then taken up by the railway industry, most notably by Kenneth Cook at Doncaster. Such was its importance to his work that he included this diagram in his presentation to the ILocoE, which shows it being applied to the setting of coupled wheels. (KN)

A physical demonstration of the way improvements have been made can be as effective as a vast number of descriptive words. This proved to be the case with Kenneth Cook's work to improve the middle big-end of Gresley's Pacifics, and help resolve a perennial problem that had dogged these engines throughout their lives. In his 1955 paper he chose to include four photos to show how he successfully introduced Churchward and de Glehn's ideas for an inside big-end (top left), but also modified Gresley's own marine type big end, significantly improving its performance in the process (lower left). To prove how successful these modifications to the Gresley big-end were he produced two more pictures. (Upper right) This shows the 'marine type brasses with complete white metal bearing surfaces and felt pad' as produced using optical measurement precision based techniques. (Lower right) The same brasses after running 50,000 miles when wear was assessed as being only 0.004 inch – a miniscule amount considering the mileage covered and the stresses imposed by heavy duty, high-speed running. (KC)

Pacific inside connecting rods and the rebuilding of the Pacifics generally with optical equipment.

For his part, Bert Spencer was more sanguine in assessing Cook's contribution, which the man himself seems to have valued so little:

Without a doubt his impact was a positive one, especially at a time when there was great uncertainty over the future of the organisation he led. Many felt their jobs were no longer secure with cutbacks and closures imminent. For this reason, recruitment was proving a challenge and retention of skilled workers was growing increasingly more difficult. The railway workshops and steam locomotives, in particular, no longer had the pulling power they once did to attract men and women of all trades. The spirit of old had gone and other more modern businesses attracted the people who had once flocked to the railways for work.

By his actions alone, which included the introduction of precision engineering, Cook managed to reverse this trend and bring back some much needed pride in what we were doing. He also fought to bring as much work as possible to the workshops, which encouraged many to view the future more optimistically. But his impact on locomotive performance, and his desire to see Gresley's Pacifics give of their best while steam lasted, was without doubt something of which he should have been justifiably proud.

After eight years at Doncaster I retired. Actually I think that going to Doncaster was a wasted effort, although Sir John Elliott, Chairman of the Railway Executive told me that he was very pleased that I had agreed to go and thought it was a very good thing.

Perhaps I was able to do a few useful things amongst which might be mentioned the overcoming of long-standing troubles with the

This was a view confirmed by the historian and writer O.S. Nock, who had the opportunity to observe Cook's work from close quarters and how his contribution greatly benefited the Western, then the Eastern Regions. In his book *The Gresley Pacifics,* Nock presented this well-considered assessment. '[Cook's appointment] could have been regarded as one of those caretaker moves designed to assist in breaking-down the old railway loyalties, and establishment of a unified British Railways…(But) at Doncaster Cook threw himself heart and soul into the atmosphere of his new surroundings with successful results.'

On taking up the reins at Doncaster, Cook inherited a rather complex situation. The 'new' Pacific engines [Thompson and Peppercorns] were not proving entirely successful. At their best they were no better than the Gresleys at their best, and were heavier coal burners. For that reason alone, they were not too popular with the running staff. On the other hand, the Gresleys, both A3 and A4, were immensely popular, but fully half the stud was around 25 years old by 1951. But Cook appreciated that in these famous engines there was still potential for high power output, and fast, economical, long distance running; and in a systematic programme of rehabilitation he set about eliminating those features of detail design that had proved sources of weakness – not only in wartime, and just after, but also in the high noon of Gresley's own career.

Now well into its peacetime stride, A4 No. 60004 *William Whitelaw* simmers while waiting to clear the Flying Scotsman, under the interested gaze of the driver or fireman on an unnamed V2 No.60883. At this stage in the mid-1950s this A4 was based at Haymarket Shed where she had been since 1941. She will remain a Scottish based engine until withdrawn from traffic in July 1966. Meanwhile the V2, which was built at Darlington in 1939, is based at nearby St Margarets Shed, where she became a resident in 1956. (THG)

When considering these conflicting views of Cook's tenure at Doncaster, and the successes to which he might justifiably have claimed credit, where does the truth lie. Certainly there was no reason for the honest and hugely experienced Spencer to exaggerate Cook's achievements or for Nock, as a knowledgeable critic of locomotives matters, to do likewise. So what exactly did the new M&EE, soon to be re-titled CM&EE, do to warrant their praise in the case of the A4s and the other Pacifics?

First of all, he was possessed of the need to introduce optical based precision techniques at a time when these were not generally recognised in the railway industry. To do this he had to convince others of its benefits, find the funds to purchase the equipment and then set up a training programme to ensure his engineers could operate it effectively. In Nock's words these new ways of working were applied with such precision that 'erection of the working parts, particularly the pin joints of the conjugated valve gear could be assembled with greatly reduced clearances, as well as having the pins themselves and the bearings machined to much finer tolerances'.

The results, as Spencer later observed 'offered an effective solution to the long running problems associated with this valve gear and greatly reduced the amount of maintenance required and reduced time out of service when under repair'. While Nock, a little more poetically perhaps, recorded that it was 'no exaggeration to say that the wildly syncopated exhaust beats that were at one time so characteristic of the Gresley three-cylinder locomotives, and a sigh audible of slogger in the pin joints of the valve gear, became a thing of the past'.

His next achievement was to tackle what many believed to be the Gresley Pacific's most significant weakness – the middle big-end and their tendency to overheat and fail. In fact, Nock referred to them as their Achilles' heel so serious did many consider the problem to be. In seeking a solution, Cook fell back on lessons learnt at Swindon by Churchward who had adapted a de

Glehn type of inside big end for use in his four-cylinder locomotives. This proved to be a wise move and Cook, after carefully considering the problem, decided to apply this hybrid solution to Gresley's Pacifics.

At the same time as this, he refused give up on the 'Gresley Marine type big-end' and sought to modify them with a completely machined bearing and felt pad lubrication inserted. In justifying this development, he argued that 'there is no doubt that the accurately machined finish is greatly superior and reduces wear' and this again proved to be the case. And to validate his argument, he produced a pair of marine brasses, during his presentation in 1955, that had run for 50,000 miles and had worn by no more than 0.004 inch. As Spencer later recalled 'there could be no clearer indication of success than this graphic

illustration of minimum wear in a big-end noted for its weakness'.

Finally, we have the work he instituted in replacing the original 3 per cent nickel-steel based connecting and coupling rods with ones containing carbon steel. The effect of this change, when matched to the reduced clearances in the big-ends and crack pins 'virtually eliminated the ring and knock to which we had been accustomed for so many years' as Nock recalled years later.' The end result of all this for the Pacifics was that 'the engines so modified, and so meticulously repaired at Doncaster, ran with the silence and precision of well-oiled sewing machines'.

At this point it would be interesting to quote some figures to back up the assessments of these two experienced engineers, but if such an exercise was carried out, any report that might have

No. 60004 again this time at rest between turns, keeping company with V2 No. 60921 a Doncaster engine throughout the 1950s, where she was cut up in 1963. The location of the photo is not recorded. (RH)

resulted does not appear to have survived. All we can assume is that the Pacifics probably spent less time in the Works and ran more effectively between general repairs. In addition, we cannot confirm whether the modifications resulted in less coal being consumed. If so, it was a figure that would surely have drawn the attention of BR's accountants ever eager to reduce costs in a time of austerity. However, if the engines ran more efficiently such a gain may have been outweighed by the poor quality of coal the engines were now required to burn. Here again Nock's observations are relevant:

I was privileged to go through the corridor tender [on a southbound Elizabethan in 1954 pulled by A4 No. 60030 *Golden Fleece*] and spend a considerable time on the footplate, and I was deeply impressed with the beautifully steady conditions of steaming, and the way in which a bright clean fire was maintained in the later stages of the journey despite coal that in pre-war days would hardly have been considered ideal for such a duty.

With Britain still struggling to meet the heavy financial burden imposed by the two world wars at the same time as fund a massive rebuilding programme and then meet the considerable costs of new health and welfare reforms, something had to give. In addition, it was essential that exports be boosted to help reduce the balance of payments deficit and so help pay for all the things society demanded. Britain was rich in coal and its export value was high, so, much of

the mines' output, particularly the better quality coal, went for export, leaving the poorer grade coal for home consumption.

As a major user of fossil fuel, the railways were vulnerable to these pressures, as footplate crew would quickly bear witness. Spencer, in his position alongside Cook at

Doncaster, captured the essence of the problem when he wrote:

The Yorkshire collieries, our traditional source of supply, still produced a great deal of coal, but much of this ended up going overseas or to the growing number of coal fired

Standing near a water trough when an express was passing through was always a spectacular sight and, occasionally, a damp one as the two young boys trespassing on the track will soon find out. The A4 is not identified though appears to be pulling a fast freight train. (THG)

The date of this photo is not recorded and the placing of two A4s side by side at Grantham both with Flying Scotsman nameplates adds an intriguing twist to the occasion. It may simply be that one engine was replacing the other due to breakdown. No. 60019 *Bittern* is in the background apparently without carriages, while 60022 *Mallard* waits on the adjoining platform. In due course, both locomotives will be preserved. (RH)

Mallard **receives** some attention at King's Cross in the late 1950s, according to notes that came with the negative. By this stage, she and her sisters were showing the benefits of Cook's work in trying to resolve the problems caused by Gresley's valve gear and middle big-end. 60022 will remain a King's Cross engine until withdrawn from service in 1963. (THG)

power stations. At the same time BR wished to economise and reduce its substantial fuel bill and this could only be achieved by purchasing poorer quality coal, which seemed to include a lot of dust. This made the fireman's job, particularly on the express services, even more difficult and it became quite common for them to be shovelling mostly dust towards the end of long journeys. It also made life on the footplate even dirtier. It was a wonder that the men on the Pacifics still managed to get the best out of their engines, especially the A4s which tended to dominate the premier services. Towards the end of the 1950s the position improved slightly, and a better quality of coal again became available, though not

The production of DP1 by English Electric in the 1950s was accompanied by a great deal of publicity material in the hope of encouraging interest at home and abroad that might lead to orders. Spencer collected many of these brochures and technical assessments including this early illustration. (BS)

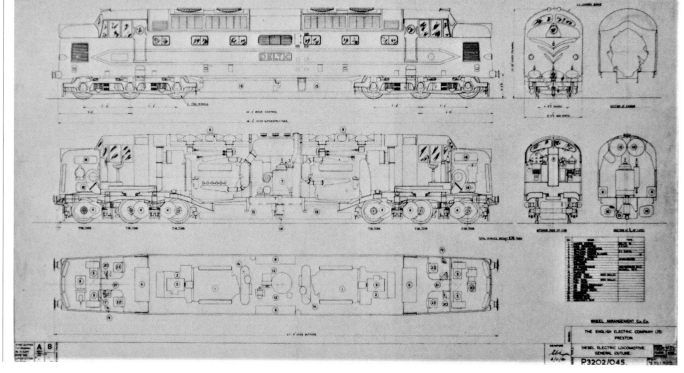

always, much to the running department's frustration.

Of course, as steam came to the end the standard of coal procured again appeared to drop, a fact that was only too evident to me when viewing locomotives from the luxury of retirement in Devon.

With the price of oil dropping and its increased availability it is little wonder that BR finally acted to produce adequate numbers of diesel engines and revive electrification.

For the Eastern Region Pacifics, and particularly the A4s, this meant that a search was on to develop a diesel capable of matching their performance on the high speed, long distance services. Electrification was the eventual aim, but in the 1950s and '60s the cost of this was deemed so high as to make it impossible to achieve in the foreseeable future. So, where could BR and Cook, in particular, find a diesel alternative that might easily be developed or procured? It was here that Spencer's growing awareness of what was happening in industry proved of great value, coupled to the work undertaken by the LMS in producing its two mainline diesels, Nos. 10000 and 10001.

For some years, Spencer had been keeping in close touch with English Electric, Napier, Sulzer and Brush, amongst others, as they developed new products and experimented with different concepts. At the same time, he viewed what was going on around the world, through the forum of learned institutions and other bodies, to see if there were ideas emerging that BR might exploit; in so doing he continued

a way of working common in the engineering world and heavily favoured and encouraged by Gresley.

Spencer's aim was a simple one – to keep abreast of the latest

developments in the field of locomotion. In some cases, he simply acquired brochures and detailed descriptions of developing products. In other cases, he seems to have become involved in the actual

Diesel Prototype No. 1 (DP1) under construction at English Electric's Preston Works. (Above) The underframes, minus fabricated steel bogies, ready to receive the superstructure then its two Napier Deltic E158 D18-12 which will produce 3300 hp and propel the engine, initially, up to a maximum speed of 90mph. This was then deemed to be too low and modifications were made that increased its potential top speed to 105mph. (Below) The underframes now married to the superstructure frames and final fitting out have begun. (BS)

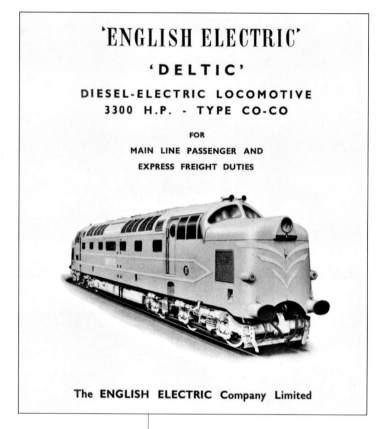

'ENGLISH ELECTRIC'

'DELTIC'

DIESEL-ELECTRIC LOCOMOTIVE
3300 H.P. - TYPE CO-CO

FOR

MAIN LINE PASSENGER AND
EXPRESS FREIGHT DUTIES

The ENGLISH ELECTRIC Company Limited

As one would expect, the production of the prototype was accompanied by an energetic PR campaign which saw brochures and photographs widely distributed and, in due course, articles in the press and performance reports. With much riding on DP1's commercial success, such an active programme was essential. The booklet reproduced here was one of a number that Spencer collected and found its way into a large folder he kept which contained papers covering all aspects of the engine's development. (BS)

production of new engines. This was particularly so with English Electric and their Diesel Prototype No. 1 which evolved into the main line Deltic class, and would come to dominate the East Coast routes for many years to come.

By 1951, the company had many years of experience in building and selling diesel and electric engines and the DP1 can be seen as a speculative venture in producing a large locomotive that might be sold to markets around the world and so expand their business. The design concept for this prototype was first explored by the company in 1950/51. Such was their confidence in the proposed design that an order for four engines to power them was raised with Napier's, a subsidiary of EE. In November this

led to an internal contract being issued by the company's Tractive Division at Bradford for a single prototype to be built at EE's Preston Works.

Production of this engine proved to be a long-drawn out affair, not unusual when a new design is being developed. In this case the project was accompanied by many revisions as other avenues were explored. Coupled to this, a lack of any customers lined up to purchase the locomotive would have encouraged a certain amount of drift in the programme, which a full order book might have helped counteract. So the project struggled on with the prototype finally being ready for trials in November 1955.

It was some time in 1953 that Spencer first enquired about this engine and received a substantial pack of material relating to its development from EE. Why he began gathering this information is unclear. It may have simply been personal interest that encouraged his actions or, more likely, he was carrying out a task delegated to him by one of several BR committees on which he sat. Either way, he seems to have become something of a focal point within BR for this project, and his papers record regular visits to Preston as DP1 slowly emerged, followed by participation in the engine's trials. In the same way, he also became involved in the projects that resulted in the Brush Type 2 (BR Class 31), the EE Type 2 (BR Class 20) and the EE Type 4 (BR Class 40) all of which began entering service in 1957/58 shortly before he retired.

Having followed its development with interest for several years, Spencer obtained permission

to travel on DP1 in March 1956 and several more times in 1957. Finally, in the few weeks before his retirement, he was invited to join the engine one last time on a run from Liverpool Lime Street to London. By this stage, a discussion between EE and BR regarding the construction of more of the type, for use on the East Coast mainline, was well underway. This resulted in a final order for twenty-two locomotives being agreed with contracts exchanged in May 1958, delivery to begin in March 1960. While this was happening, the prototype remained with the LMR until January 1959. After a major overhaul, the Deltic was sent to Hornsey depot for testing by staff on the Eastern Region in anticipation of the first of the new engines being delivered. Although by now departed, one wonders whether Spencer's expert assessments of the Deltic played any part in the development programme and their use along the East Coast, where they would soon begin to displace the A4s. Of this programme and the slow speed of its evolution Spencer later wrote:

The Deltics could have entered service much earlier than they did. Luckily there were companies prepared to invest and experiment in new technologies which meant that when BR finally bit the bullet they could tap into their work.

I did find the Deltics interesting and enjoyable and rode in the cab of the prototype on a number of occasions, most notably on 26th March 1958 when running from Liverpool to London. A detailed report of which I submitted to John Harrison at Derby, soon to be BR's CME.

Well before DP1 was considered for service on the East Coast Mainline, it had undergone extensive testing on the West Coast route, beginning in the autumn of 1955. In fact, she remained under wraps when undergoing static tests at Netherton in Lancashire then carrying out braking and wheel slip checks at Speke. Main line working soon began and here a veil of secrecy was ensured by assigning her to freight trains running between Liverpool and London at night, where all was shrouded by darkness. As confidence in the engine slowly grew, she undertook a first passenger turn pulling the up Merseyside Express on 13 December 1955, then returning to Liverpool the same day. And for the

first time the prototype, in its most striking livery of powder blue with aluminium mouldings on the body sides, with chevrons at each end and the name 'Deltic' on each side, could be observed by the wider

public with dramatic results. It was an image of modernity that steam locomotives would find impossible to equal.

As with any new machine, the first few months in service can be

Spencer did not record time or place (but thought to be King's Cross) when archiving this photograph in his collection, one of many that went the same way. However, from the limited information available it seems to have been taken when the engine was allocated to the Eastern Region in 1959 for testing purposes, twenty-two production models having being ordered the year before at an estimated cost of £3,410m. When first built, the engine was painted in English Electric's house colours of green and cream, but this was soon changed to a more striking powder blue. Its impact was immediate and probably helped sell the concept to press and potential customers. (BS)

DP1 under test with the LMR and captured pulling the Merseyside Express in 1956. (BS)

challenging as teething problems come to the fore and modifications and adjustments become necessary. DP1 was no different. This long period of testing and fine-tuning led Spencer to reminisce about the A4 development programme:

Looking back I could not help but remember how quickly these engines were developed with little or no testing taking place before they entered service on the most arduous of duties possible. They then ran very successfully at high speed with few if any problems of any great significance occurring. True, they were, for the most part, working with well-established technology and were part of a programme that began in 1922 with Gresley's A1s, whereas DP1 was a prototype using technology still at a very early stage of development. Despite this the A4 programme was still without parallel in the industry and one never likely to be repeated in the modern world.

With regard to the Deltic project Spencer added an interesting aside hinting at some of the issues that lay behind the types selection by BR and its eventual use on the Eastern Region:

A clear case of out with the old and in with the new is captured in these two photographs taken at about the same time, on virtually the same spot, at King's Cross. Despite the sleek modern appearance of No. 60030 *Golden Fleece*, her technology is Victorian in nature and the A4s position at the apex of this science is soon to be usurped by this twentieth century phenomenon. (RH)

I couldn't understand why the LMR having spent so long testing DP1 didn't then select it for use on their lines. 'Freddie' Harrison, who was CM&EE at Derby, for reasons not entirely clear to me came down against them and that could have been an end to the matter. However, Gerry Fiennes, who was the Line Traffic Manager at King's Cross at the time, came to their and English Electric's rescue.

If Spencer couldn't fathom Harrison's reasons for rejecting the design, having been so close to the project and to Harrison himself over many years, it is difficult for us to do so now. There has been some speculation that he believed that high-speed diesel engines, producing, 1500 rpm, were unsuitable for railway applications. This may be so, but was outright rejection a fair response, when so few other alternatives existed to replace his aging fleet of Pacifics? Whatever his reasons, and the forthcoming plans for electrifying the West Coast Mainline cannot be ignored, passing up the chance of acquiring the Deltics did open the door for Fiennes to take advantage of the situation.

Gerard Francis Gisborne Twisleton-Wykeham-Fiennes, to give him his full name, was born in June 1906 and became a Traffic Apprentice with the LNER in 1928, after studying for a degree at Oxford University. He quickly rose through the ranks of the London and North Eastern Railway, and later British Rail. In 1957, he was appointed to the prestigious Traffic Manager post at King's Cross, having served at Cambridge, York, London Liverpool Street Station and Edinburgh, then Operating Superintendent Eastern Region for BR, along the way. Until 1961 his word would become law at King's Cross and, with it would come the right to recommend suitable motive power to work the main express

services and, in the process, replace steam locomotives.

Unlike many of his contemporaries in BR, Fiennes was a deep thinker, with a strong academic bent, who 'believed strongly in growing traffic and using resources intensively through aggressive scheduling and that, in order to compete with air and road, the average end-to-end speed of passenger trains had to be at least 75 miles per hour', as he wrote later. He quickly realised that these speeds required engines with a much higher power output than British Railways were currently considering and purchasing at the time. The Deltic seemed the only design currently available capable of filling this gap and, it seems, he was largely responsible for pushing BR's top managers to acquire sufficient numbers for his

purposes. By this stage of testing, it was believed that they were capable of prolonged running at 100 miles per hour on the East Coast route, with a level of service equally as good as the West Coast Mainline

(Left) Gerard Fiennes, as the Eastern Region's Traffic Manager, who was largely responsible for bringing the Deltics to that Region when the LMR rejected them after several years of testing. During his career Fiennes would rise to become Chairman of the Eastern Region Board and General Manager, Eastern Region, BR, 1965–67, but then be sacked for being too critical of his employers in print. (Below) DP1 in 1959 or early 1960 at Newcastle Central Station whilst undergoing tests on the East Coast Mainline, by which time an order for twenty-two had been raised on English Electric. (BS)

when electrified (an incremental programme beginning in 1960 that would not be completed in 1974).

In selecting a suitable diesel locomotive, Fiennes and his team had looked at the alternatives and concluded that there were only two options, other than retaining steam for another ten or fifteen years, that is. The first of these was the 2000 hp English Electric type 4 diesel. Two hundred had been ordered by BR and they began appearing in 1958, but Fiennes soon concluded that they were underpowered for the planned timings. As a result, he appears to have had few qualms about choosing the other alternative – a Deltic type locomotive. But in following this course of action he did face some opposition, as he later related:

Objections to the order included those arising from: a limited permitted top speed due to the mass of the locomotive; the potential for the order to delay a proposed (1957) electrification scheme of the line; as well the size which required modifications to the King's Cross platforms. Nevertheless my arguments prevailed and an order was placed in 1959 for 22 Class 55s to replace 55 steam locomotives.

Despite his advocacy, it took some time for BR's managers to feel sufficiently confident to commit the Ministry of Transport to this programme, ever conscious of Harrison's concerns over the prototype. His objections possibly

became even more pointed after his promotion to Chief Mechanical and Electrical Engineer to BR in 1958, but, finally, the deal was done and EE could press ahead with the development and construction of their long conceived Deltics. In truth, there were general concerns about the reliability and cost of all the new diesels, not simply the new Class 55s.

Ever conscious of the problems and the debate Spencer recorded that, 'any new technology generally takes a longish period of time to bed in and be accepted. And so it was with all the diesels. When they failed, which in reality was no more frequently than steam, there were many sage comments, especially when a steam locomotive was substituted'. But the Railway

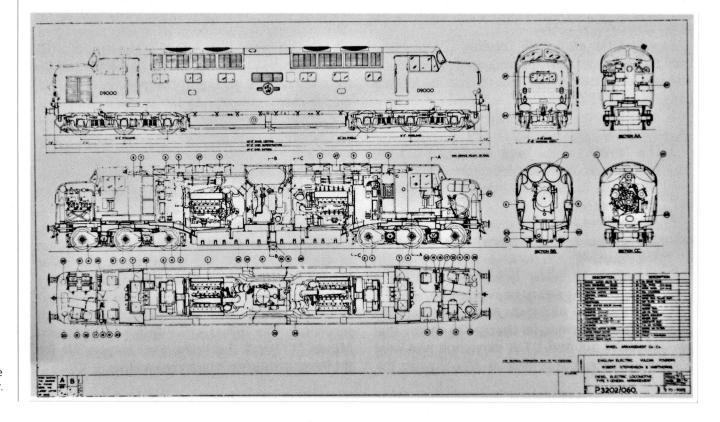

The layout of the Class 55s ordered in 1958 by BR. Deliveries were due to begin in 1960, but many design issues had to be resolved first and so the engines only began to arrive in February 1961 and the last twelve months later. (BS)

Engines installed in Class 55 during construction at Vulcan Foundry in 1961.
Key:
1. Control cubicle
2. No 2 engine and generator group
3. Steam generator
4. Air intake for scavenge blower
5. No 1 engine and generator group
6. Framework for cooling group under construction

(Above right) A numbered photo produced by English Electric showing the key features of a Class 55 when under construction. (Above left) The production line at Vulcan Foundry is up and running in late 1961 with eight of the class captured in this photo in various states of construction. (BS)

Executive, having finally committed itself to true modernisation after going down the blind alley of building many more steam engines, were not pre-disposed to stopping now. Nevertheless, delivery of the first engine, No. D9000, did not take place until early 1961 and the last would arrive twelve months later. This long and complex programme had one saving grace, though. For those enamoured by steam, it gave the A4s, in particular, a few more years to dominate the main line and draw some final headlines, before obsolescence finally overtook them.

It was certainly a time to savour before the inevitable happened. Yet the A4s were only one part of the picture. In the background lay the culture that went with steam and the way of life it had established over a century or more. This too will soon be gone, being replaced by a more functional, less intensive 'switch on and go' way of life that diesel then electric powered trains symbolised. Some might say more efficient in the way it did its business, but what it gained in efficiency it seemed to lose in soul and in the sense of commitment that made steam locomotives work. This despite the poorest working conditions imaginable for footplate crew and the sheer, exhausting physical effort it took to keep the trains running on time – in peace and war.

All this would soon be swept away, leaving only fading memories and somewhat anodyne, de-sensitised images captured on film to remind us of this unique part of our heritage. Luckily, some of the footplate crew did put pen to paper to record how they lived their lives and coped with the strain of such hard work. Here there were none better than Norman McKillop who served both the LNER and BR at Haymarket and was someone who knew how to work Gresley's Pacifics and the A4s in particular.

His writings, although a little flowery and contrived at times,

For the moment the A4s still dominate and the late 1950s and early 1960s were a great time to see them 'rule the roost' at King's Cross, which I did on many occasions. Here 60017 *Silver Fox* quickly pulls away with the Elizabethan seemingly without any great effort. (RH)

The Queen of Scots service as Norman McKillop would have remembered it as it pulls away from Queens Street Station in Glasgow on its way to King's Cross. By this stage, the BR emblem on the A4s' tender has changed from the lion atop a wheel to a lion holding a wheel with a crown beneath. (RH)

do provide a fitting memorial to this lost world. In this case, he is recalling one particular run as a driver of an A4 pulling the Queen of Scots. This was a luxury Pullman train, with table service, that ran between London King's Cross and Glasgow Queen Street on weekdays and Saturdays from 1 May 1928 until June 1964. It was a turn that McKillop described as 'greatly sought after by footplate crew and was entrusted to very few'. The account that follows takes some elements from his book *Top Link Locomotives* and several long letters, probably written in preparation for the book, that described life with an A4. His story begins when

60009 *Union of South Africa*, which he refers to simply as 'Nine', is being made ready for departure from Waverley on the first stage of the journey to Newcastle, where another engine and crew will take over:

When you enter the cab of Nine and close the side-doors you are in a world of your own … master of your own destiny for the next three hours. Even as you sit on the driving seat, you make a 'long arm' and slap the tender hand-brake to make sure it's off. You glance at the water scoop indicator to see that the scoop is up and the catch is securing it firmly. Your eyes sweep across the dials on the storm board in front of you and your mind registers what the needles on the vacuum brake, boiler steam pressure and heater gauges tell you.

And even as you light your pipe or cigarette you are studying the boiler water level, the reversing gear indicator and listening to the sound of the air valve letting in a breath of air to prevent the ejector creating more than 21 inches of vacuum as it works to fill up the tiny leaks on that long brake pipe-line stretching to the last vehicle on your train.

Behind you Bob McKerchar's shovel is slithering and clinking on the Firehole shovel-plate, and that a glance at the chimney was to verify that no more than a blue haze was all the indication that a good few hundred-weights of coal were being plugged into the firebox. You also hear Bob's slap on the

heater governor and the quick hiss and click of its spring-loaded response. He knows the tricks of the heat governor does Bob and his slap was to make sure it was working properly.

No matter how long you have been at this game, you never open the throttle on a high-capacity engine without marvelling at the swaggering ease it displays. Here with 250 pounds to the square inch of boiler pressure, all that Nine needed on this level start was a bare 150 pounds to lift her 320 ton train along with her own 168 ton weight from a dead stand – and this as soon as the throttle was opened. Now that you are in the cab and hear the hiss stopping before Nine has gone a hundred yards, you know it was only the piston rods being cold that caused it. As soon as it warmed up and

expanded it becomes as steam-tight as the proverbial 'bottle'.

So you settle down comfortably in your seat as Nine drops her nose down the 1 in 70 gradient through the Calton tunnel, and you pat the throttle almost shut before winding the reverser until the pointer travelling down the brass plate reaches 15 per cent and a mere whiff of steam drifting over the boiler is the only indication that the throttle is open at all. As Nine sweeps on a main line which traverses the centre of St Margaret's motive power depot, you know that the sound of her chime whistle is more than a warning to clear her path. It's a daily salute and farewell… Then you settle back in your seat and gently tug the throttle handle to increase the speed to 40mph on the nearly level stretch to

No. **60017** *Silver Fox* awaits departure from King's Cross with the down Talisman as A1 Pacific No. 60139 Sea Eagle gets underway on an unidentified service towards the end of the 1950s. The Peppercorn A1 acquired its name in 1950, having been previously allocated to A4 No. 4487/60028 and then discarded when that engine became *Walter K. Whigham* in 1947. (THG)

Portobello, then a right hand glide round the bend to Joppa where you realise you are on an engine which not only looks well bred, but proves it in her actions.

Gradually you pull the throttle wide open and slowly wind the reverser until the pointer reaches 20 and you sense the surge in power, but still you keep the pointer moving. 25 and the cough at the chimney top assumes a distinctly business like note and you feel Nine's 'drivers' biting into the rails, but still you keep the pointer moving. The cough becomes a bark, and you can feel her sinews and muscles really in action as the pointer passes 30 and you finally push in the reversing lever catch and sit back with the pointer at 37 per cent.

Nine is really giving her tongue now – a full throated roar – and accelerating as if there is neither train behind her or rising gradient under her wheels. She kicks that rise as if

it was merely the springboard from which to leap into the dip that is Monktonhall Junction.

At Prestonpans you have wound her back to 20 and by the time she's passing Longniddry, the pointer is at 15 and she's doing near 70mph. Presently she takes a short hill as if it wasn't there, rips through a couple of well-spaced bridges as if they were tied together, and is tearing down the gradual slope into the hollow of Drem at 75mph. As you come out of the protection of the trees a near gale reaches a hand from the sea, and Nine thinks another hundred tons have been hung on behind her. You can feel her start with surprise, a brief hesitancy which wouldn't have registered if you knew her less well. It doesn't stop Nine at all and with full throttle once more she fights back at the detaining wind.

What about the 7-mile bank ahead. It's 1 in 90 you know! 'That's better', the exhaust shouts back at the wind and at

72mph hits the foot of the rise and seems to lean forward to tackle the long ascent. As the gradient steepens you give her the necessary encouragement, but just enough to keep her breathing easily. Even at the steepest, she doesn't ask for more than 25 per cent of the power she has at her disposal. But you pull out enough to satisfy your planned timing, well aware that you have reserve enough to cover up almost anything.

So, thinking of that sudden gale which seems to have died out, you settle back comfortably as you pass Granthouse, over 41 miles from Edinburgh, in 44 minutes 45 seconds: which isn't too bad, you reflect, when you remember Nine's style was cramped by those first four miles, which by reason of restrictions to speed filched no less than 6 ½ minutes from the total time she has taken so far.

You have been more or less concerned with driving Nine and been tied to the driving

Another day, another duty. On this occasion A4 No. 60030 *Golden Fleece* is pulling 'The Norseman', which ran between King's Cross and Newcastle to link with shipping services to Norway. (RH)

seat, and now, after 100 minutes of thus confinement, you're starting to envy Bob McKerchar in his freedom and movement. 'It's easy, this firing,' you've been thinking. Bob has never turned a hair, though by the look of the hole he's made in that tender-full of coal, he's bound to have shovelled a ton or two. You do a quick calculation, and your arithmetic is quite good when you make it three tons, and while this rather daunts you, nevertheless you carry on with the bright idea. You will have a turn at firing.

You turn the heater just a mite shut to stop the hiss of steam which suddenly escapes from the safety valves. Then, not till then you stretch out your hand for the shovel. The first shovel-full of coal you attempted to shoot into the firebox as Nine switched herself round the Morpeth curve told more than thousands of words could have done. It told you that the firehole door was just wide enough to allow the narrow shovel blade through, with little to spare, and that, even at 40mph, Morpeth isn't the best place to start learning how to fire.

As your first attempt struck the side frame of the door and the coal scattered everywhere except in the firebox, you could have sworn Nine deliberately jinked when you were in mid-swing. So you have another go and this time you find the firehole door, but only just... And now you start to pay attention to what has been going on beside you for over 100 miles. You find that it is infra dig to

keep your feet wandering all over the place. Your legs are planted wide apart and the weight is carried on the balls of your feet. As you bend to jab the shovel into the tender coal-hole you also find that this action jams your lower regions into contact with the seat on which you sit when not firing. Even the way you bend down has a bearing on how you can last the pace, but believe me, this firing on a long road 'fast' can be tough if you don't know how.

On the finishing stretch (between Morpeth and Newcastle) there are certain things to do before Nine comes off and another engine ties on for the run to Leeds. First at full throttle, then at three-quarters, Nine is literally straining at the leash. On the

toughish bit between Morpeth and Stannington you feel her drive biting into the springs with a slight side-to-side roll as each of her three-pistons does its job. Stannington – and she's clocking 51mph and on passing Plessey does Bob sing out that your firing can stop. You grin with satisfaction at the steam gauge. You have kept the pointer as near full pressure as doesn't matter, but you are quite pleased to desist and rest while Bob puts in a strong finish.

Cramlington, then Annitsford and Nine has settled to a comfortable 71mph and is riding like a dream. The throttle is shut and the first lap is in the bag. After Annitsford is passed Bob sweeps the cab floor, Nine does a quiet 70mph with the sun shining on the gleaming

No. **60011** *Empire of India* at Waverley with the Elizabethan. This engine, which at the time this photograph was taken was based at Haymarket, would survive in service until 1964, having first migrated to Aberdeen. (RH)

King's Cross A4 No. 60033 *Seagull* on duty with a mixed rake of carriages towards the end of the 1950s. This Pacific remained a King's Cross's books until condemned in December 1962 having been superseded by the Class 55s. For her there will be no transfer to Scotland and a few more years of running. Instead, she will go to Doncaster and be cut up in the early part of 1963. (THG)

A classic 1950's scene as 60027 Merlin works her express train through Edinburgh. (THG)

steel ribbons winding under her … Long before we come to the slow round the bend at Heaton South box Nine has had her pace curbed and time is given to the train ahead to clear. With the green showing,

the Queen of Scots needs little inducement to negotiate the curve at Manors and, to the unmistakable clickity-click of this one of the largest crossings in the world forming the approach to the station, she

glides like a wraith along the main platform.

Before the wheels have actually come to a rest, Bob is off the engine and away to the front as hard as he can go. He returns with one of the headlamps, sticks it on the lampholder at the tender end, and has Nine uncoupled from the train. Even before he reaches the cab there's a blast on the whistle and Nine is away to Gateshead.

McKillop's words capture the professional pride he took in being a driver of such a locomotive. At the same time, he makes light of the hard physical work that was required by many people for him to demonstrate his prowess. Even the effort to prepare the engine that morning is glossed over. In truth, the loco had probably been kept in light steam overnight and then had her fire slowly built up by 'junior' staff, as Spencer called them, until she was ready for the day's work. He then added that:

They would have spent a lot of time oiling the engine, clambering underneath in the process to check all was well, raking out ashes from the smokebox and much more. Whilst they did this, a posse of cleaners would have been at work polishing everything in sight with oily rags so giving the engine a high gloss finish that these premier services demanded. When all this was complete the tender would be filled with water and coal carefully shovelled and neatly stacked so that it didn't spill over. Then it was a case of

awaiting the arrival of the Top Link crew. Some of these old chaps were real sticklers and woe betide the youngsters if the engine wasn't as they wished to see it – everything ready, a good fire burning, pressure up to scratch, clean all over, plus a swept and polished cab. And even though the engine was ready to go the footplate crew would begin their own checks.

There is little doubt that many had a strong sense of pride in their work, especially those working on the Pacifics, but there were few who did not welcome the arrival of diesels and the saving of all those hours of hard work. They might remember steam locomotives with affection, but those who transferred over did so with some relief.

With new motive power becoming firmly established in the last few years of the 1950s, it was only a matter of time before steam gave

way to diesel, its death knell being sounded by the authors of the 1954 Modernisation Plan. But in these final years you might be forgiven for thinking that such a change programme was so much political

'kite flying' and steam would go on for many more years yet simply because the cost of its replacement would prove prohibitive. Inevitably, such ambitious plans will invariably attract a jaundiced reaction from commentators grown used to politician's sweet words and then poor delivery. But in this case, the promise of change seems to have been sincerely held and funds continued to be found, even for the final stage of Riddles' Steam Standardisation Plan, in all its misguided efficiency.

As the decade came to an end, all this was becoming clear to those who worked the A4s, with their main Nemesis, the Class 55s, soon to roll off the production line and enter service on the East Coast line. Now was the time, for those who could see it coming to an end, to stretch their mounts and enjoy the last years of steam on Britain's railways.

Trying to keep a Pacific clean could be a thankless task and towards the end of steam, with staff shortages, even more difficult. In this case a team of three make progress on polishing 60001 *Sir Ronald Matthews*, a Gateshead engine throughout her life. (RH)

As No. 60022 *Mallard*, now with later style BR emblem, on her tender, thunders past with the Tyne-Tees Pullman service while something ahead, now lost to time, attracts the attention of the driver and fireman. (THG)

Chapter 4

ALL GLORY IS FLEETING

The last years of the A4s were a sad time for those intrigued by steam. Perhaps, it was less so for the general public, many of whom would have been eager for the cleanliness of diesel and electric trains; though even here, amongst the more practical souls, their going might invoke a touch of nostalgia for the past. But change once embraced is rarely stalled and by 1966 the last of A4s were gone.

A gradual migration northwards, as the Class 55s and Type 4s took over their duties, provided only temporary relief from the inevitable trip to scrapyards and a lucky few into preservation. Before this happened there was much for the enthusiast to enjoy and the men who stood on their footplates could push these engines a few more times before they were gone.

By the early 1960s, steam had become even more of

an anachronism in a rapidly modernising, nuclear powered world. When they were first launched in 1935 even the most advanced aircraft could barely touch 300mph and the heaviest could carry bombloads of little more than 4,000lb. Now Mach 2 and higher speeds could be reached, and one well-placed missile could destroy a major city, with nuclear arsenals on both sides of the Iron Curtain capable of laying waste

To the end, steam held fascination for some, though in a modernising world its allure was fast fading as car and lorry sales boomed and the railways continued to lose custom and struggle to break even without government subsidies. Nevertheless, the old steam sheds and their inmates still drew a small, but willing audience and boys of varying sizes still congregated on the end of platforms to watch steam engines when given the opportunity to do so. Here two A4s (one unidentified and the other 60017 *Silver Fox*, a King's Cross engine until 1963) and B1 No. 61291 make a pleasing sight as they are made ready for work. (RH)

to the whole planet making it uninhabitable for a millennium or two. To make this nightmare seem more real, the Cuban Missile Crisis of 1962 acted as a timely reminder that Armageddon was only one small step away, though this didn't stop the build-up of arms, both atomic and conventional, on both sides of this great divide.

After a while, this terrible impasse faded into the background as people got on with their lives, although there were occasional reminders that all was not well. But by the 1960s much in society was changing, in part because post–war austerity was gradually becoming a distant memory and a consumer boom that fuelled many ambitions had taken hold. Many households could boast more money, a car, a TV and much more, with holidays in the UK and, increasingly, overseas becoming more commonplace. Changes that had gradually become more apparent in the late 1930s, but stifled by war and loss, were awakened and pursued with even greater vigour and determination, fuelled by banks more eager to lend. This was clearly reflected in the way the 1960s quickly became the 'Swinging Sixties', with fashion and music reflecting the changes. As Britain moved forward, so the steam engines that still dominated the network seemed increasingly out of place. In 1935, the 'streaks' appeared ultra-modern, now they were simply relics from a distant world. People wanted a great deal more. No vague assurances of a better future, but something tangible in return for the sacrifices of two world wars, and decades of hardship.

And yet the A4s continued to perform well and, though a

throwback to a different age, they did so with verve and something to spare, as Spencer later confirmed when he wrote:

> Discussions about the top speed an A4 could reach went on throughout the engines' lives and many drivers were

tempted to give them their head when the opportunity arose. I was told that towards the end of their time at King's Cross that some of the bolder drivers were determined to let one really go and take it well past the 1938 record and even speculated that 140mph might

Its number shrouded in smoke and steam, an anonymous A4 gets underway in a flurry of activity from King's Cross in 1962, its distinctive gas tanks providing a familiar backdrop. (THG)

A sign of a rapidly modernising world overlooking the crowning glory of the old world. A4 No. 60019 *Bittern* simmers gently at St Rollox as things change around her, although in this case preservation awaits followed by years of active running. In all probability she will still be working when this high rise slab of concrete and steel nonsense is but a distant memory. To the left of 60019 sits Stanier Black 5 No. 45084 which will be withdrawn from service in 1966. (THG)

be topped. If they did try they kept very quiet about it not wishing to suffer the wrath of BR's more safety conscious managers. Did they do it? I like to think they did before the end came. Certainly, I took a ride behind one when returning from Doncaster to Devon, via London, in the early 1960s and we came down Stoke Bank at very high speed – undoubtedly faster than usual. However, I did not have any accurate means of recording timings between mileposts, so I shall never know the true speed.

By this stage, with so short a time remaining for A4s on the mainline, there was little or no need to test a steam hauled train with a dynamometer car attached. So we are left with the unofficial work of the likes of Cecil Allen and O.S. Nock to fall back on and they could not be everywhere, so who knows what really went on.

It is certainly interesting to ponder the mysteries of footplate life when there were no inspectors around. For the most part, the drivers had a freedom of action that today's crew would find alien, every aspect of their working lives being carefully monitored and controlled by automated systems. For a steam driver and a fireman there were few prying eyes – human or machine – and if they so wished, they could push their locomotives or not as the mood took them. Some, as Spencer related, may have allowed professional pride or simply a devil may care attitude to govern their actions and 'go for it', keeping their efforts within a looser bound of safety. Years later I was privileged to interview a number of Southern Region drivers and each admitted that in the last two years of life with their Merchant Navy Pacifics they did just this and pushed their locomotives to the limit, with at least one suggesting that 'Mallard's 1938 record was probably bested on a number of occasions'. If they did, it seems likely that Eastern Region's drivers would have tried too, perhaps with more serious intent because of their region's history of fast running.

With the A4s' demise so close, care and maintenance had been reduced to something described as minimum essential and cannibalisation of parts from some laid-up engines was being practised to keep others going. As this happened, the inevitable call of the cutter's torch could be silenced no more and slowly but surely engines were condemned and scrapped. But before this happened there was much to observe and much to relish in a final burst of action. And to this end, shed staff did their best to keep the A4s in as good a condition as possible, despite the problems they faced in doing so.

In addition to Allen and Nock, we have one other author and railway observer to thank for recording these last few years of operation. R.A.H. Weight wrote many articles for the *Meccano Magazine* and produced a regular 'Railway Notes' page or two describing the decline of steam and the arrival of the diesels. Much of this he observed from Welwyn Garden City Station and occasionally he took his notebook

No.60024 *Kingfisher* ready for her next turn of duty at Haymarket in 1962. A year earlier, I travelled behind this engine and would do so again in 1964. Over the years I had seen her many times and was once, very briefly, allowed on to her footplate by the driver, whose name I did not record. For this reason, she became my personal favourite. (THG)

and timepiece and ventured out on the line, most notably with the A4s. He clearly relished what he was doing and his words capture the essence of this dying world and the excitement he felt in witnessing its final flourish. On this occasion he was taking the Elizabethan from Edinburgh behind A4 No. 60033 *Seagull*:

Nearly all first and third class seats were booked in the beautiful and spotless Elizabethan train, which I boarded that morning with a rather thrilled feeling of anticipation. It is a unique and outstanding express in several respects running during the summer in advance of the Flying Scotsman. It is not only scheduled to make the longest non-stop run in the World, over the 393 miles each way between the English and Scottish capitals, but it is also decidedly

the fastest Anglo-Scottish express. By a long margin it is the only one to average over 60mph for such a long distance, as the allowance is only 390 minutes or 6½ hours.

Our train also included two through carriages from Aberdeen and Dundee. It had first and third restaurant cars, a buffet lounge car of novel design and other very complete

Mallard **towards** the end of her operational life in 1963, but still in clean condition and still a thoroughbred. (THG)

With such a busy display of steam power at King's Cross shed its hard to believe that in a few short years all will be gone. Meanwhile this part of London still echoed to the sounds of steam locomotives and the air was heavy with the smell of smoke, steam and oil. (Left to right) No. 60007 *Sir Nigel Gresley*, ex A1 now A3 No. 60062 *Minoru*, No.60033 *Seagull*, Thompson A2/3 Pacific No. 60524 *Herringbone* and ex-War Department 2-8-0 No. 90613, which at this time was based at New England shed. (THG)

R.A.H. Weight, the railway commentator, took the opportunity, while steam lasted, to record many locomotive movements and on one occasion travelled on the southbound Elizabethan so he could record his thoughts for readers. On this occasion the service was pulled by 60033 *Seagull,* which, he reported, turned in a fine performance that day. This photo captures 60033 at about the same time, looking in good condition, while pulling another service. (THG)

amenities, including some air-conditioning, and the heavy 11 coach set weighed 403 tons empty or 423 tons including passengers, luggage, staff and stores.

It is usual for King's Cross and Haymarket A4s to work the train each way on alternate days, with crews from those depots sharing each journey, using the corridor tender to do so. When off duty they travel in a reserved compartment, take a meal in the restaurant car and are free to change into ordinary clothes.

Space permits only a brief summary of this splendidly steady, fast run. We were soon up to 70mph as we wound round the coast, passing Dunbar 29¼ miles in 30 minutes, and topping Cockburnspath bank,

1 in 90 and the steepest on the route, at 40mph. We enjoyed grand sea views and fine cliff and woodland scenery as we crossed the border, passed cautiously through Berwick-on-Tweed and over the curved and lofty Royal Border Bridge.

Fast travel again and a mile-a-minute average was being maintained as we approached Tyneside industrial belt with its electric trains, many branch lines and more great bridges. At much reduced speed we passed outside the platforms of the Newcastle Central Station – 124½ miles in 127 minutes. Uphill we went at 60-58mph, and soon came the imposing view from the elevated railway embankment in Durham at the Cathedral and University high on another rocky hill.

Again, another speed restriction. But we were soon pelting away towards the Tees and the great plain of York, passing Darlington Station at 65mph, along the fast tracks, about 30 seconds late. The almost level 44 miles on to York, that busy high-speed section of the main line, provided an opportunity to get a valued minute or two in hand, and to secure the preponderance of miles over minutes essential to keep time. They were reeled off in 35¾ minutes with a sustained maximum of 82-83mph to take the Elizabethan slowly through the big, curved York Station, two minutes before time at 1.5 pm, or in 200 minutes for 204½ miles from Edinburgh.

In recent years many improvements have been made to the East Coast route to permit the running of faster trains on tighter schedules, one of which is the new one-million-pound dive-under at Retford to carry the Eastern Region lines from Grimsby to Sheffield underneath the East Coast main line. A very large proportion of the five million tons of coal needed by the Central Electricity Generating Board at West Burton will have to pass over the crossing at Retford. This new dive-under scheme will avoid considerable congestion of trains travelling through the junction.

Meanwhile the drivers and firemen had changed. We passed the northbound sister express approximately halfway to London. With much of railway and other interest flashing by, we went impressively on through Doncaster and Grantham. Owing to a long stretch of track in hand for relaying, with a restriction imposed, there was no chance of reaching an exciting high speed down that part of Stoke Bank which has seen most of the A4 and other records achieved. As a result our maximum was 79mph. Through Peterborough we went slowly at 2.56, 316½ miles in 312¼ minutes, followed by some grand locomotive work over undulating gradients and level track, so that as we approached Hatfield at 66mph we had covered 375 miles in 366 minutes.

The hard work was over. *Seagull* was eased and was still in splendid form, with plenty of steam and coal left in the tender as an indication of efficient and economical performance. Operating efficiency, too, had ensured that the hundred signals for which the driver must watch closely had all been at clear in the country, as well as the big stations and numerous junctions for 387 miles, and the all-important water supply for the boiler had been replenished five or six times from the tracks troughs.

In the London suburbs adverse signals did slow us, twice, we kept moving and glided to a stop in No. 2 Platform, King's Cross, at 4.14, minutes early. We had run almost 393 miles in 389 minutes overall, or 384 net when allowing for extra speed

60024 *Kingfisher* appears to have been a regular on the Elizabethan, as this photo taken at Waverley in the late 1950s, bears witness. (BS)

restrictions. The world record run had been achieved once more on its fastest ever timing and with a little in hand.

As the months passed, there was an increase in the number of through engine workings, which placed an even greater demand on engines and footplate crew. It was an issue Peter Townend, then Shedmaster at King's Cross, raised in his fascinating book *Top Shed*. He reported that this led to the number of locomotives rostered for these duties being increased from nine to seventeen Pacifics in 1957. And in terms of manning, these duties were shared by thirty-four drivers at King's Cross alone, with the number of engines reaching a peak of forty-two for a time in

the last few months of 1957. With diesels waiting in the wings, this high point was soon followed by an inevitable decline. However, this large number of Pacifics stabled in London created significant operational problems for shed staff whose numbers were already in decline. Nevertheless, they coped well for a time helped, it would seem, by the improvements to the Pacifics introduced by Kenneth Cook, to whom Townend gave much credit. In his view, these modifications meant that 'remarkably little difficulty was experienced at Top Shed in covering the main line services during the prolonged transitional period'. High praise indeed from a very experienced and knowledgeable man whose career and reputation

New for old on the Eastern Region, though in this case the old, in the form of Peppercorn A1 No. 60129 *Guy Mannering*, is only ten years or so old and will only be fifteen when cut up in 1965. Behind the Pacific sits one of ten EE Type 2 diesels, that became known as the Baby Deltics, each being powered by a Napier T9-29 engine producing 1,100hp. They were procured to cover outer suburban duties from King's Cross and worked passenger services to Cambridge amongst other destinations. However, they proved unreliable in service and even though modifications improved their performance, a rationalisation exercise led to their withdrawal between 1968 and 1971. (THG)

rested on meeting so many pressing demands in the face of customers growing more critical of the service BR offered.

By the late 1950s, the transition period to which he refers was well underway. The gestation period for diesels may have been a long one, but finally BR's managers had begun to get their act together. By degrees they harnessed the effort of companies eager to do business having, like English Electric, invested heavily in diesel technology. We have seen how DP1 evolved into the Class 55 and a single order for twenty-two eagerly-awaited locomotives. But there was much more coming along, some of which would impact on the A4s and the other Eastern Region Pacifics.

Peter Townend recorded the early arrivals in 1958 at King's Cross and, as he described it, 'the beginning of the end' that this presaged. First up in the large diesel stakes was the EE Type 4s, later to become the Class 40s, though, as we have seen, these were quickly condemned by Gerry Fiennes for their lack of power. This was a view shared by Sir Brian Robertson, then chairman of the British Transport Commission, who was also unimpressed by their performance, believing that the locomotives lacked the power to pull heavy loads at high speed for long distances and were too expensive to double-head in an effort to increase range and capacity – a view judged by many to be correct.

And yet on paper they seemed to offer much more and should have been an adequate replacement for the Pacifics, especially with 200 being built between 1958 and 1962. Nevertheless, the LMR appears to have had no such qualms and used them on their main line services, although they had electrification on the horizon. As a result, they might have been seen at Derby as a short term measure only, to allow the old LMS Pacifics to be discarded, which they were, the last being withdrawn in 1964.

As we have seen, Fiennes had a preference for the Class 55s and so undoubtedly used Robertson's comments about the Type 4s in gaining support for Deltics on the Eastern Region. Here Bert Spencer, now retired but still observing what was happening, probably revealed the truth of the matter when he wrote:

I think it likely that Fiennes, being a dyed in the wool LNER man, wanted something to replace the A4s that had a spark of glamour about it. Prestige and good headlines were still important and the Deltics brought something distinctive and unique to the East Coast Mainline. Plus they could do the job better than any alternatives, except the A4s. However, a better option than either the Class 40s or 55s was probably waiting in the wings with the Brush Type 4 Co-Co (Class 47) diesels, which began appearing in 1962.

So the Type 4s were side-lined and the Pacifics continued to carry the

burden until the Deltics began to arrive in 1961, but Spencer's view of the Class 47s is an interesting one because, in his mind, it offered a viable alternative.

These Co-Co diesel-electric locomotive were developed by Brush Traction and a total of 512 Class 47s were built between 1962

and 1968 at the company's Falcon Works in Loughborough and at British Railways' Crewe Works. Such a large number made them the most numerous class of British mainline diesel locomotive built and probably one of the most successful. The design was based on the D0260 Lion prototype which

The **distinctive** emblem of a highly polished Silver Fox on each side of its boiler made identification of this A4 the easiest of all. When I saw No. 60017 working for the last time, near Hadley Wood, she was still in a highly polished state and in good mechanical order and, to my mind, capable of many more years of service. Yet a few months later she had been condemned and scrapped. (THG)

A **comparison** of styles and technologies at Doncaster. Workmanlike and blunt nosed but easy to handle beside sleek, fast but much harder to operate. The Brush Type 2 (BR Class 31s) diesel-electric No. D5625 was one of two hundred and sixty-three built between 1957 and 1962 and here is posed beside 60009 soon to join the preservation movement. (RH)

Where the A4s had once held sway, the diesels now dominated, as this photo taken at Peterborough in the mid-1960s demonstrates. Gone are the long hours of preparation before an engine enters traffic and the hard work of firing each day. Now, as this driver pulling himself up into the cab of this Class 47 diesel will verify, footplate crew are in a switch on, warm up and move world where power is much easier to control and, it must be said, much more comfortable and better for their health. (RH)

was developed by a consortium of the Birmingham Railway Carriage and Wagon Company, Associated Electrical Industries and Sulzer. In the bidding process for new engines, they offered a production version of Lion, with both steam and electric heating.

The Type 4 was powered by a Sulzer 12LDA28C twin-bank twelve-cylinder engine producing 2,750bhp. This was later cut to 2,580bhp in an effort to reduce the number of breakdowns thought to have been caused by excessive stresses on the power plant. The change seemed to work and by all accounts did not cause any appreciable fall-off in their

performance and, in due course, they found wide employment on BR's network pulling passenger and freight trains. With a designed top speed of 95mph and good pulling power, they could easily undertake fast express work when required to do so. This was probably why Spencer saw them as a possible alternative to steam, or even the Deltics, on the Eastern Region. In the event, they did become a regular feature on these lines, but did not displace the Class 55s.

In early 1961 the first of the Deltics, No. D9000, which was named *Royal Scots Grey* on 18 June 1962, was ready for service. By this time, many of the drivers had

footplate experience of the type with DP1 which remained in the Region until March 1961 when an engine failure led to its withdrawal and eventual display in London's Science Museum. But they had also been given the opportunity of working with a smaller version, the EE Type 2, which the company were commissioned to build by BR in 1955, under the auspices of its Modernisation Plan. Construction of ten engines, powered by Napier T9-29 engines producing 1,100hp, was completed in 1959. In due course, they were allocated to the Eastern Region and were employed on outer suburban duties from King's Cross and worked short haul passenger services to Cambridge and other destinations. However, they proved unreliable in service and even though modifications improved their performance somewhat, a rationalisation exercise led to their early withdrawal between 1968 and 1971. Despite this, they helped the Eastern Region drivers and maintenance staff adapt to diesel motive power at a difficult time and so helped smooth the path to this modern world and the Deltics in particular.

When entering service in 1961 the decision to paint these engines in a distinctive two-tone colour scheme has been taken, making the 55s, as Spencer reported 'stand out from the crowd' though adding an interesting footnote in that he 'personally would have continued with the more striking DP1 blue scheme'. He, of course, clearly remembered the impact the grey and then blue A4s had made before the war and saw the commercial and aesthetic benefits of doing so again. But corporate identity

Left and below: **As the** end of steam on the Eastern Region approached those with a sense that history was passing grew in their determination to record all aspects of a way of life that was disappearing. As a result, the number of photographers and those simply observing steam locomotives seemed to multiply as the months passed and much was recorded, not simply A4s rushing by as they had always done. Sheds, though generally out of bounds, became very popular destinations for those with cameras. Good vantage points were chosen and day to day life recorded in some detail as here, where 60006 *Sir Ralph Wedgwood* was recorded going through the simple act of being turned and serviced ready for her next duty. (THG)

was more important now and BR were looking for a collective brand that better reflected the aims of a nationalised industry.

D9001 arrived at Doncaster in February 1961 for acceptance trials to begin and went into traffic on the 23rd. She was the first of the class to be delivered and was assigned to Haymarket after some initial problems had been ironed out. A few months later she was christened at Doncaster taking the name St Paddy after the 1960 Derby winner. To followers of Nigel Gresley's career the decision to choose racehorse names harked back to the 1920s and the decision to name many of the A1s and A3s in the same way. As a nod to Britain's military history, fourteen of the new engines would also be given the names of famous regiments – those with a geographic link to the old LNER network.

And so the change programme got underway and the East Coast Mainline began hum to the sound

of Napier engines as the sound of steam slowly died away. But the Class 55s were not without their teeting problems and the transition wasn't as easy or as simple as the powers that be might have wished it to be. For those who could remember the virtually trouble-free arrival of the A4s in the mid-1930s, this was something to look back on with relish and savour. But the new diesels embraced a more complex technology, so problems were inevitable. Nevertheless, many would have nodded sagely at a famous Giles cartoon of the time which showed up the fallibility of diesels in the face of BR's promises of a better more efficient service. A diesel has failed, and the driver looks over his shoulder to see an ancient steam locomotive in the distance coming to his rescue. He turns to a colleague and utters the words 'He'd better not ask if the rubber band is broken again .....'. As always, Giles caught the mood of the nation and in a

In the shadows but not yet forgotten would seem to be an appropriate caption for this photograph. In the background, and out of the limelight, 60028 *Walter K. Whigham* prepares to depart with the Elizabethan during 1961 from King's Cross while Class 55 No. 9003 *Meld*, which was named at Doncaster in July that year, sits waiting for an unrecorded duty. (BS)

Although failure rates were high in their first year of operation, and they suffered from a number of niggling problems, the Deltics did at least look splendid at the head of a train, in this case a highly publicised run with the Flying Scotsman. Here D9020 *Nimbus*, which entered service in early 1962, is captured at Newcastle. Spencer's notes suggest that this picture was taken in June that year during celebrations of the centenary of this service, on which he was a passenger (BS).

rapidly becoming something of an embarrassment, and many looked back at the pre-nationalised companies and wished to return to those days. While they lasted, the A4s provided this link and were probably celebrated even more because of it.

A great fuss was made of the Deltics when they were finally put into service, but it rang hollow when they did not quite meet expectations. Between March 1961 and April 1962 there were seventeen failures all told, caused by problems with connecting rods, fractured liners and dephasing amongst other things. Perhaps not a particularly high rate for such new technology but concerning nonetheless, considering they had been in development for many years. But besides the complete breakdowns came a whole host of other problems that made the Deltics far from popular. Noise levels in the cab were too high for drivers to bear comfortably. They produced too much smoke because lubricating oil was allowed to carry over into the exhaust system. As a result, dense fumes would often engulf the engines and infiltrate the carriages, much to the discomfort of passengers. Steam customers were long used to this but expected better from these new locomotives.

And so the list went on. The Barber-Coleman spline assemblies began failing, the overspeed shut-down mechanism kept tripping and the underspeed switch proved less than reliable. Then problems with radiator fans and the engine load control system cropped up. The engines' electrical equipment developed a number of defects,

whimsical way revealed many truths. By poking fun at the new diesels, he was highlighting a growing disenchantment with British Railways and the way they were doing their business. Whether it be the state of the trains or the poor food on offer, BR was

due to design deficiencies and the effects of hard running, a condition that could hardly be avoided considering the nature of rail operations. To resolve these problems there were a number of 'get well' programmes in operation at any one time. As a result, confidence in the Deltics soon dropped and relationships between BR and English Electric were probably sullied, though not irrevocably.

For the A4s, this meant a stay of execution and a final flourish of activity before the East Coast line moved away from steam entirely. In response, the 'Streaks' and the other Pacifics appear to have worked well and didn't disappoint, despite fewer staff to maintain or even clean them. Once again R.A.H. Weight recorded many of the comings and goings:

Considerable changes were made to services from King's Cross to the North of England and Scotland. A new train, The Fair Maid replaced the morning Talisman and, for the first time, provided an early morning service in both directions on Mondays to Fridays between London and Perth, calling at Darlington, Newcastle and Edinburgh. The new train is timed to run the 232 miles from King's Cross to Darlington at an average speed of 60mph.

He added in a separate note, 'These changes were introduced in expectation of diesels becoming available, though stream engines, particularly the A4s, seem to have had no difficulty in meeting these revised times.'

The principal expresses, running with lighter loads, now run faster. Many intermediate stops have been cut out and additional trains run to serve intermediate passengers. These revisions provide a more orderly timetable and better use of engines, coaches and crews.

Notable changes are reductions of 37 minutes for the down Flying Scotsman and 39 minutes in the opposite direction. The Aberdonian sleeper now leaves King's Cross at 10.15 pm instead of 7.00 pm and has been accelerated by 92 minutes, while the corresponding train from Aberdeen now leaves the city at 8.35 pm and its running time reduced by 85 minutes. The 1.20 pm King's Cross to Leeds has also been speeded up by 42 minutes and the 10.45 pm train by 35 minutes.

Meanwhile with numerous additional holiday trains, the Elizabethan has often been hauled by A4s *Mallard* and *Commonwealth of Australia* from King's Cross and Haymarket respectively – timekeeping was remarkably good in both directions.

A new duty for the A4s – the Fair Maid – was introduced to run between King's Cross and Perth and took the morning slot normally occupied by the Talisman service on Mondays to Fridays. (RH)

Towards the end of steam on the East Coast Mainline, the A4s would often be seen pulling fast freight trains, making light work of these more mundane loads, and they were still in a good, clean state as befits a King's Cross engine. In this case it is No. 60032 *Gannet* which, shortly after this photo was taken in 1963, was condemned and scrapped at Doncaster. (THG)

Around Waverley Station was the perfect spot to photograph the A4s and this summer's day in 1963 was no different as 60016 *Silver King* departs Edinburgh with her tender fully loaded with coal, but apparently with her dome missing from atop her boiler – seemingly not regarded as a crucial omission. This engine, Gateshead based since 1945, will move northwards St Margaret's for a few weeks in October 1963 then to Aberdeen. (THG)

From Welwyn, Weight observed and recorded many passing trains particularly during August when many A4s, and occasionally diesels, went flying past. He wrote:

The Fair Maid, 6.6 from Leeds and the 6.40 from Glasgow, were worked respectively by streamlined Pacifics *Miles Beevor*, *Wild Swan* and *Seagull*, while. the Northumbrian was hauled by a 2,000 hp diesel–electric No. D207. The Elizabethan was late that day, but A4 No. 60013 *Dominion of New Zealand* appeared in good condition. With an extra coach, ten on, the northbound Talisman topped Potters Bar summit in fine style hauled by A4 *Lord Faringdon*.

And occasionally he seems to have found time to travel behind an A4, or used accounts prepared by a friend, in this case Norman Harvey, when unable to travel himself:

A summer day in 1962 and this immaculately turned out A4, in this case 60025 *Falcon*, flashed past pulling the Flying Scotsman with barely a whisper of steam and smoke, making very light of her twelve carriage train in the process. She will, in October 1963, be condemned and scrapped at Doncaster three months later. (THG)

With streamlined A4 No. 60013 at the head of the northbound Talisman and in the expert hands of Driver Hoole, the smart 8 coach set weighing nearly 300 tons full, recorded some fast travel. Some slower trains ahead caused a number of signal delays while there were three track repair slowings. High speed stretches had therefore to be exploited, so the 14½ miles between Grantham and Newark was covered in 10 minutes. While the 30¼ miles of nearly level country between York and Darlington was covered in 21½ minutes. These represented 87 and 83½mph respectively. Though Newcastle was not quite reached to time owing to a signal stop and other slacks, due to a special train in front, the overall time from King's Cross had not been more than 4½ hours – a mean speed of 63mph.

60042 *Kingfisher* now took over, with Driver Nairn from Haymarket Shed, from the King's Cross engine and crew and soon set out to make-up time. It was another splendid performance, faster on balance than my recent Fair Maid run. In this case Edinburgh was reached in only a few seconds more than 2 hours for 124½ miles, including a slowed approach from Inveresk, and with a number of maxima in the 80 to 85mph range.

Southbound, A4 60003 *Andrew K. McCosh*, driven by Drive Clowes, King's Cross, gained 9½ minutes on a brisk timing from Durham to York, arriving well ahead of schedule

with a Sunday morning eleven coach express. An A8 4-6-2T banked us in the rear for a short distance to aid our start on the curved rise out of Durham. Then Darlington was passed on the through line at 74mph in no more than 21¾ minutes. Then along the regularly very fast stretch to the outskirts of York 77mph was averaged, with a maxima of 87, in spite of a signal check at Thirsk.

These are only snapshots of life then, but they convey so much in terms of the daily load that fell on engines and the people who

kept them going. But these notes barely hint at all the work that was going on on the train, at stations, signal boxes, workshops and sheds and much more. The footplate crew were the head of the arrow, but much lay behind, unseen, unrecognised and unrewarded except in pay packets each week or month. The diesels would see these numbers greatly reduced and with them would go the spirit of the old LNER. The individuality of the Deltics might briefly echo this sense of history, but it was no more than a shadow of a former glory that would soon fade away. But change came and was celebrated by Weight

60010 *Dominion of Canada* is given a slight gloss as pouring rain cascades over her body. In reality she is in a very mucky condition as she awaits her next turn of duty. She will shortly be withdrawn from service, but avoid the cutter's torch and be presented to a railway museum near Montreal, after being externally restored at Crewe. (THG)

BR are modernising, after many years of apparent stagnation, and a gleaming Deltic seems to highlight the changes as it powers along with the Flying Scotsman, now with thistle crest on the front. (RH)

for one and he wrote at length about the coming of the Class 55s and the impact they were making, though on this occasion the Deltic's 'glory' was spoilt by an unexpected incident:

Although I am a veteran railway traveller I still feel the thrill of anticipation when joining one of the 'top' British long-distance trains. So it was on a sunny day in June when I climbed aboard a northbound Flying Scotsman express now

on a timing cut from seven to six hours in each direction, including a call at Newcastle. Now one of the extremely powerful Deltic diesel-electric locomotives is usually in charge south of Edinburgh. For my run it was D9017, *The Durham Light Infantry*, manned as far as Newcastle by my friends Driver Arthur Davis, who was making his last run before retirement, assisted by Brian Graves. It was a handsome 11-coach train with most seats reserved. Its

running was most comfortable over new-type Commonwealth or B4 type bogies on track largely re-fettled and including considerable stretches of long-welded rails.

After leaving King's Cross at 10 am travel was very fast. After three extra slowings en route we passed Peterborough at the usual sedate pace, 76½ miles in 68 minutes, having touched a maximum of 98mph before Sandby. Peterborough to Grantham

29 miles in 22½ minutes, was my quickest ever; so overall on the way, was the ascent of the long rise to Stoke Box entirely at 85-83mph. The Scotsman was through Grantham in just over one and a half hours; Retford (severe signal slack) in two hours and was punctual at Doncaster – 156 miles in 137 minutes.

A sudden and prolonged stop just beyond the double main line junction north of Doncaster destroyed expectations of a 268 mile, 4 hour non-stop run to Newcastle. An observant signalman a little way back had thought he saw smoke coming from one of the coaches, possibly indicating a fire or an overheated axle box and

had sent the emergency bell signal 'Stop and examine train' to Doncaster signal box. As a result the first available colour light beyond was reversed to show red. Examination by the guard however, proved it to have been a false alarm – perhaps smoke coming from the kitchen window – and all was well. The first service of lunch was just being completed at the time, and most passengers had no idea why the train had stopped.

The delay was considerable, and we were out of our path and so encountered some adverse signals. On a 67½mph overall schedule with about 420 tons to haul, and facing a number of speed restrictions,

there was not much margin, even with a Deltic. After a cautious passage of York, however, beyond Tollerton we regained a little time along the very fast stretch towards to Darlington, 93.95mph being sustained for a considerable distance. I alighted at Newcastle 20 minutes late, but it might have been more!

Perhaps the Gateshead crew who took over the driving cab were able to snatch a few minutes from the tight timing on past Berwick. The entire journey in six hours requires a mean speed of 65mph, necessitating a good deal of over 80mph travel, with fast uphill work and rapid acceleration.

An A4, rendered anonymous by dirt but still capable of great speed and effective running. Enthusiasts often ask how long could they have gone on. Everyone will have an opinion, but it seems that if serviced regularly and effectively they could easily have lasted well into the 1970s. (THG)

60022 *Mallard* presents a sorry picture in the middle of the yard in early 1963, her future apparently uncertain. However, this famous engine will soon undergo some restoration work and be preserved as part of the national collection. (THG)

The tone of these words suggests that the world has changed, for better or worse, and it is time to embrace the future and let steam go. For most people its passing was of little consequence, and few had yet begun to grow dewy-eyed at seeing a locomotive wreathed in smoke pass by. This would come later, although some forward-thinking people were quick to see that preservation and conservation of elements of this culture and its technology were important and acted accordingly. BR were far less concerned and sometimes practiced tokenism but generally were quick to obliterate the last vestiges of the old. But it is the role of industry to look ahead, not backwards and unless preservation can be seen to have some commercial purpose, which in most cases BR's managers could not envisage, it was best to let it go and move on. This is what they did and then quickly began culling steam locomotives by the thousand as diesels took over, keeping a few examples for posterity. So *Mallard*, as the World Record Holder, found a home in the national collection and was cosmetically restored for public display, while the rest struggled on, through the early 1960s, into an uncertain future. However, for a few, salvation was at hand as some concerned individuals marshalled their resources to ensure more locomotives survived, along with carriages, wagons and the paperwork that defined their lives.

For some A4s, the end came quickly as the Deltics and the other diesels began to dominate the East Coast line, with the first locomotives becoming reserves to take over from any failing engine, diesel or steam, then being condemned and scrapped. It could be a hit or miss affair and some survived longer because they were in the right place at the right time, others because they were in better condition so might better survive a regime of declining maintenance. It may also have helped that as diesel numbers increased, so some A4s moved to Scotland to help service the lines there. But it was a demand that would eventually diminish and disappear as BR sought to modernise and eradicate the old and remove the labour-intensive

infrastructure that supported steam locomotives.

The cull began in December 1962, when five King's Cross A4s were condemned, a sure sign that the Deltics were finally coping with demand. And so 60003 *Andrew K. McCosh*, 60014 *Silver Link*, 60028 *Walter K. Whigham*, 60030 *Golden Fleece* and 60033 *Seagull* were despatched to Doncaster where all were reduced to scrap by the end of January. With hindsight, it seems to have been very remiss not to preserve *Silver Link*, the first member of the class, but these were unemotional, cold days and it was just another locomotive amongst thousands that needed to be ditched as easily and as quickly as possible.

During 1963, many others followed them, including three more from King's Cross – 60013 *Dominion of New Zealand*, 60015 *Quicksilver* and 60022 *Mallard* - but here the running department nearly miscalulated, or so it seems. During the busy summer season that followed, they were in danger of running short of suitable motive power and could probably have made use of these three engines as an active reserve at least. But BR survived and the disposal programme continued, with both 60013 and 60015 finding their way to Doncaster to be cut up while *Mallard*, of course, entered a well earned retirement in preservation. She was joined in this envious state by 60008 *Dwight D. Eisenhower* which was presented to the US Ambassador, David Bruce, having been condemned in July 1963 at New England. After some cosmetic restoration, Dr Beeching, BR's 1961 appointed Chairman, very publicly handed the engine over and shortly

afterwards she was shipped to the States for display in the 1956 founded American National Railroad Museum in Wisconsin.

Sadly, five sister engines from New England fared less well that year – 60017 *Silver Fox*, 60021 *Wild Swan*, 60025 *Falcon*, 60029 *Woodcock* and 60032 *Gannet* – all being scrapped at Doncaster. In June, they were joined by 60018 *Sparrow Hawk* from Gateshead to make a yearly total of ten. The pace of disposals only eased slightly in 1964, with seven more added. Four of these came from Aberdeen – 60005 *Sir Charles Newton*, 60011 *Empire of India*, 60012 *Commonwealth of Australia* and 60023 *Golden Eagle* – and three from Gateshead –

60001 *Sir Ronald Matthews*, 60002 *Sir Murrough Wilson* and 60020 *Guillemot*. Destruction of these engines now spread from Doncaster to other yards. Six went either to G.H. Campbell of Airdrie, Darlington Works, the Motherwell Machinery and Scrap Co, Hughes Bolckow's of North Blyth or Cohen's of Middlesborough to be cut up that year with only 60012 surviving into 1965.

There is something about the way a large bureaucratic organisation operates that seems to encourage vacillation and dithering in the name of prudent management. BR was no different and having spent considerable time and money in the late 1940s and early '50s to

60004 *William Whitelaw* apparently held in reserve in case of motive power shortages, but still looks in remarkably good condition. From June 1963, she was based at Aberdeen and was condemned in 1966. (THG)

With such a famous name as *Dwight D. Eisenhower* A4 No. 60008 was bound to attract the attention of enthusiasts and patriots in the United States and this proved to be the case. The engine was withdrawn from service in 1963 and, after some restoration work, was presented by BR's Chairman Dr Richard Beeching to the US Ambassador and Harold Fuller, Chairman of the American National Railroad Museum (above left). A little while later the locomotive was shipped to the States (above right). (RH)

perpetuate the myth that steam could go on for many decades, it now moved to destroy this heritage with such haste that it seemed to have become an anathema to them. So one poor decision followed another and thousands of engines, many with a considerable asset value and remaining life left to them, were hurriedly, and indecently scrapped in an orgy of destruction. For the A4s, this meant that as 1965 dawned there were only twelve active survivors, all based in Scottish sheds, left – ten at Aberdeen Ferryhill and one each

at St Margarets and St Rollox in Glasgow.

Six of these engines would be withdrawn in 1965, with five – 60006 *Sir Ralph Wedgwood*, 60016 *Silver King*, 60026 *Miles Beevor*, 60027 *Merlin* and 60031 *Golden Plover* – being scrapped and 60010 *Dominion of Canada* being presented to the railway museum near Montreal, once restored externally. Then, in 1966, the last six followed suit, now all based at Aberdeen's Ferryhill shed, with the first to go being 60007 *Sir Nigel Gresley* in February. For this famous engine

a better future beckoned and three months later her sale to the A4 Preservation Society was completed. A little later, she appeared in a freshly applied garter blue coat of paint to begin work again in preservation and on specials where the authors found her in 1967 operating out of Waterloo.

This was an act of providence that gathered in two more from this group with 60009 *Union of South Africa* and 60019 *Bittern* also being saved from the scrapyard. But for 60004 *William Whitelaw*, 60024 *Kingfisher* and 60034 *Lord Faringdon*,

Once proud steam locomotives always presented a sad picture when discarded and consigned to remote parts of a yard awaiting scrapping. Sometimes they didn't look in too bad a state and may even have kept their nameplates for a time, but generally they had been stripped for spare parts and had an air of dereliction about them. (Top) 60034 *Lord Faringdon*, the second to last A4 to be withdrawn in August 1966 when based at the last bastion of operation, Aberdeen. She is surrounded by diesels as one final insult. (BS) (Left) Gateshead's 60020 *Guillemot,* condemned in March 1964, was scrapped a month later at Darlington. (THG) (Bottom left) 60002 *Sir Murrough Wilson*, photographed at Cohen's of Middlesborough in late 1964 having been withdrawn in May 1964 and briefly placed in store at Heaton, a sub-shed of Gateshead where the engine had been based since October 1943. (NS) (Bottom right) The cutting up of 60001 *Sir Ronald Matthews* at North Blyth's Hughes Bolckow's yard has begun and will be completed during January 1965. (EL)

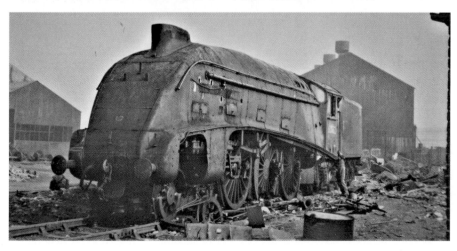

In March 1966, when nearing the end of her life, 60024 *Kingfisher* came south from her home at Ferryhill, where for the most part she appears to have been employed pulling express trains between Aberdeen and Glasgow, to work over Southern metals. With her 'LCGB A4 Commemoration Rail Tour', headboard she made her way to Weymouth and Exmouth and was photographed at every stage of her journey and received quite wide press coverage. Sadly, this tour did not include one last visit to King's Cross. This photo captures the engine at Waterloo during the tour, without her headboard. (THG)

The last A4 to serve at St Margarets, No. 60027 *Merlin*, is captured by the photographer shortly before withdrawal from service in September 1965, but still, apparently in steam. The cab sides have been emblazoned with crossways yellow stripes apparently painted when the engine was assigned to St Rollox in Glasgow between May 1962 and September 1964. These markings showed that the engine was precluded from working under the electrified wires south of Crewe when working on the London, Midland Region lines. (RH)

there were no saviours and they were consigned to scrapyards in Motherwell, Blyth and Renfrew for disposal, and cut up the same year. Strangely enough, these three were survived, briefly, by 60026. Her execution was delayed until late 1967, her sale to Motherwell Machinery and Scrap having been cancelled and the engine cannibalised at Crewe for spare parts to be used on 60007. What was left was then taken to Hughes Bolckow for disposal.

Any sadness there may have been at the passing of these giants was alleviated, to a certain extent, by a late burst of activity and some 'specials' in 1966, all carefully followed by enthusiasts, including the authors. Perhaps the most noteworthy of these duties found 60024 *Kingfisher* heading south of the Border during March, but this

time to run from Waterloo along Southern lines taking members of the Locomotive Club of Great Britain to such places as Exmouth and Weymouth. For some, it harked back to the 1948 Interchange Trials when the A4s appeared at Waterloo to be set against the best the SR and LMR could offer. For others, it seemed strange that this East Coast worthy did not run similar tours from King's Cross. In fact, the last recorded departure from there by an A4 was on 24 October 1964 when 60009 hauled the 'Jubilee Requiem' on a return trip to Newcastle, according to records kept by the RCTS. However, the Southern rather surprisingly played host to an A4 again, in June 1967, when newly preserved 60007 *Sir Nigel Gresley*, resplendent in blue and restored to its old number 4498, worked from Waterloo to

Bournemouth and Weymouth. With the end of steam only days away on the Southern, she was an interesting interloper because of the obvious Bulleid connection between the LNER Pacifics, on which he worked with Gresley, and the Southern Pacifics which he brought to life during the war.

This was in many ways a final farewell to a time of great

endeavour in which the A4s had delivered all their design team hoped they might, and more. It was the end of an era but, thanks to the preservation movement, six remain and can be seen in steam, when time and money allowed. How long they can continue to delight us in this way is difficult to predict, but whatever happens, we can still see them, albeit in a static, highly polished state. Whilst 4472 *Flying Scotsman* quite rightly has acquired legendary status and draws large crowds wherever she goes, even to the risk of life and limb, the A4s are worthy of the same status and accolades. The huge crowds that came together for the Great Gathering of 2013, when all six survivors were brought together for possibly the last time, is perhaps the clearest indication of their enduring appeal and the high esteem in which they are held.

60009 *Union of South Africa* has been a star of main line running since withdrawal from BR service in 1966. In 2022 she is slated for static display for the time being. Will she steam again? I sincerely hope so. I have ridden behind her on numerous occasions, each memorable, and wish to do so again. Here she draws a smaller crowd than usual on Cupar Station in Fife, but hopefully an equally appreciative one. The driver who is leaning out of his cab appears to be sounding his distinctive chime whistle for the benefit of the child. (THG)

60024 at Ferryhill and still in business for a little bit longer. During the last year of steam's life in Scotland, a group called Scottish Railfans, which had strong links with BR, produced a booklet which gave details of all steam hauled trains. The A4s seemed to have been focussed on the Aberdeen to Glasgow Buchanan Street route morning and afternoon, plus returns, but also worked each way once a day from Glasgow to Dundee, a late night run from Glasgow to Perth apparently with the mail train, two early morning runs from Perth to Aberdeen and a Sunday afternoon service from Perth to Carstairs. Around them ran a host of other classes of engine, including BR Standard Class 7s, Class 4 and 4MTTs, LNER B1s, LMS Black 5s. (THG)

Epilogue

THE SUM OF ALL ITS PARTS

A Summer Saturday or Sunday near Hatfield in 1961 was a good place to spot A4s in full flow heading north or south. This day in July was no different. 60007 *Sir Nigel Gresley* was captured when going particularly fast. Later on, the author would follow the Deltics, in particular, from the same spot but it wasn't the same. (THG)

My own memories of A4s date back to the early 1950s, when they still had a decade or more of life left in them. For the most part, I saw them at King's Cross with my uncle, but occasionally we might venture to a station in the city's outer reaches to see a Gresley Pacific, and hopefully a 'Streak', in full flow as it headed north. Those heading south were interesting, but with King's Cross fairly close, the drivers were 'easing off', their job nearly done. After hours of hard work, this was hardly surprising, though frustrating for a child eager for thrills.

One of our favourite haunts turned out to be Barnet, a short drive from my uncle's home in North London and Bert Spencer's old stamping ground when working for Gresley in London. As I grew older, aided by family friends who lived near Hadley, I saw them running at speed and then, finally, rode behind six members of the class as they worked their magic. Of these events I mostly remember the sense of excitement I felt to be hurtling along behind one of these engines. Yet it was tinged with frustration that I couldn't see the locomotive until we had arrived at our destination. Oh, to be omnipresent and be everywhere at once!

By comparison, my late uncle observed them closely from *Silver Link*'s first day of service in 1935 until 1967 aboard 4498 *Sir Nigel Gresley* when pulling a special train from Waterloo to the South Coast. In between times, he followed them on a regular basis, gathering views, impressions and information about them, as well as the LNER's other Pacifics. To him they were without equal, but he realised that to some, even other ardent admirers of the LNER, this was not always the case, and they could become like Marmite – you either loved or hated them. He would often recall conversations with other enthusiasts that began with the words 'not those horrible streamliners again, give me the A1s or A3s any day'. It was a frame of mind of which Bert Spencer was only too aware. He wrote that:

Bulleid and many others at King's Cross, Doncaster and Darlington were not overly enamoured with the A4s, detesting and rejecting, like Stanier at Euston, the whole aerodynamic shaping of these engines and the Princess Coronation.

'It's nothing more than just a passing fancy' seemed to sum up their views. And even when faced with exceptional performances as a matter of course every day they rarely if ever changed their minds.

In many ways, it may simply have been a matter of aesthetics – beauty in the eye of the beholder and all that. Nothing wrong with this of course, because when it comes to looks, defining appeal will always be a subjective judgement where little is right or wrong. Then there is the issue of tradition to consider. Some people find change difficult and seek comfort in the familiar and for the steam enthusiast this often meant well-established and widely appreciated lines to the locomotives. Then there are others who are attracted by the new and embrace the radical and the unusual, especially if it is linked to some scientific discovery which gives it added appeal.

In some ways, this divergence of opinion over design can best be demonstrated by studying the careers of Gresley and Stanier and how their natures and their engineering backgrounds effected the paths they took and the opinions they expressed.

In engineering there is a clear difference between those who specialise in design and those

60016 *Silver King* slips into Waverley Station in 1963 making light of her load and with a tender full of coal ready for the onward journey to an unrecorded destination. (THG)

60026 *Miles Beevor* filling in between passenger turns with this 'Conflat' train near Welwyn Garden City on Monday, 12 August 1961. (THG)

60026 *Miles Beevor* with a wonderfully impromptu head board advertising the LNER Society, though there is little else to say that this might be a 'special' rather than a scheduled service. The sooty strip along the engine's top suggests that whoever was cleaning the loco was too short or had insufficient time to complete the job. On this rather wet day, the pouring rain has given the rest of the engine a slightly glossy look, a reminder of better days before the engine was withdrawn in 1965. (THG)

in production. One is creative and conceptual in nature and is concerned with scheming out possible solutions to meet a specific need – in essence, changing a specification into a working machine. Production engineering complements the designer's work by turning these concepts into reality through the application of sound workshop practices. As this happens, they test out the design's effectiveness, machine and manipulate all individual parts to the greatest accuracy and seek modifications where necessary, to ensure smooth and efficient operation. When trials are complete and the item is proven, these engineers then manage production lines and flow rates

through the workshops and then in life maintenance and modification programmes.

While both CMEs were exemplary, talented leaders and understood both these areas of work, Gresley was recorded as being, first and foremost, a creative thinker who revelled in the exploration of scientific principles and their application to locomotives in particular. Stanier came from the other, equally important, engineering world and was a specialist in production management and how to get the best out of his workshops. Within this framework some might see the designer as less practical and liable to flights of fancy that can become distractions. And yet this

is countered by others who have argued that this is the way that scientific boundaries are pushed back and real progress made to better, more advanced solutions. In truth, a successful industry needs to combine both disciplines and achieve a balance that is speculative where necessary but always effective and affordable.

And it is the issue of streamlining, and the aerodynamic principles that underpinned it, that best demonstrates the attitudes, instincts and skills of each man, and each discipline, when approaching the question of design and how advanced or experimental it might be. I will leave their sense of aesthetics to one side, because in both cases these men had an eye for good lines, although the end result of their work could differ somewhat.

For the ever practical, but perhaps more traditional Stanier, it seems that streamlining was no more than a fashion with little to enhance or benefit steam locomotive design. He allowed himself to be persuaded by, amongst others, his Chief Draughtsman Tom Coleman, to give the Coronations a form of air-smoothing recommended and tested by Frederick Johansen, the expert in this field. Yet he did so with little enthusiasm and when the opportunity arose, as it did when the third batch of these Pacifics (numbers 6230 to 6234) were built, he reverted to a more traditional form before the powers that be authorised another fourteen streamliners, possibly with an eye to their publicity value. However, Coleman was, like Gresley, a scientist at heart and believed that better performance at high speed

and reduced running costs would follow if fluid flow principles, to aid the passage of speeding objects, were adopted.

For the academic Gresley there was no such conflict, once the principles of streamlining had been fully explained and demonstrated to him. He was quick to see the benefits and quick to experiment when Johansen had shown him a way forward. Nevertheless, he did not simply accept the younger man's theories but approached them in a measured and questioning way. He studied the principles, sought evidence to underpin the concept and only advanced when reasonably certain that there were benefits to be gained by speculating. And so, he

began a programme of live, full-scale testing. To do this, of course, he had to build an engine that fully absorbed these ideas from the beginning, not simply toying with them as he did with the W1 and the first two P2s. The A4s were the result of this work, for good or bad, and led to a critical debate, in engineering circles at least, that has rarely slackened. Namely, was the streamlined shape of the A4s, P2s, W1 and the Coronations simply a gimmick, as the effort to streamline two B17 4-6-0s for the East Anglian service seemed to be, or did their development hold true scientific intent?

For such a serious-minded scientist and engineer as Gresley, who passed all he did through

the filter of very strong business instincts, it is hard to make the case that his efforts to introduce the science of aerodynamics to the railway industry were not soundly and economically based. Was it worth the effort? In answering this question, you have to set his and Johansen's ideas in an historical context and not apply a veneer of beneficial hindsight, which is very easy to do when all the outcomes are known. And here Tom Coleman and Bert Spencer's words are pertinent, because they sum up the prevailing attitude to such things in the latter part of the 1930s. Coleman wrote:

By this time our understanding of air resistance was improving

One of the more interesting duties that the A4s picked up during the last two years of their service involved overnight Royal Mail trains, as witnessed here with 60004 *William Whitelaw* in charge. The last scheduled mail service they were rostered to was, apparently, the 23.00hrs Glasgow Buchanan Street to Aberdeen on weekdays and Perth on Saturdays. (RH)

An interesting comparison of styles between Gresley's A4 60004 *William Whitelaw* and Peppercorn's last A1 60162 *Saint Johnstoun* which appeared in December 1949, twelve years after this 'streak'. I have always thought that even at rest A4s seemed to be moving fast such was the dynamism of their shape. When set beside a more upright Pacific, this illusion is even more apparent – a low slung racy sports car versus a more practical, but elegant top of the range saloon. (THG)

and there seemed much to be gained if we persevered in building high speed trains capable of cutting through the air more cleanly … I believe some [including Stanier] thought streamlining was just a publicity exercise, with little practical value. I didn't agree because the science was in a very early stage of development and so we still had much to learn and understand. With other forms of locomotion [diesel, electric and turbine where higher speeds might be possible] being developed it was likely that the idea might be better suited to them than

steam engines … Still the high speed Pacifics were fast enough for us to explore the science and rehearse solutions for the future. After all, science is a matter of experimentation, research, testing and measured, incremental advances.

To which Spencer added:

Streamlining was seen by many as a meaningless fashion and condemned it for that reason. Yet it was a science still in its infancy with future application barely glimpsed. Gresley saw its potential, as he did many things, and began the process of

experimentation with the A4s proving its worth.

In each case, these men recognised there were limitations to what could be achieved with streamlining, as did Gresley, but were eager to explore what was possible in the short term as a path to a more expansive, accomplished future. Sadly, only Spencer lived long enough to see some of these performance predictions being fully realised. Amongst his papers were many articles and photographs relating to the high speed trains that entered service in Japan during the early 1960s. The launch of the Tokaido Shinkansen service between Tokyo and Osaka in 1964 saw the streamlined O Class twelve car sets reduce journey times from 6 hours and 40 minutes to 3 hours and 10 minutes within a year – safely and economically.

In collecting and keeping this material, plus so much more about streamlining, Spencer was clearly making a link between the high speed Bullet trains, as they became known, and the developmental work pursued by Gresley in the late 1920s through to the 1930s and '40s. But for the war and ill-health, he, supported by Spencer and Johansen, would undoubtedly have pursued these ideas much further if his outline designs for a 4-8-4 and 4-8-2 are anything to go by, let alone his plans for a larger 'super' A4. Thompson also seems to have been imbued with similar ideas and actively commissioned research into the streamlining of Pacifics produced during his watch, but these came to naught under Peppercorn. Was this a case of commercial necessity,

Purely by chance, I came across 60004 more often than any other A4 in the late 1950s and early '60s, undoubtedly helped by the fact that she survived until 1966. I was never fond of the name *William Whitelaw*, or for that matter all the other notable figures whose names crept in, and would have liked to see her returned to *Great Snipe*. (THG)

personal preference based on looks or rejection of the streamlining principles by those unconvinced of their benefits where steam express locomotives were concerned? It does not matter which it was, because the result was just the same. And so the streamlining experiment virtually came to an end in Britain, only to be revived much later by BR when developing its Advanced Passenger Train and then the High Speed Train in the 1970s.

With Mallard having achieved the world speed record for steam in 1938, the A4s' important position in railway history is assured, but do they deserve such vaunted status? Critics, or so it seems to me, are divided on this question, their

views often formed by a like or dislike of streamlining. John Clay, when writing in the *Stephenson Locomotive Society Journal* in 1960, probably captured the essence of this debate when he wrote that:

As long as the steam locomotive is remembered, men will talk of the A4s. Agreement will never be reached because partisanship is eternal … Rejecting all legends, and sincerely trying to avoid emotional thinking, how good were the A4s? They emerge as one of the best of the larger British express engines. There is no reason to consider them significantly better or worse than the best of their contemporaries. Like other

engines they may be criticised for some detailed features of their design. Like other Pacifics they are, at times, prone to slipping troubles. Sometimes they have appeared to be erratic steamers and in this respect again they have a distinct resemblance to other engines.

They have been given opportunities for achieving the spectacular in greater measure than other British locomotives and thanks to skilled and hard-working footplate crew, they have amply fulfilled all reasonable expectations. If such an assessment disappoints those who love superlatives, it may be of some consolation to reflect that no higher praise

60029 *Woodcock* just coasting along without a puff of smoke or a swirl of steam and soon to be condemned and scrapped, which may be why she was in a particularly dirty, unkempt state. (RH)

60022 *Mallard* photographed, according to notes with the negative, shortly before being withdrawn from service. (RH)

can, in justice, be given to any possible British rivals. The myth of the perfect engine is the most tenaciously held of all railway myths.

I read this when travelling behind *Bittern*, dressed up as 4492 *Dominion of New Zealand*, in garter blue with side valances restored, for the occasion, and was intrigued by John Clay's perceptive assessment. His article was far longer than the two paragraphs quoted here and presented a solid argument to support his views. Although more than sixty years have passed since he wrote these words, they still hold true today, especially the myth of a perfect engine. But such an aim must be the driving force behind any good designer's work, if it is not, why bother to try? Science and engineering are primarily concerned with pushing back boundaries within the limitations imposed by time, money and circumstances. Rarely is anyone master of their own destiny or work without boundaries, so have to temper ambition and scientific curiosity with pragmatism. This is nowhere more apparent than in the design of a locomotive and this is something Gresley realised. And yet he was prepared to argue and push for better and seek out perfection however and wherever he could.

Once again it was Spencer who captured the essence of how his CME pursued such an issue to a successful conclusion, making best use of everything that was available to him:

He had the ability to think broadly and absorb a great deal of information before reaching conclusions. He sought the advice of those he respected and would always consider other possibilities, modifying his own plans accordingly if the arguments put forward held value. But once a decision was made, he pursued a course of action with great determination, taking stock and reviewing progress all the time.

And later he added a slightly more reflective note:

He always considered an issue calmly, dispassionately and, more often than not, in private. He thought in the manner of a scientist – of definition and analysis and pursuing research that took into account developments in many related fields. In doing so he sought the advice of men with specialist knowledge and minds as keen as his own and then reached conclusions based on demonstrable evidence. Once convinced of the way forward, and the gains and risks involved, he had the management skills to argue his case, gain approval and proceed.

It seems that experience had shown Gresley never to be the pawn of events but to dominate them and adopt the maxim 'the will is reason acting'. If so, the evolution of the A4s captured his methods perfectly and the results were plain for all to see – love them or hate them.

When alighting from 4492 (or 4464 in disguise), I had an hour or so to look at this wonderful, so carefully preserved engine and consider how closely Gresley came to achieving his ambition. I also had to put to one side the fact that I have and will always be a big fan of the 'streaks' and will search them out whenever I can. But I am also a realist and, by inclination and training, stand back and assess an issue without prejudice. So I began with an assessment of their streamlining, which for many is the nub of the issue, before moving on to consider their success as high profile steam locomotives.

In *Gresley's Silver Link*, I quoted my uncle's words when recalling seeing 2509 *Silver Link* for the first time in September 1935. 'Such an advanced shape must have had something special inside, especially

I saw A4s running fast many times, their image often blurred by their speed and rain and mist, which were the lot of those following them in the 1950s and '60s. Nevertheless, in these conditions they left an indelible mark on many memories of a machine unrestrained and fighting the elements. Here the passing engine is the evergreen 60007 *Sir Nigel Gresley*, running at speed. (RH)

In 1961 and early 1962 I saw 60003 *Andrew K. McKosh* on a number of occasions each time at something near full speed. The sounds she made did not speak of an engine at the end of her life but one of smooth and effective running, with no leaking steam to betray worn parts or poor maintenance. On 10 June 1961, she was photographed near Hatfield with an Up sleeper. (THG)

when news of its high-speed runs appeared. It was easy to forget that it was just another steam locomotive and its modern form may not have reflected the aging and soon to be obsolescent state of its engineering.'

In essence, the engine's shape distracted the onlooker from the obvious – namely that it was still only a steam locomotive. Admittedly, it had advanced a long way from Stephenson's Rocket and been considerably refined in the process, but its lineage was only too clear. The obvious conclusion to be drawn from this was that the A4s had probably taken steam design as far as it could go, with a modernistic metal shroud on an obsolete body giving it the veneer of being a cutting-edge design. And when they first appeared, two other truly modern alternatives had already presented themselves – electric and

diesel – advanced considerably and were ripe for exploitation. Cost was a key factor here, but so was the inability of some locomotive engineers to embrace the future and think deeply about these alternatives. Not so Gresley, who, while advancing his steam designs, never lost sight of Raven's earlier electrification work and actively and enthusiastically advocated its continuance whenever he could.

However, it was the restrictions imposed by the state of Britain and the LNER's finances that stopped him moving these ideas forward until the mid-1930s. By then, as hard times began to give way to better times and the National Grid had grown in strength, the government's active support and funding of electrification projects had enabled progress to be made. And with Gresley's influence and advocacy brought to bear, through his work on various government

committees, the LNER was one of the first companies to benefit from this support. As a result, the Shenfield and Sheffield/Manchester electrification projects carefully advanced. But for the war, the company would probably have extended this work to other main line projects, with their newly developed Bo Bo and Co-Co electrics locos providing the impetus and the motive power. So, in many ways the A4 programme can be seen as a stop gap measure between steam and electric; a transitory step that made best use of the old, allowing Gresley to experiment one last time with the technology that had dominated his working life. Being a pragmatist, a good engineer and a moderniser, he advanced the new and wrung the last scraps of potential from the old.

It is against this background that the A4s must be considered when assessing how successful they were and how close they came 'to perfection'. And here the issue of streamlining is of importance, because it sought to link design to the rapidly developing world of fluid flow research and aerodynamics, not simply as a publicity exercise, but in a genuine search for greater efficiency. Here the basic issue is one of speed. All specialists in this field seem to agree that anything over 70mph is where a streamlined shape begins to attract aerodynamic benefits – better fuel economy, greater efficiency and better riding qualities as the engine cuts rather than bludgeons its way through the atmosphere and adhesion improves. And while there were many sections of the East Coast Mainline where high

60003 again but now pressed into a more mundane service pulling freight. On this occasion, neither date nor place are recorded. (RH)

Looking for all the world like an A4, the sole W1, unless viewed from the side, still looked good when photographed shortly before withdrawal in June 1959 when based at Doncaster. Although a singleton, she performed effectively and, according to various accounts that have survived, was well-liked by footplate crew. It is a shame that this unique engine was not preserved. (RH)

speed running was possible, other parts were a much harder slog. This imbalance caused difficulties even for the fleet of foot A4s and meant that average speeds over an entire journey hovered in the 60s to 70s. It was a position not helped by the need to force a path through heavy traffic and the stop/start nature of any high speed run.

In France, the solution to these problems was to build dedicated, well-engineered lines for such trains. There is little doubt that if such a system had been adopted in Britain, then the A4s' full potential might have been exploited more fully. But in the 1930s, there was little enough money to keep the existing system running efficiently and safely, let alone meet the high costs of such a venture. Nevertheless, the Sheffield to Manchester and Shenfield

electrified lines were a promising start and allowed these new concepts to be explored more fully. But then the war came, and with it an end of meaningful or explorative investment, with expenditure on such things curbed for 15 years or so.

Nevertheless, and despite the operating difficulties experienced when moving around a heavily congested network, the A4s demonstrated their ability to maintain high average speeds, despite the restrictions imposed, and could quickly accelerate away when required to do so and keep delays to a minimum. It was here that Johansen believed streamlining proved most beneficial and confirmed his theory that 'the air resistance of a train of conventional British type represents upwards of half the total train resistance at

speeds above 80mph'. From this he had deduced, through extensive research and trials that 'it can be reduced by 50 per cent without drastic departure from conventional design, and by 75 per cent by ideal streamlining … [but] the full benefit of measures to reduce air resistance can be realised only if the locomotive and the coaches are all streamlined.'

These were views that Gresley very publicly supported in 1936 and continued to explore with his high speed locomotives and carriage designs and found them, in practice, to be true. Spencer later verified this when comparing the performance of conventional LNER Pacifics with the A4s when running on comparable services. In 1947, he recorded that streamlining was likely to reduce the horse power exerted by these engines, in speeds ranging from 60 to 100mph, by approximately 42 per cent. This, if true, and I have no reason to doubt it, resulted in two main benefits – enhanced fuel economy and an ability to sustain higher speeds consistently and effectively. In service, according to Spencer, this appears to have been the case, and validated the exercise. However, it has to be said that some engineers, including Bulleid, questioned these figures. They found them to be too generous and made the case that the performance gap between streamlined and conventional trains was far narrower and barely made a difference over long non-stop runs.

Who was right and who was wrong? With such an issue there will always be opposing and well-considered views for and against. This is often the case until evidence, one way or another,

Of the original four 'silver' A4s, 60016 *Silver King* was the last to remain in service by nearly a year, to March 1965. She spent her last eighteen months based at Ferryhill and, as seen here, was by the end in quite a sorry state. (RH)

piles up and proves impossible to ignore. In the 1930s and '40s this was far from being the case for locomotive engineers. Yet it could have been very different then if testing methods had been more advanced and allowed these complex issues to be analysed and assessed more completely. As it was, engineers and scientists were, as Spencer later put it, 'searching in the dark for answers before they fully understood what the questions were. Nevertheless, Gresley, as good scientists do, was prepared to experiment and explore ideas that might have significant benefits and streamlining clearly had great potential where high speed running was concerned.'

This was a view that Tom Coleman also supported:

We still had much to learn as far as aerodynamic modelling was concerned. It was a science with many potential benefits some of which the A4s and Coronations began to reveal, whether it simply be improved smoke lifting or the more complex issue of improving performance at high speed. Nevertheless, it was a worthy effort and the A4s did, in my view, come very close to validating the theories.

However, it is true to say that they might have benefitted from the replacement of Gresley's 2 to 1 valve gear with a third set of Walschaerts, but they still did their job well despite this perceived weakness.

Coming from the chief designer of the Coronations and the LNER's main rival this is high praise indeed, but he does touch on one thorny issue, which itself leads into a wider assessment of the A4s' overall worth.

If streamlining divides opinion, Gresley's adherence to three-cylinders and conjugated valve

60032 *Gannet*, a King's Cross engine until June 1963, in a polished state for an important turn with the Tyne Tees Pullman. (BS)

All too frequently, the 'streaks' found themselves on ignominious freight duties in their last few years, but they still managed to look good even when undertaking these more modest tasks, as 60015 demonstrates here. (RH)

gear can be equally divisive, though opinion then and now tends to view it as a flawed solution. But for his single-minded determination, and possible obstinacy, some of his fellow engineers have said that such a talented engineer should have seen its weaknesses and tried other solutions. He didn't, of course, and it was left to others to do this, led by Edward Thompson and then Arthur Peppercorn. However, neither felt it necessary to apply these changes to Gresley's Pacifics which remained largely unaltered to the end of their lives, except for No. 1470 *Great Northern* which was rebuilt in 1945. Was this out

of respect for Gresley – they were after all his widely recognised masterpieces – or did they feel that, despite their reservations, these engines were working well, even under wartime conditions? For such hard-headed engineers, the latter is more likely to be the case, but so might lack of money and workshop capacity to undertake rebuilding during the war and the years of austerity that followed.

This was an issue Spencer touched on late in life when recalling a debate that took place in 1945 over the future of the Pacifics and the A4s in particular when Thompson was CME and Edward Windle his Chief Draughtsman

and not, or so it seems, overly enamoured with the streaks:

The future of the A4s also came up and Windle was keen to de-streamline them when removing Gresley's conjugated valve gear. Thompson was not prepared to sanction these changes and preferred to keep them as they were. Statistically they had performed well during the war, this, despite the very difficult working conditions. In fact, the valve gear had held up well, far better than on other engines. This convinced the CME that all they needed was remedial work to help overcome the detrimental effects of poor maintenance in the war and nothing else. This may simply have been a business decision, but I was left with the impression that he regarded the A4s as being too good to touch. He even made reference to them in the standardisation plan as worthy members of the new fleet.

As life returned to something near normal in the 1950s, it could have been the time to tackle the A4s' perceived weakness. But first John Harrison then Kenneth Cook chose to leave them largely unaltered, relying on more effective maintenance routines to keep them operating efficiently. It was here that Cook's application of GWR-learnt precision engineering techniques proved crucial. For thoroughbreds such the A4s this was crucial and probably ensured that they lasted so well and could have gone on much longer if required. But if the design was not inherently strong and reliable, even the processes Cook introduced would have been of little use. In natural sciences there is a saying that 'you can't put in what nature hasn't provided' and this, I believe, applies in many ways to the engineering world. A poor machine will always be a poor machine no matter how much it is tweaked because the concept is inferior and incapable of improvement short of an entire rebuild. The A4s would never fit into this category and always displayed their good pedigree no matter what they were asked to do. And as we have seen, in war the demand was excessive and tested them to the limit. Yet they still coped and came back for more.

In some ways the three-cylinder, conjugated valve gear issue is

something of a distraction because as the ever faithful and hugely talented Bert Spencer recorded during his 1947 presentation to the ILocoE, the engines so equipped 'Did their jobs very well and proved economical and effective in practice. Three cylinders had many advantages over two and these outweighed the complications introduced.'

This may be an oversimplification of a complex issue and the views of one of Gresley's closest aides and strongest supporters will always be open to question. But this was 1947 and his master long dead, so he had no need to dissemble or solemnise the CME's work. He was free to speak his mind and yet he chose to remain faithful to Gresley's memory and his ideas. And he was not one to keep quiet when

he felt something was wrong, as witnessed by his successful long-term campaign in the 1920s to get Gresley to modify his ideas on the 'long lap valve' issue. So here was a man of honesty and integrity, yet an independent thinker who by the weight of his arguments and exercise of patience was able to influence events. He was no 'yes' man and so his opinion is of even greater value in assessing Gresley but also the A4s. For him they were:

Without equal which is not surprising because they came at the end of a long development programme that had begun to take shape in Gresley's mind before the Great War. Its antecedents were, as a result, excellent, so it was, perhaps unsurprisingly, that they should

The Flying Scotsman, once the province of the A4s but something of a rare sight after the Deltics began entering service in numbers. When this photo was taken in the mid-1950s they still reigned supreme (in this case the engine's number is obscured, but it may be 60018 *Sparrow Hawk*). (RH)

Pacific had to be substituted for part of the journey. Of course, the crew would be fresh and perhaps determined to show what their engine could do, but they were known on occasions to turn in slightly better times than the esteemed streamliners. If they could have managed this over the entire route is quite another matter though.

However, the A4s were not perfect, as the CME would have been the first to acknowledge, but the refinements introduced, particularly the double chimney and Kylchap exhaust, brought them closer to this ideal. They had their limitations of course, as does any machine, but these tended to be the limitations inherent in steam designs – labour intensive in operation, too many moving parts needing constant attention and lubrication, poor visibility and so on. And yet they still performed wonders and did all that was asked of them, day in and day out, year after year. By any standards they were remarkable engines and were equal to or even better than any other contemporary design of high speed steam locomotive in this country and possibly overseas."

Once again rain comes to the aid of an engine soon to be scrapped and gives it a highly polished look, though in 60021 *Wild Swan's* case, she already seems quite clean. (RH)

have been so good. Streamlining added a final touch to a good design and certainly enhanced their performance on those long, fast non-stop services for which they were built. Yet even when running more mundane duties the A4s performed impeccably and with minimum fuss.

They were better than the A1s and A3s as one would expect, especially when accelerating away and climbing gradients, but the gap was not as large as you might think. This was best demonstrated when an A4 occasionally failed on a long run and one of the other types of

In addition to performance issues, there is no denying that the A4s were a glamorous breed which turned heads, attracted many flattering soubriquets and filled many column inches from their inception to the present day. In assessing the success of a machine this is not a quantifiable or, to some, a valid or relevant issue to include in any detailed analysis. And yet in pursuing commercial success such an image is often a godsend. It captures the attention of the press and the public and so influences the way someone wishes to travel. 'Getting bums on seats' is a crude maxim but true nonetheless and the image projected by the A4s was very effective in doing this. Even in his hard-headed technical appreciation written in 1960, John Clay felt moved to give voice to this issue, before adding a brief note about their effectiveness:

The pre-war LNER streamliners have had no equals in this country. They raised the reputation of their own company and the railway industry in general at a time when the need for public esteem was great. Despite the operational difficulties of threading such trains through ordinary traffic their punctuality record was good by contemporary standards and by today's standards fabulous.

The A4s were born at a time when the value of good PR was being appreciated and aggressively exploited for the first time. As a result, their modern streamlined image proved so powerful that they achieved global recognition even before *Mallard*'s record run in 1938. And it was an appeal that lasted beyond the time when BR no longer needed them. For evidence of this you only have to watch the 1954 film *The Elizabethan*, which was given wide release in cinemas at the time and boosted trade if reports from the time are to be believed. Even today it still gets

an occasional airing on television and has been viewed on YouTube nearly 600,000 times, so confirming a continuing fascination with these singular engines today. Apart from the equally iconic Pacific *Flying Scotsman*, there are probably no other engines that have maintained such a prominent position so well. Would this have been the case if they had not been streamlined? For myself, I think not, although 126mph on Stoke Bank in 1938 would probably still have echoed loudly even if the streaks had been given a conventional shape.

In bringing this story to a end I looked for words to sum up the contribution made by the A4s. I believe that gauging

success or failure is often best left to competitors or people uninvolved in a particular project. As the LMS's Chief Designer, and someone who led in creating the A4s' main rival, Tom Coleman's thoughts on the subject are of immense value here. He could so easily have played down their success or damned them with faint praise, but instead he wrote, 'They were remarkable engines – basically of traditional design, but engineered to their limits. They proved to be exceptional high speed, long distance performers year after year in the most difficult of circumstances … There was no doubting that they were fine, good looking engines.'

Silver King in the precincts of Waverly, rushing to pick up her next train still with no dome on her boiler. (THG)

This was a view shared by another stalwart of the LMS, the talented and vastly experienced Roland Bond, who became British Railway's CME and had responsibility for the streaks. He simply wrote of the A4s 'what magnificent engines they were'.

Then there is a typically understated assessment by Andre Chapelon, which he included in his seminal work *La Locomotive a Vapeur*. He begins by describing some of the engineering issues he believed contributed to their success before giving his final judgement:

The A4 class locomotives were derived from the well-known Gresley Pacifics. Apart from streamlining they differed from these in their higher working pressure of 17.6 atm, compared with15.4 atm and by the provision of main steam pipes with a cross sectional area virtually doubled and branch steam pipes to cylinders with cross section increased to 22 per cent.

Contrary to the preceding Gresley Pacifics the three-cylinders were cast separately and their steam passages were particularly well designed.

The reciprocating masses were balanced at the wheel rims to 40 per cent of their weight. All wheels, including those of the tender, were dynamically balanced with great care to provide equilibrium at 161 km/hr (approximately 100mph).

The streamlining of the locomotive front end had a specific profile designed not only to reduce air resistance but also achieve effective smoke lifting.

These locomotives have given excellent results. On July 3rd 1938, *Mallard,* fitted with double Kylchap draughting, attained the world speed record for steam.

No matter how closely a locomotive engineer observes the work of another designer, the people who come to know an engine best are probably the men who have to coax a good performance out of them every day and in every conceivable

Silver Link, once so proudly heading the inaugural run of the Silver Jubilee service, now awaits the cutter's torch at Doncaster. Being the first A4 she was worthy of preservation and should still be with us today. (RH)

condition. To do this successfully you have to understand the design and all its nuances. For this reason, the footplate crew are probably the most astute judges of an engine and so to one of their number, Norman McKillop, goes the final words and very poetic they are too:

Dressed in blue when she [in this case 60009] was built, this creation of a superb engineer is something more than merely a railway engine. From her streamlined nose to the bustle at her back (the prosaic call it the vestibule to her corridor tender)

she is unique. To an engineman she is beautiful in all her 71 feet of her stately length.

No one is going to tell me that Sir Nigel Gresley was an engineer and nothing more. Only an artist could have thought up that combination of a blue and silver Coronation train in 1937 and set at the head this kind of engine.

Luckily for us, the story of the A4s didn't end in 1966. With the help of the preservation movement, it continues to this day giving us six to observe, if we are lucky, in steam.

The Great Gathering of 2013 was undoubtedly a high point in this story, though one that is unlikely to be repeated. But the interest seems to show few signs of diminishing even though the number of people who knew them in their prime grows smaller each year. However, younger generations seem to be equally interested, undoubtedly helped by Thomas the Tank Engine and his friend Spencer the silver A4. If so, the Gresley streaks are worthy of remembrance and worthy of their place in railway history. We are unlikely to see their charismatic like again.

This photo which Bert Spencer kept and transcribed with the words '60015 (*Quicksilver*) makes an effortless start from King's Cross' makes a fine end piece to this book. (BS)

INDIVIDUAL HISTORIES OF THE A4s
(in order of construction)

Name: *Silver Link*.

Numbers: 2509, 14 and 60014.

Works Number: 1818.

Date to traffic: 7/9/35

Withdrawn from service: 12/62 (cut up at Doncaster 1/1963).

Total mileage: 1,527,412.

General Repairs/Heavy Repairs: Oct/Dec 1936, Oct/Dec 1937, Aug/Oct 1938, Oct/Nov 1939, Oct/Dec 1941, Jan/Feb 1944, Aug/Oct 1945, July/Aug 1947, May/June 1949, Aug/Sept 1950, Dec '51/Jan 1952, June/July 1953, Nov/Dec 1954, Mar/April 1956, Sep/Oct 1957, Sep/Nov 1959, Feb/April 1961.

Modifications: 1936 – longer buffers fitted; 1937 larger coal space provided; 1941 side valancing removed; 1947 – to 75% cut-off; 1950 – experimental Automatic Train Control fitted; 1953 – long guard irons removed; 1957 – double chimney fitted; 1961 – speed indicator fitted.

Boilers fitted: 8905 in 1935, 9031 in 1941, 9022 in 1945, 9023 in1949, 29272 in 1950, 29315 in 1952, 29323 in 1953, 29310 in 1954, 29273 in 1956, 29286 in 1957, 29273 in 1959 and 29330 in 1961.

Tenders attached: 5589 in 1935, 5590 in 1939, 5592 in 1939, 5590 in 1945, 5649 in 1945, 5590 in 1955, 5330 in 1955 and 5590 in 1955.

Colour schemes: Grey – from new; Garter Blue – 12/37; Black – 12/41; Garter Blue – 6/46; BR Blue – 6/49; Green – 1/52.

Sheds:1935 to 1944 – King's Cross, 1944 to 1948 – Grantham, 1948 King's Cross for two weeks then back to Grantham until 1950, King's Cross from 1950 to 1962.

Name: *Quicksilver*

Numbers:2510, 15 and 660015.

Works Number: 1819.

Date to traffic: 21/9/35.

Withdrawn from service: 4/63 (cut up at Doncaster 5/1963).

Total mileage: 1,529,463.

General Repairs/Heavy Repairs: Feb/Mar 1937, April/June 1937, April/May 1948, Feb/April 1939, June/July 1940, Sep/Nov 1941, Aug/Oct 1943, Jan/Feb 1945, Mar/April 1946, Aug/Oct 1947, Oct/Nov 1949, Oct/Nov 1951, Mar/May1953, Sep/Oct 1954, Jan/Feb 1956, June/Aug 1957, Mar/May 1959, Sec '60/Jan 1961.

Modifications: 1936 – longer buffers fitted; 1937 – larger coal space provided; 1941 – side valancing removed; 1946 – to 75 per cent cut-off; 1953 – experimental ATC fitted and long guard rods removed; 1957 – double chimney fitted; 1961 – speed recorder fitted.

Boilers fitted: 8906 in 1935, 8908 in 1940, 8906 in 1941, 9021 in 1943, 9127 in 1947, 29297 in 1951, 29324 in 1953, 29318 in 1954, 29324 in 1956, 29324 in 1956, 29304 in 1957, 29332 in 1959 and 29325 in 1961.

Tenders attached : 5590 in 1935 and 5589 in 1963.

Colour schemes: Grey from new; Garter Blue – 5/38; Black – 10/43; Garter Blue – 10/47; BR Blue – 11/49; Green – 11/51.

Sheds: 1935 to 1936 – King's Cross, 1936 to 1937 – Gateshead, 1937 to 1944, 1944 to 1951 – Grantham, 1951 to 1963 – King's Cross.

Name: *Silver King*

Numbers:2511, 16 and 60016.

Works Number: 1821.

Date to traffic: 5/11/35.

Withdrawn from service: 3/65 (cut up at Doncaster 5/65).

Total mileage: 1,490,852.

General Repairs/Heavy Repairs: Dec '36/Feb 1937, Aug/Sep 1937, June/Aug 1938, Aug/Oct 1939, Feb/Mar 1940, Feb/April 1941, Mar/April 1943, May/July 1944, April/June 1946, April/

May 1947, Sep/Oct 1949, Dec '50/Jan 1951, June/July 1952, Dec '53/Jan 1954, Aug/Oct 1955, Apr/June 1957, Sep/Oct 1958, May/July 1960, May/Aug 1962.

Modifications: 1936 – longer buffers fitted; 1938 – larger coal space provided; 1943 – side valancing removed; 1944- to 75 per cent cut-off; 1954 – long guard irons removed; 1957 – double chimney fitted; 1959 – AWS fitted, 1960 – speed indicator fitted.

Boilers fitted: 8907 in 1935, 9126 in 1940, 8907 in 1941, 9031 in 1946, 9026 in 1949, 29275 in 1950, 29283 in 1951, 29302 in 1952, 29313 in 1954, 29304 in 1955, 29285 in 1957, 290303 in 1958, 27966 in 1960 and 29338 in 1962.

Tenders attached: 5591 in 1935 and 5636 in 1948.

Colour schemes: Grey – from new; Garter Blue – 8/38; Black – 4/43; Garter Blue – 10/49; Green – 7/52.

Sheds: 1935 (for a few days) – King's Cross, 1935 to 1939 – Gateshead, 1939 to 1943 – Heaton, 1943 (for 1½ months) – Gateshead, 1943 to 1945 – Heaton, 1945 to 1963 – St Margarets, 1963 to 1965 – Aberdeen.

Name: *Silver Fox.*

Numbers: 2512, 17 and 60017.

Works Number: 1823.

Date to traffic: 18/12/35.

Withdrawn from service: 10/63 (cut up at Doncaster 12/63).

Total mileage: 1,596,459.

General Repairs/Heavy Repairs: Aug/Oct 1936, Sep/Nov 1937, Nov/Dec 1938, Apr/May 1940, Oct/Nov 1941, June/Aug 1943, Oct/Nov 1944, Mar/May 1946, Aug/Sep 1947, Mar/ April 1949, Aug/Sep 1950, Nov/Dec 1952, May/June 1953, Sep/Nov 1954, Nov/Dec 1955, April/May 1957, Dec '58/Jan 1959, Sep/Oct 1960, Mar/April 1963.

Modifications: 1936 – longer buffers fitted; 1937 – larger coal space provided; 1941 – side valancing removed; 1950 – experimental ATC fitted; 1953 – long guard irons removed; 1955 – to 75 per cent cut-off; 1957 – double chimney fitted; 1960 – speed indicator fitted.

Boilers fitted: 8908 in 1935, 9128 in 1940, 8958 in 1944, 9025 in 1949, 29270 in 1950, 29295 in 1953, 29324 in 1954, 29285 in 1955, 29270 in 1957, 29325 in 1959, 27971 in 1960 and 29321 in 1962.

Tenders attached: 5592 in 1935, 5642 in 1939 and 5592 in 1939.

Colour schemes: Grey – from new; Garter Blue – 11/37; Black – 11/41; Garter Blue – 9/47; BR Blue – 9/50; BR Green – 12/51.

Sheds: 1935 to 1963 – King's Cross, 1963 – New England.

Name: *Golden Eagle.*

Numbers: 4482, 23 and 60023.

Works Number: 1847.

Date to traffic: 22/12/36.

Withdrawn from service:10/64 (cut up at M,M & S Wishaw 12/64).

Total mileage: 1,450,000 approx (official figure of 1,902,372 queried).

General Repairs/Heavy Repairs: Dec '37/Jan 1938, Mar/May 1939, Mar/April 1940, June/July 1941, July/Sep 1943, Aug/Oct 1944, Aug/Sep 1946, Feb/Mar 1948, July/Aug 1949, Jan/Feb 1951, Aug/Sep 1952. Jan/Mar 1954, June/July 1955, Jan/Feb 1957, July/Sep 1958, Apr/June 1960, Nov '62/Jan 1963.

Modifications: 1938 – larger coal space provided; 1940 Hudd ATC fitted; 1941 Hudd ATC removed and side valances removed; 1949 – to 75 per cent cut off; 1954 – long guard irons removed; 1958 – double chimney fitted; 1959 – AWS fitted; 1960 – speed indicator fitted.

Boilers fitted: 8945 in 1936, 9126 in 1941, 9125 in 1944, 9029 in 1949, 29285 in 1951, 29276 – 1952, 29292 in 1954, 29303 in 1955, 29298 in 1957, 29328 in 1958, 29337 in 1960 and 29281 in 1963.

Tenders attached: 5323 in 1936 and 5667 in 1941.

Colour schemes: LNER Green – from new; Garter Blue – 1/38; Black – 9/43; Garter Blue – 9/46; BR Blue – 8/49; BR Green – 9/52.

Sheds: 1936 to 1938 – King's Cross, 1938 to 1941 – Haymarket, 1941 to 1942 – Heaton, 1942 to 1963 – Gateshead, 1962 to 1963 – St Margarets, 1963 to 1964 – Aberdeen.

Name: *Kingfisher.*

Numbers: 4483, 585, 24 and 60024.

Works Number: 1848.

Date to traffic: 26/12/36.

Withdrawn from service: 5/65 (cut up by Hughes Bolckow 9/66).

Total mileage:1,566,961.

General Repairs/Heavy Repairs: Nov'37/Jan 1938, Feb/Mar 1939, Apr/June 1940, Sep/Nov 1941, Dec '42/Feb 1943, May/June 1944, Feb/Apr 1945,July/Aug 1946, Sep/Nov 1947, May/June 1948, Feb/Mar 1949, July/Aug 1950, Feb/Mar 1952, Dec '53/Jan 1954, My/ July 1955, Feb/Mar 1957, July/Aug 1958, Dec '59/Jan 1960, Apr/June 1961, Apr/Sep 1964.

Modifications: 1938 – larger coal space provided; 1940 – Hudd ATC fitted; 1941 – side valances removed; 1946 – to 75 per cent cut off; 1954 – long guard irons removed; 1958 – double chimney fitted; 1960 –AWS fitted; 1961 – speed indicator fitted.

Boilers fitted: 8946 in 1936, 8949 in 1941, 9028 in 1943, 8945 in 1947, 29299 in 1952, 29319 in 1954, 29303 in 1957, 29326 in 1958, 27961 in 1960, 29319 in 1961.

Tenders attached: 5331 in 1936, 5329 in 1957 and 5640 in 1966.

Colour schemes: LNER Green – from new; Garter Blue – 1/38; Black – 2/43; Garter Blue – 8/46; BR Purple – 6/48; BR Blue – 8/50; BR Green – 3/52.

Sheds: 1936 to 1937 – Haymarket, 1937 to 1938 – King's Cross, 1938 to 1939 – Doncaster, 1939-1963 – Haymarket, 1963 – Dairy Road, 1963 to 1965 – Aberdeen.

Name: *Falcon.*

Numbers: 4484, 586, 25 and 60025.

Works Number: 1849.

Date to traffic: 23/1/37.

Withdrawn from service: 10/63 (cut up at Doncaster 1/64).

Total mileage: 1,548,928.

General Repairs/Heavy Repairs: Nov/Dec 1937, Jan/Mar 1939, Jan/Mar 1940, Oct/Nov 1941, June/July 1943, Aug/Oct 1944, Mar/May 1946, Nov/Dec 1947, Dec '49/Jan 1950, June/July 1951, Nov/Dec 1952, Mar/ Apr 1954, Aug/Oct 1955, Apr/May 1957, July/Sep 1958, May/June 1960, Apr/June 1962.

Modifications: 1937 – larger coal space provided; 1941 – side valancing removed; 1950 – to 75 per cent cut off and experimental ATC fitted; 1952 – long guard irons removed; 1955 – ATC fitted; 1958 – double chimney fitted; 1960 – speed indicator fitted.

Boilers fitted: 8947 in 1937, 8953 in 1943, 8961 in 1950, 29291 in 1951, 29273 in 1954, 29282 in 1955, 29278 in 1957, 29295 in 1958, 29338 in 1960 and 29331 in 1962.

Tenders attached: 5327 in 1937, 5330 in 1945, 5590 in 1955, 5330 in 1955, 5648 in 1958.

Colour schemes: Green – from new; Garter Blue – 12/37; Black – 11/41; Garter Blue – 12/47; BR Blue – 1/50; BR Green – 10/63.

Sheds: 1937 to 1939 – Haymarket, 1939 to 1948 – King's Cross, 1948 to 1950 – Grantham, 1950 – King's Cross, 1950 – Grantham, 1950 to 1963 – King's Cross, 1963 – New England.

Names: *Kestrel/Miles Beevor.*

Numbers: 4485, 587, 26 and 60026.

Works Number: 1850.

Date to traffic: 20/2/37.
Withdrawn from service: 12/65 (cut up at Hughes Bolckow 9/67).

Total mileage: 1,349,578.

General Repairs/Heavy Repairs: Oct/Dec 1937, Nov '38/Jan 1938, Mar/May 1940, Dec '41/Jan 1942, Aug/Sep 1943, Nov '44/Jan 1945, Mar/Apr 1946, Feb/Mar 1947, Sep/Nov 1947, Aug/Sep 1949, June/July 1951, Sep/Oct 1952, Aug/Sep 1954, Jan/Mar 1956, June/Aug 1957, Nov '58/Jan 1959, Sep/Oct 1960, June/Aug 1962.

Modifications: 1937 – larger coal space provided; 1942 – side valancing removed; 1949 – to 75 per cent cut off; 1950 – experimental ATC fitted; 1953 – long guard irons removed; 1957 – double chimney fitted; 1960 – speed indicator fitted.

Boilers fitted: 8948 in 1937, 9127 in 1940, 8955 in 1946, 8948 in 1949, 29310 in 1951, 29314 in 1954, 29318 in 1956, 29282 in 1957, 29327 in 1959, 27972 in 1960 and 29327 in 1962.

Tenders attached: 5324 – in 1937, 5329 in 1943, 5675 in 1952, 5329 in 1953, 5642 in 1954.

Colour schemes: Green – from new; Garter Blue – 12/37; Black – 1/42; Garter Blue – 11/47; BR Blue – 9/49; BR Green – 1/53.

Sheds: 1937 Haymarket, 1937 to 1938 – Gateshead, 1938 to 1939 – King's Cross, 1947 – Doncaster, 1947 to 1948 – King's Cross, 1948 to 1951 – Grantham, 1951 to 1963 – King's Cross, 1963 – New England, 1963 to 1964 – St Margarets, 1964 to 1965 – Aberdeen.

Name: *Merlin.*

Numbers: 4486, 588, 27, E27, and 60027.

Works Number: 1851.

Date to traffic: 13/3/37.

Withdrawn from service: 9/95 (cut up at G H Campbell of Shieldhall 12/65).

Total mileage: 1,556,803.

General Repairs/Heavy Repairs: Nov/Dec 1937, Apr/May 1939, May/July 1940, Nov/Dec 1941, Feb/Mar 1942, May/June 1943, June/Aug 1944, Dec '45/Jan 1946, Dec '46/Jan 1947, Jan/Mar 1948, Feb/Apr 1949, May/July 1950, Apr/June 1952, Jan/Feb 1955, June/July 1956, Jan/Feb 1958, May/June 1959, Apr/May 1960, Nov/'61/Jan 1962.

Modifications: 1937 – larger coal space provided; 1940 – Hudd ATC fitted; 1941 – side valances

removed; 1950 – to 75 per cent cut off; 1953 – long iron guards removed; 1958 – double chimney fitted; 1960 – AWS and speed indicator fitted.

Boilers fitted: 8949 in 1937, 8948 in 1940, 9020 in 1941, 9129 in 1946, 29274 in 1950, 293116 in 1952, 29300 in 1955, 29301 in 1956, 29277 in 1958, 29304 in 1959, 29316 in 1960 and 29336 in 1962.

Tenders attached: 5332 in 1937, 5642 in 1948, 5652 in 1948.

Colour schemes: LNER Green – from new; Garter Blue – 12/37; Black – 12/41; Garter Blue – 1/47; BR Purple – 6/48; BR Blue – 7/50; BR Green – 6/52.

Sheds: 1937 to 1962 – Haymarket, 1962 to 1964 – St Rollox, 1964 to 1965 – St Margarets.

Names: *Sea Eagle/Walter K. Whigham.*

Numbers: 4487, 28 and 60028.

Works Number: 1852.

Date to traffic: 20/3/37.

Withdrawn from service: 12/62 (cut up at Doncaster 1/63).

Total mileage: 1,471,623.

General Repairs/Heavy Repairs: Jan/Feb 1938, Dec '38/Jan 1939, Mar 1939, June/July 1940, June/July 1941, Sep/Nov 1941, Dec '43/Jan 1944, Aug/Oct 1945, Aug/Oct 1947, Feb/Apr 1949, Sep/Oct 1950, Jan/Feb 1952, July/Aug 1954, Jan/Feb 1956, Sep/Nov

1957, Apr/June – 1959, Mar/Apr 1961.

Modifications: 1938 – larger coal space provided; 1941 – side valancing removed; 1944 – to 75% cut off; 1950 – experimental ATC fitted; 1953 – long guard irons removed; 1957 – double chimney fitted; 1961 – speed indicator fitted.

Boilers fitted: 8950 in 1937, 9125 in 1939, 9027 in 1944, 8951 in 1949, 29276 in 1950, 29318 in 1952, 29289 in 1954, 29302 in 1956, 29307 in 1957, 29324 in 1959 and 29282 in 1961.

Tenders attached: 5330 in 1937, 5327 – in 1945, 5642 – in 1951 and 5649 in 1952.

Colour schemes: LNER Green – from new; Garter Blue – 2/38; Black – 11/41; Garter Blue – 10/47; BR Purple – 6/48; BR Blue – 10/50; BR Green – 2/52.

Sheds: 1937 – Haymarket, 1937 to 1938 – Gateshead, 1938 to 1939 – Doncaster, 1939 – Haymarket, 1939 to 1945 – King's Cross, 1945 to 1948 – Grantham, 1948 to 1962 – King's Cross.

Name: *Osprey/Union of South Africa.*

Numbers: 4488, 9 and 60009.

Works Number: 1853.

Date to traffic: 29/6/37.

Withdrawn from service: 6/66 – sold for preservation.

Total mileage: 1,582,593.

General Repairs/Heavy Repairs: May/June 1938, June/July 1939, Sep/Nov 1940, Jan/Mar 1942, July/Aug 1943, Nov '44/Jan 1945, Jan/Feb 1946, Jan/Feb 1947, Mar/May 1948, June/Aug 1949, Oct/Nov 1950, Aug/Oct 1952, Mar/Apr 1954, May/June 1955, Mar/Apr 1957, Oct/Nov 1958, Jan/Feb 1960, June/July 1961, July/Nov 1963.

Modifications: 1938 – larger coal space provided; 1939 – Hudd ATC fitted; 1942 – side valances removed; 1949 – to 75 per cent cut off; 1952 – long guard irons removed; 1958 – double chimney fitted; 1960 – AWS and speed indicator fitted.

Boilers fitted: 8951 in 1937, 9129 in 1940, 8955 in 1945, 9128 in 1946, 8957 in 1948, 9027 in 1949, 29279 in 1950, 29285 in 1954, 29278 in 1955, 29319 in 1957, 29310 in 1958, 27965 in 1960, 27961 in 1961 and 29337 in 1963.

Tenders attached: 5325 in 1937, 5636 in 1948, 5591 in 1948, 5332 in 1963, 5484 in 1966.

Colour schemes: Garter Blue – 1937; Black – 3/42; Garter Blue – 2/47; BR Blue – 8/49; BR Green – 10/52.

Sheds: 1937 to 1962 – Haymarket, 1962 to 1966 – Aberdeen.

Names: *Woodcock/Dominion of Canada.*

Numbers: 4489, 10 and 60010.

Works Number: 1854.

Date to traffic: 15/6/37.

Withdrawn from service: 5/65 (to Canada for preservation).

Total mileage: 1,366,378.

General Repairs/Heavy Repairs: Feb/Mar 1938, Jan/Mar 1939, Mar/May 1940, Jan/Feb 1942, Oct/Nov 1943, Dec '44/Jan 1945, Mar/May 1946, Oct/Nov 1947, Mar/Apr 1949, Aug/Sep 1950, Apr/May 1952, July/Aug 1953, Jan/Feb 1955, Apr/June 1956, Nov/Dec 1957, May/July 1959, Aug/Oct 1960, Oct/Dec 1962.

Modifications: 1937 – larger coal space provided; 1942 – side valancing removed; 1950 – experimental ATC fitted; 1953 – long guard irons removed; 1957 – double chimney fitted; 1960 – speed indicator fitted.

Boilers fitted: 8952 in 1937, 8908 in 1942, 9126 in 1946, 9018 in 1949, 29273 in 1950, 29321 in 1955, 29323 in 1955, 29312 in 1956, 29272 in 1957, 29307 in 1959 and 27970 in 1962.

Tenders attached: 5326 in 1937, 5328 in 1937, 5647 in 1953, 5639 in 1953, 5328 in 1953, 5326 in 1960.

Colour schemes: Primer grey with green coupled wheels – from new; Garter Blue – 1937; Black – 2/42; Garter Blue – 11/47; BR Blue – 9/50; BR Green – 5/52.

Sheds: 1937 – King's Cross, 1957 – Grantham, 1957 – King's Cross, 1963 – New England, 1963 – Aberdeen.

Name: Empire of India

Numbers: 4490, 11 and 60011.

Works Number: 1855.

Date to traffic: 26/6/37.

Withdrawn from service: 5/64 (cut up at Darlington).

Total mileage 1,538,829.

General Repairs/Heavy Repairs: Mar/May 1938, May/June 1939, July/Sep 1940, Sep/Nov 1941, Sep/Oct 1942, Mar/Apr 1944, May/July 1945, Sep/Oct 1947, Feb/Mar 1949, Apr/June 1950, Mar/Apr 1952, June/July 1953, Dec '54/Jan 1955, Mar/May 1956, Dec '57/Jan 1958, Apr/May 1959, Sep/Oct 1960, Mar/May 1962.

Modifications: 1938 – larger coal space provided; 1940 – Hudd ATC fitted; 1941 – side valences removed; 1946 – to 75 per cent cut off; 1953 – long guard irons removed; 1958 – double chimney and AWS fitted; 1960 – speed indicator fitted.

Boilers fitted: 8953 in 1937, 8957 in 1942, 8905 in 1947, 9022 in 1950, 29300 in 1952, 29277 in 1955, 29321 in 1956, 29274 in 1958,29334 in 1959, 29331 in 1960 and 29326 in 1962.

Tenders attached: 5328 in 1937, 5326 in 1937 and 5328 in 1960.

Colour schemes: Garter Blue – from new; Black – 10/42; Garter Blue – 11/46; BR Blue – 6/50; BR Green – 5/52.

Sheds: 1937 to 1938 – King's Cross, 1938 to 1962 – Haymarket, 1962 to 1964 – Aberdeen.

Name: *Commonwealth of Australia.*

Numbers: 4491, 12 and 60012.

Works Number: 1856.

Date to traffic: 22/6/37.

Withdrawn from service: 8/64 (cut up by M M & S of Wishaw – 3/65) Total mileage: 1,534,607.

General Repairs/Heavy Repairs: May/June 1938, May/June 1939, Sep 1939, Mar/May 1941, Aug/Sep 1942, July/Sep 1943, Oct/Dec 1944, Apr/May 1946, June/Aug 1947, Apr/ May 1948, July/Aug 1949, Jan/Feb 1951, Oct/Nov 1952, Feb/Mar 1954, Nov/Dec 1955, Mar/Apr 1957, June/July 1958, Oct/Nov 1959, Sep/Oct 1961.

Modifications: 1938 – larger coal space provided; 1939 Hudd ATC fitted; 1942 – side valances removed; 1947 – to 75 per cent cut off; 1954 – long guard irons removed; 1958 – double chimney fitted; 1959 – AWS fitted; 1961 – speed indicator fitted.

Boilers fitted: 8954 in 1937, 8950 in 1939, 9026 in 1943, 8958 in 1949, 29284 in1951, 29286 in 1952, 29274 in 1954, 29270 in 1955, 29326 in 1957, 29316 in 1958 and 27963 in 1959.

Tenders attached: 5646 from 1937 to 1964.

Colour schemes: Garter Blue – from new; Black – 9/42; Garter Blue – 8/47; BR Blue – 8/49; BR Green – 11/52.

Sheds: 1937 to 1963 – Haymarket, 1963 to 1964 – Dairy Road, 1964 – Aberdeen.

Name: *Dominion of New Zealand.*

Numbers: 4492, 13 and 60013.

Works Number: 1857.

Date to traffic: 27/6/37.

Withdrawn from service: 4/63 (cut up at Doncaster – 4/63).

Total mileage: 1,459,904.

General Repairs/Heavy Repairs: Feb/Mar 1938, Dec '38/Jan 39, Dec '39/Feb 1940, Sep/Nov 1941, Oct/Nov 1943, Jan/Mar 1945, June/Aug 1946, Jan/Feb 1947, Apr/May 1949, Sep/Nov 1950, Aug/Oct 1952, Feb/Mar 1954, Apr/June 1955, Feb/Mar 1957, May/July 1958, Nov/Dec 1959, May/June 1961.

Modifications: 1937 – larger coal space provided; 1941 – side valances removed; 1952 – experimental ATC fitted; 1954 –long guard irons removed; 1957 – to 75 per cent cut off; 1958 – double chimney fitted; 1961 – speed indicator fitted.

Boilers fitted: 8955 in 1937, 8950 in 1943, 8908 in 1949, 29277 in 1950, 29271 in 1952, 29178 in 1954, 29283 in 1955, 29310 in 1957, 29314 in1958, 29286 in 1959 and 27969 in 1961, Tenders attached: 5647 in 1937, 5670 in 1951 and 5647 in 1955.

Colour schemes: Garter Blue – from new; Black - 11/41; Garter Blue – 8/46; BR Blue – 5/49; BR Green – 10/52.

Sheds: 1937 – King's Cross, 1937 to 1938 – Haymarket, 1938 to 1948 – King's Cross, 1948 to 1950 –

Grantham, 1950 to 1963 – King's Cross.

Name: *Woodcock.*

Numbers: 4493, 29 and 60029.

Works Number: 1858.

Date to traffic: 26/7/37.

Withdrawn from service:10/63 (cut up at Doncaster – 1/64).

Total mileage:1,489,772.

General Repairs/Heavy Repairs: June/July 1938, Aug/Sep 1939, Jan/Mar 1941, July/Sep 1942, Nov/Dec 1943, July/Sep 1945, Apr/June 1947, May/July 1948, Nov '49/Jan 1950, Apr/June 1951, Sep/Oct 1952, Mar/Apr 1954, July/Aug 1955, Jan/Feb 1957, Aug/Oct 1958, Feb/Apr 1960, Nov/Dec 1961.
Modifications: 1938 – larger coal space provided; 1942 – side valances removed; 1948 – to 75 per cent cut off; 1950 – experimental ATC fitted; 1954 – long guard irons removed; 1958 – double chimney fitted; 1960 – speed indicator fitted.

Boilers fitted: 8956 in 1937, 8960 in 1947, 8946 in 1948, 8947 in 1950, 29289 in 1951, 29290 in 1954, 29292 in 1955, 29313 in 1957, 29298 in 1958, 29336 in 1960 and 29302 in 1961.

Tenders attached: 5648 in 1937 and 5323 in 1953.

Colour schemes: Green – from new; Garter Blue – 7/38; Black – 9/42; Garter Blue – 6/47; BR Purple – 7/48; BR Blue – 1/50; BR Green – 10/52.

Sheds: 1937 to 1938 – Gateshead, 1938 – Doncaster, 1938 to 1943 – King's Cross, 1943 – Gateshead, 1943 to 1963 – King's Cross, 1963 – New England.

Names: *Osprey/Andrew K. McKosh*

Numbers: 4494, 3 and 60003.

Works Number: 1859.

Date to traffic: 12/8/37.

Withdrawn from service: 12/62 (cut up at Doncaster – 1/63).

Total mileage: 1,348,732.

General Repairs/Heavy Repairs: Sep/Oct 1938, Feb/Mar 1940, July/Aug 1942, Apr/May 1944, Sep/Oct 1945, May/June 1947, Jan/Mar 1949, Feb/Apr 1950, Sep/Oct 1951, Dec '52/Jan 1953, May/June 1954, Sep/Oct 1955, May/July 1957, Dec '58/Feb 1959, Dec '60/ Feb 1961.

Modifications: 1938 – larger coal space provided; 1942 – side valances removed; 1943 – to 75 per cent cut off; 1950 – experimental ATC fitted; 1953 – long guard irons removed; 1957 – double chimney fitted; 1961 – speed indicator fitted.

Boilers fitted:8957 in 1937, 8952 in 1942, 9023 in 1947, 8946 in 1949, 9488 in 1950, 29312 in 1951, 29291 in 1954, 29286 in 1955, 29284 in 1957, 29313 in 1959, 27974 in 1961.

Tenders attached: 5649 in 1937, 5584 in 1945, 5649 in 1945, 5642 in 1952, 5329 in 1954 and 5670 in 1955.

Colour schemes: Green – from new; Garter Blue – 10/38; Black – 8/42;

Garter Blue – 6/47; BR Blue – 4/50; BR Green – 10/51.

Sheds: 1937 to 1938 – Heaton, 1938 – Doncaster, 1938 to 1939 – Grantham, 1939- Doncaster,1939 to 1941 – King's Cross, 1941 – Grantham, 1941 1957 – King's Cross, 1957 – Grantham, 1957 to 1962 – King's Cross.

Names: *Great Snipe/Golden Fleece.*

Numbers: 4495, 30 and 60030.

Works Number: 1860.

Date to traffic: 30/8/37.

Withdrawn from service: 12/62 (cut up at Doncaster – 1/63).

Total mileage: 1.419,855.

General Repairs/Heavy Repairs: Oct/Nov 1938, Feb/Apr 1940, Nov/Dec 1941, Oct/Nov 1942, Aug/Sep 1943, Feb/Mar 1945, Noc/Dec 1946, June/July 1948, Sep/Nov 1949, Feb/Mar 1951, Aug/Sep 1952, Mar/Apr 1954, Aug/Oct 1955, Dec '56/Jan 1957, Apr/May 1958, Oct/Nov 1959, June/July 1961.

Modifications: 1937 – larger coal space provided; 1941 – side valances removed, 1953 – experimental ATC fitted; 1954 – long guard irons removed; 1957 – to 75 per cent cut off; 1958 – double chimney fitted; 1961 – speed indicator fitted.

Boilers fitted: 8958 in 1937, 9019 in 1943, 9024 in 1948, 29286 in 1951, 29303 in 1952, 29286 in 1954, 29313 in 1955, 29316 in 1957, 29300 in 1958, 27962 in 1959 and 29286 in 1961.

Tenders attached: 5650 in 1937, 5652 in 1945, 5642 in 1948 and 5327 in 1951.

Colour schemes: Green – from new; Garter Blue – 9/37; Black – 12/41; Garter Blue – 12/46; BR Blue – 11/49; BR Green – 9/52.

Sheds: 1937 – Doncaster, 1937 to 1939 – King's Cross, 1939 to 1942 – Grantham, 1942 – King's Cross, 1942 to 1950 – Grantham, 1950 to 1957 – King's Cross, 1957 – Grantham, 1957 to 1962 – King's Cross.

Names: *Golden Shuttle/Dwight D. Eisenhower.*

Numbers: 4496, 8 and 60008.

Works Number: 1861.

Date to traffic: 4/9/37.

Withdrawn from service: 7/63 (to USA for preservation).

Total mileage: 1,409,000.

General Repairs/Heavy Repairs: Oct/Nov 1938, Feb/Apr 1940, Dec '41/Jan 1942, Feb/Mar 1943, Apr/June 1944, July/Sep 1945, Oct/Nov 1946, Sep/Oct 1948, May/June 1950, Oct/Nov 1951, Feb/Mar 1953, May/June 1954, May/July 1955, Nov/Dec 1956, July/Aug 1958, May/June 1960, Mar/May 1962.

Modifications: 1937 – larger coal space provided; 1941 – side valances removed; 1952 – experimental ATC fitted; 1954 – long guard irons removed; 1957 – to 75 per cent cut off; 1958 – double chimney fitted; 1961 – speed indicator fitted.

Boilers fitted: 8959 in 1937, 8945 in 1942, 8906 in 1946, 8955 in 1950, 29314 in 1951, 29303 in 1954, 29296 in 1955, 29308 in 1956, 29312 in 1958, 27964 in 1960 and 29335 in 1962.

Tenders attached: 5651 in 1937 and 5671 in 1957.

Colour schemes: Garter Blue – from new; Black – 1/42; Garter Blue – 9/45; BR Blue – 6/50; BR Green – 11/51.

Sheds: 1937 – Doncaster, 1937 to 1939 – King's Cross, 1937 to 1950 – Grantham, 1950 to 1957 – King's Cross, 1957 to 1963 – New England.

Name: *Golden Plover.*

Numbers: 4497, 31 and 60031.

Works Number: 1862.

Date to traffic: 2/10/37.

Withdrawn from service: 10/65 (cut up at Campbell's of Renfrew)

Total mileage: 1,523,805.

General Repairs/Heavy Repairs: Nov/Dec 1938, Nov/Dec 1939, Dec '40/Feb 1941, Apr/May 1942, Oct/Dec 1942, Dec '43/Jan 1944, Feb/Mar 1945, Apr/May 1946, June/Aug 1947, Apr/June 1948, May/July 1949, Nov/Dec 1950, June/July 1952, Feb/Mar 1953, Dec ;53/Jan 1954, Mar/Apr 1955, July/Aug 1956, Feb/March 1958, May/July 1959, Jan/Mar 1961, Apr/June 1963.

Modifications: 1939 – Hudd ATC fitted; 1942 – side valances removed; 1947 – to 75 per cent cut off; 1954 – long guard irons removed; 1958 – double chimney fitted; 1961 – speed indicator fitted.

Boilers fitted: 8960 in 1937, 8948 in 1942, 8956 in 1947, 29283 in 1954, 29306 in 1955, 29323 in 1956, 29321 in 1958, 29277 in 1959, 29313 in 1961 and 29333 in 1961.

Tenders attached: 5652 in 1937 and 5650 in 1945.

Colour schemes: Garter Blue – from new; Black – 5/42; Garter Blue – 8/47; BR Blue – 7/49; BR Green – 7/52.

Sheds: 1937 to 1962 Haymarket, 1962 to 1965 – St Rollox.

Name: *Sir Nigel Gresley.*

Numbers: 4498, 7 and 60007.

Works Number: 1863.

Date to traffic: 30/10/37.

Withdrawn from service: 2/66 (sold for preservation – 5/66).

Total mileage: 1,328,734.

General Repairs/Heavy Repairs: Nov '39/Jan 1940, Jan/Feb 1942, Sep/Oct 1943, Mar/May 1945, Jan/Mar 1947, Aug/Oct 1948, Aug/Sep 1950, Mar/Apr 1952, Sep/Oct 1953, Feb/Mar 1955, Feb/Apr 1956, Nov/Dec 1957, Mar/Apr 1959, Aug/Oct 1960, Aug/Oct 1962.

Modifications: 1938 – larger coal space provided; 1942 – side valances removed; 1950 – experimental ATC fitted; 1953 long guard irons removed; 1955 – to 75 per cent cut off; 1957 – double chimney fitted; 1959 speed indicator fitted.

Boilers fitted: 8961 in 1937, 8946 in 1942, 9489 in 1947, 29271 in 1950,

29319 in 1952, 29306 in 1953, 29321 in 1955, 29314 in 1956, 29324 in 1957, 29331 in 1959, 27970 in 1960 and 27966 in 1962.

Tenders attached: 5329 in 1937 and 5324 in 1943.

Colour schemes: Garter Blue – from new; Black – 2/42; Garter Blue – 3/47; BR Blue – 9/50; BR Green – 4/52.

Sheds: 1937 – King's Cross, 1944 – Grantham, 1950 – King's Cross, 1963 – New England, 1963 – St Margarets, 1964 – Aberdeen.

Names: *Great Snipe/William Whitelaw.*

Numbers: 4462, 4 and 60004.

Works Number: 1864.

Date to traffic: 10/12/37.

Withdrawn from service: 7/66 (scrapped by MM&S at Wishaw – 10/66).

Total mileage: 1,463,692.

General Repairs/Heavy Repairs: Jan/Feb 1939, Feb/Apr 1940, June/July 1941, Sep/Oct 1942, Mar/Apr 1944, Sep/Oct 1945, Oct/Nov 1946, Dec '47/Jan 1948, Mar/Apr 1949, July/Oct 1950, Jan/Feb 1952, Apr/May 1953, Aug/Oct 1954, Feb/Mar 1956, Nov/Dec 1957, Mar/apr 1960, Dec '60/Jan 1961, Nov/Dec 1962.

Modifications: 1938 – larger coal space provided; 1941 – side valances removed and Hudd ATC fitted; 1944 – to 75 per cent cut off;

1953 long guard irons removed; 1957 – double chimney fitted; 1959 speed indicator fitted.

Boilers fitted: 9018 in 1937, 9029 in 1942, 9126 in 1950, 9129 in 1950, 29311 in 1952, 29289 in 1956, 29302 in 1957, 29330 in 1959, 29333 in 1961 and 29307 in 1962.

Tenders attached: 5667 in 1937, 5323 in 1941, 5639 in 1948 and 5484 in 1948.

Colour schemes: Garter Blue – from new; Black – 10/42; Garter Blue – 11/46; BR Blue – 8/50; BR Green – 2/52.

Sheds: 1937 – King's Cross, 1938 – Gateshead, 1940 – Heaton, 1941 – Haymarket, 1962 – Aberdeen, 1962 – Haymarket, 1963 – Aberdeen.

Name: *Sparrow Hawk.*

Numbers: 4463, 18 and 60018
Works Number: 1865.

Date to traffic: 27/11/37.

Withdrawn from service: 6/63 (cut up at Doncaster – 7/63).

Total mileage:1,288,947.

General Repairs/Heavy Repairs: Jan/Feb 1939, Mar/May 1940 Sep/Nov 1941, July/Aug 1943, Nov/Dec 1945, Nov/Dec 1946, Aug/Oct 1948, Jan/Apr 1950, Aug/Oct 1951, Mar/May 1953, Oct/Nov 1954, Mar/Apr 1956, Aug/Oct 1957, Jan/Mar 1959, Jan/Feb 1961.

Modifications: 1941 – side valances removed; 1953 long guard irons removed; 1956 – to 75 per cent cut

off; 1957 – double chimney fitted; 1961 – speed indicator fitted.

Boilers fitted: 9019 in 1937, 8949 in 1943, 9020 in 1948, 9028 in 1950, 29295 in 1951, 29294 in 1953, 29312 in 1954, 29311 in 1956, 29320 1957, 29282 in 1959 and 29270 in 1961.

Tenders attached: 5668 in 1937.

Colour schemes: Garter Blue – from new; Black – 8/43; Garter Blue – 12/46; BR Blue – 4/50; BR Green – 10/51.

Sheds: 1937 - Gateshead, 1940 - Heaton, 1943 - Gateshead, 1943 – Heaton, 1945 – Gateshead.

Name: *Bittern.*

Numbers: 4464, 19 and 60019.

Works Number: 1866.

Date to traffic: 18/12/37.

Withdrawn from service: 9/66 (sold for preservation – 9/66).

Total mileage: 1,260,870.

General Repairs/Heavy Repairs: Mar/May 1939, July/Aug 1939, Sep/Oct 1940, Dec '40/Jan 1941, Sep/Nov 1941.Apr/May 1943, June/July 1945, Aug/Oct 1947, Aug/Oct 1948, June/July 1950, Jan/Feb 1952, May/June 1953, Oct/Nov 1954, Apr/May 1956, July/Sep 1957, Oct/Dec 1958, Feb/ Mar 1960, Mar/Apr 1962, Feb/Mar 1965.

Modifications: 1941 – side valances removed; 1950 – to 75 per cent cut off; 1957 – double chimney fitted; 1960 – speed indicator fitted.

Boilers fitted: 9020 in 1937, 9025 in 1941, 9018 in 1943, 8952 in 1948, 8905 in 1950, 29317 in 1952, 29317 in 1952, 29298 in 1953, 29279 in 1954, 29320 in 1956, 29315 in 1957, 29319 in 1958 and 29335 in 1060.

Tenders attached: 5638 in 1937.

Colour schemes: Garter Blue – from new; Black – 11/41; Garter Blue – 3/47; BR Blue – 7/50; BR Green – 2/52.

Sheds: 1937 – Heaton, 1963 – St Margarets, 1963 – Aberdeen.

Name: *Guillemot.*

Numbers: 4465, 20 and 60020.

Works Number: 1867.

Date to traffic: 8/1/38.

Withdrawn from service: 3/64 (cut up at Darlington – 4/64).
Total mileage: 1,311,352.

General Repairs/Heavy Repairs: Dec '38/Feb 1939, Mar/May 1940, Sep/Oct 1941, June/Aug 1943, Jan/Feb 1945, Sep/Oct 1946, Aug/Oct 1947, Aug/Oct 1948, Mar/Apr 1950, Oct/Nov 1951, Mar/Apr 1953, June/July 1954, Apr/May 1956, Oct/Nov 1957, July/Aug 1959, Apr/May 1961.

Modifications: 1941 – side valances removed; 1953 long guard irons removed; 1956 – to 75 per cent cut off; 1956 – double chimney fitted; 1958 – AWS fitted; 1961 – speed indicator fitted.

Boilers fitted: 9021 in 1938, 8951 in 1943, 8907 in 1948, 9020 in 1950,

29298 in 1951, 29320 in 1953, 29277 in 1956, 29273 in 1957, 27960 in 1959 and 29273 in 1961.

Tenders attached: 5669 in 1938.

Colour schemes: Garter Blue – from new; Black – 8/43; Garter Blue – 10/46; BR Blue – 4/50; BR Green – 11/51.

Sheds: 1937 – Gateshead, 1944 – Heaton, 1945 – Gateshead.

Names: *Herring Gull/Sir Ralph Wedgwood.*

Numbers: 4466, 605, 6 and 60006.
Works Number: 1868.

Date to traffic: 26/1/38.

Withdrawn from service: 9/65 (cut up by M M & S of Wishaw).

Total mileage: 1,295,453.

General Repairs/Heavy Repairs: Jn/Feb 1939, Mar/Apr 1940, Jan/Feb 1942, Dec '43/Jan 1944, Aug/Oct 1945, Feb/Apr 1947, Oct/Dec 1948, Apr/May 1950, Sep/Oct 1951, Apr/MAY 1953, Sep/Oct 1954, Dec '55/Jan 1956, Aug/Sep 1957, July/Aug 1959, Nov/Dec 1960, Aug/Oct 1962.

Modifications: 1942 – side valances removed; 1944 – to 75 per cent cut off; 1950 – experimental ATC fitted; 1953 – long guard irons removed; 1957 – double chimney fitted; 1960 – speed indicator fitted.

Boilers fitted: 9022 in 1938, 9030 in 1944, 8907 in 1950, 29296 – 1951, 29322 – 1953, 29302 in 1954, 29274 in 1956, 29318 in 1957, 29320 in 1959, 29334 in 1960, 27972 in 1962.

Tenders attached: 5670 in 1938, 5647 in 1953, 5647 in 1964 and 5675 in 1965.

Colour schemes: Garter Blue – from new; Black – 2/42; Garter Blue – 4/47; BR Blue – 5/50; BR Green – 10/51.

Sheds: 1938 – King's Cross, 1938 – Grantham, 1944 – King's Cross, 1963 – New England, 1963 – St Margarets, 1964 – Aberdeen.

Name: *Wild Swan.*

Numbers:4467, 21, E21 and 60021.

Works Number: 1869.

Date to traffic: 19/2/38.

Withdrawn from service: 10/63 (cut up at Doncaster – 1/64).

Total mileage: 1,361,527.

General Repairs/Heavy Repairs: Jan/Feb 1939, June/Aug 1940, Feb/Apr 1942, Jan/Feb 1944, Apr/June 45, Mar/Apr 1947, Dec '47/Feb 1948, Jan/Mar 1950, July/Aug 1951, Oct/Nov 1952, Jan/Mar 1954, May/June 1955, Jan/Feb 1957, Mar/Apr 1958, Nov/Dec 1959, Oct/Nov 1961.

Modifications: 1942 – side valances removed; 1950 – experimental ATC fitted; 1954 – long guard irons removed; 1955 – to 75 per cent cut off; 1958 – double chimney fitted; 1961 – speed indicator fitted.

Boilers fitted: 9023 in 1938, 8905 in 1942, 9488 in 1947, 8950 in 1950, 29293 in 1951, 29277 in 1952, 29299 in 1954, 29298 in 1955, 29306 in

1957, 29323 in 1958, 29321 in 1959 and 29300 in 1961.

Tenders attached: 5671 in 1938, 5651 in 1957 and 5330 in 1962.

Colour schemes: Garter Blue – from new; Black – 4/42; Garter Blue – 4/47; BR Blue – 3/50; BR Green – 8/51.

Sheds: 1938 – King's Cross, 1939 – Doncaster, 1941 – King's Cross, 1943 – Grantham, 1944 – King's Cross, 1948 – Grantham, 1950 – King's Cross, 1963 – New England.

Name: *Mallard.*

Numbers: 4468, 22, E22 60022.

Works Number: 1870.

Date to traffic: 3/3/38.

Withdrawn from service: 4/63 (for preservation).

Total mileage: 1,422,000.

General Repairs/Heavy Repairs: Mar/May 1939, Dec '40/Jan 1941, May/June 1942, Sep/Oct 1943, Feb/Mar 1945, June/Aug 1946, Jan/Mar 1948, July/Sep 1949, Dec '50/Jan 1951, May/July 1952, Mar/Apr 1954, Oct/Nov 1955, Apr/June 1957, July/Aug 1958, Jan/Mar 1960, June/Aug 1961.

Modifications: 1942 – side valances removed; 1948 – to 75 per cent cut off; 1953 – long guard irons removed; 1960 – speed indicator fitted.

Boilers fitted: 9024 in 1938, 8959 in 1942, 8907 in 1946, 8948 in 1948,

8957 in 1949, 29282 in 1951, 29301 in 1952, 29315 in 1954, 29328 in 1957, 29308 in 1958, 29310 in 1960 and 27965 in 1961.

Tenders attached: 5642 in 1938, 5639 in 1939, 5323 in 1948, 5648 in 1953, 5330 in 1962, 5651 in 1963 and 5670 for preservation.

Colour schemes: Garter Blue – from new; Black – 6/42; Garter Blue – 3/48; BR Blue – 9/49; BR Green – 7/52.

Sheds: 1938 – Doncaster, 1943 – Grantham and 1948 – King's Cross.

Names: *Gadwall/Sir Ralph Wedgwood.*

Number: 4469.

Works Number: 1871.

Date to traffic: 30/3/38.

Withdrawn from service: 6/42 (cut up at Doncaster – after 6/42).

Total mileage: Not known but estimated to be excess of 200,000 miles

General Repairs/Heavy Repairs: Jan/Mar 1939, Feb/Apr 1940, Sept/Oct 1941, Feb 1942.

Modifications: 1941 – side valancing removed.

Boilers fitted: 9025 in 1938 and 8954 in 1940.

Tenders fitted: 5672 in 1938.

Colour schemes: Garter blue from new; Black – 4/42.

Sheds: 1938 – Gateshead.

Comment: Shortly after completing a General Repair, and repainting in wartime black, 4469 returned to service in April 1942 and was performing running in duties in preparation for her return to main line service. In between these turns she was stabled overnight in York's North Shed and it was there, in the early hours of 29 April, where she was blown from the track during a Blitz on the city. The locomotive was badly damaged by blast and shrapnel and her remains were later returned to Doncaster where any repairable items were removed, such as the tender which was eventually repaired and attached to Thompson A2/1 Pacific No. 3696. Anything that could not be salvaged was cut up at the Works having been condemned in June 1942.

Names: *Pochard/Sir Murrough Wilson.*

Numbers: 4499, 2 and 60002.

Works Number: 1872.

Date to traffic: 12/4/38.

Withdrawn from service: 5/64 (cut up by G Cohen – 7/64).

Total mileage: 1,270,010.

General Repairs/Heavy Repairs: Feb/Apr 1939, May/June 1940, Dec '41/Feb 1942, Feb/Mar 1943, Nov '44/Jan 1945, Aug/Oct 1946, Apr/May 1948, Dec '49/Feb 1950, July/Aug 1951, Jan/Feb 1953, Mar/May 1954, Aug/Sep 1955, May/July 1957, Feb/Mar 1959, Dec '60/Jan 1961.

Modifications: 1942 – side valances removed; 1953 – long guard irons removed; 1957 – double chimney fitted; 1959 – AWS fitted; 1961 – speed indicator fitted.

Boilers fitted: 9026 in 1938, 8956 in 1943, 9020 in 1946, 9128 in 1948, 9487 in 1950, 29294 in 1951, 29305 in 1953, 29282 in 1954, 29272 in 1955, 29275 in 1957, 29270 in 1959 and 29320 in 1961.

Tenders attached: 5673 in 1938.

Colour schemes: Garter Blue – from new; Black – 6/42; Garter Blue – 10/46; BR Blue – 2/50; BR Green – 8/51

Sheds: 1938 – Gateshead, 1943 – King's Cross and 1943 – Gateshead.

Names: *Garganey/Sir Ronald Matthews.*

Numbers: 4500, 1 and 60001.

Works Number: 1873.

Date to traffic: 26/4/38.

Withdrawn from service: 10/64 (cut up by Hughes Bolckow at Blyth – 12/64).

Total mileage: 1,504,409.

General Repairs/Heavy Repairs: Jan/Mar 1939, Apr/June 1940, Oct/Dec 1941, Sep/Oct 1943, Mar/May 1945, Oct/Nov 1946, May/July 1948, Dec '49/Feb 1950, June/July 1952, Dec '53/Feb 1954, Apr/Aug 1955, Nov/Dec 1956 Mar/Apr 1958, Nov/Dec 1959, July/Oct 1961.

Modifications: 1941 – side valances removed; 1943 – to 75 per cent

cut off; 1954 – long guard irons removed; 1958 – double chimney fitted; 1959 – AWS fitted; 1961 – speed indicator fitted.

Boilers fitted: 9027 in 1938, 9025 in 1943, 9028 in 1948, 9128 in 1950, 29292 – in 1951, 29284 in 1954, 29316 in 1955, 29295 in 1956, 29290 in 1958, 29300 in 1959 and 29311 in 1961.

Tenders attached: 5674 in 1938.

Colour schemes: Garter Blue – from new; Black – 12/41; Garter Blue – 11/46; BR Blue – 2/50; BR Green – 8/51

Sheds: 1938 – Gateshead.

Name: *Gannet.*

Numbers: 4900, 32 and 60032.

Works Number: 1874.

Date to traffic: 17/5/38.

Withdrawn from service: 10/63 (cut up at Doncaster – 12/63).

Total mileage: 1,351,887.

General Repairs/Heavy Repairs: June/Aug 1939, Feb/Mar 1941, July/Aug 1942, Aug/Sep 1944, Dec '45/Jan 1946, Mar/May 1947, May/June 1949, Feb/Mar 1951, Sep/Oct 1952, Feb/Mar 1954, Sep/Oct 1955, Feb/Mar 1957, Oct/Nov 1958, Mar/Apr 1960, Feb/Mar 1962.

Modifications: 1942 – side valances removed; 1953 – ATC fitted; 1954 – long guard irons removed; 1958 – double chimney fitted; 1960 – speed indicator fitted.

Boilers fitted:9028 in 1938, 9023 in 1942, 8959 in 1947, 29287 in 1951, 29285 in 1952, 29308 in 1954, 29291 in 1955, 29325 in 1957, 29285 in 1958, 29326 in 1960 and 29316 in 1962.

Tenders attached: 5675 in 1938, 5329 in 1952, 5675 in 1953, 5647 in 1954, 5670 in 1955, 5329 in 1955 and 5331 in 1957.

Colour schemes: Garter Blue – from new; Black – 9/42; Garter Blue – 5/47; BR Blue – 6/49; BR Green – 10/52.

Sheds: 1938 – Doncaster, 1938 – Grantham, 1938 – King's Cross, 1939 – Doncaster, 1943 – Grantham, 1950 – King's Cross and 1963 – New England.

Names: *Capercaillie/Charles H Newton/Sir Charles Newton.*

Numbers: 4901, 5 and 60005.

Works Number: 1875.

Date to traffic: 4/6/38.

Withdrawn from service: 3/64 (cut up by G H Campbell of Airdrie – 6/64).

Total mileage: 1,330,582.

General Repairs: June/July 1939, Oct/Nov 1940, July/Aug 1942, Aug/Sep 1944, Dec '44/Feb 1945, June/Aug 1946, Nov '47/Jan 1948, Oct/Nov 1949, May/June 1951, Oct/Nov 1952, Feb/Mar 1954, July/Sep 1955, Mar/May 1957, Oct/Dec 1958, May/July 1960, Aug/Nov 1962.

Modifications: Modifications: 1942 – side valances removed; 1952 – long guard irons removed; 1957 – to 75 per cent cut off; 1958 – AWS fitted; 1960 – speed indicator fitted.

Boilers fitted: 9029 in 1938, 8961 – 1942, 9021 in 1948, 29290 in 1951, 29304 in 1952, 29272 in 1954, 29284 in 1955, 29327 in 1957, 29278 in 1958, 29312 in 1960 and 29334 in 1962.

Tenders attached: 5641 in 1938.

Colour schemes: Garter Blue – from new; Black – 8/42; Garter Blue – 8/46; BR Blue – 11/49; BR Green – 11/52.

Sheds: 1938 – Gateshead, 1963 – St Margarets and 1963 – Aberdeen.

Name: *Seagull.*

Numbers: 4902, 33 and 60033.

Works Number: 1876.

Date to traffic: 28/6/38.

Withdrawn from service: 12/62 (cut up at Doncaster – 1/63).

Total mileage: 1,384,729.

General Repairs: Sep/Nov 1939, Nov '40/Jan 1941, Mar/May 1942, July/Sep 1943, Dec '44/Jan 1945, Mar/May 1946, Oct/Dec 1947, Mar/May 1949, Oct/Nov 1950, May/June 1952, Oct/Dec 1953, Mar/May 1955, Apr/June

1956, Jan/Mar 1958, May/July 1959, Apr/June 1961.

Modifications: Modifications: 1942 – side valances removed; 1948 – to 75 per cent cut off; 1953 long guard irons removed and ATC fitted; 1961 – speed indicator fitted.

Boilers fitted: 9030 in 1938, 8947 in 1943, 8949 in 1949, 29278 in 1950, 29313 in 1952, 29296 in 1953, 29301 in 1955, 29290 in 1956, 29301 in 1958, 29302 in 1959 and 27967 in 1961.

Tenders attached: 5636 in 1938, 5325 in 1948 and 5332 in 1954.

Colour schemes: Garter Blue – from new; Black – 5/42; Garter Blue – 12/47; BR Blue – 11/50; BR Green – 6/52.

Sheds: 1938 – King's Cross, 1944 – Grantham, 1948 – King's Cross.

Names: *Peregrine/Lord Faringdon.*

Numbers: 4903, 34 and 60034.

Works Number: 1877.

Date to traffic: 1/7/38.

Withdrawn from service: 8/66 (cut up by Hughes Bolckow of Blyth – 10/66).

Total mileage: 1,246,748.

General Repairs/Heavy Repairs: Apr/June 1939, Nov/Dec 1940, Aug/Sep 1942, June/July 1944, Sep/Oct 1945, Jan/Feb 1946, Oct/Dec 1947, Mar/Apr 1949, Oct/Dec 1950, June/Aug 1952, Nov '53/Jan 1954, April/May 1955, Oct/Nov 1956, Dec '57/Jan 1958, Apr/May 1959, Sep/Nov 1960, Apr/June 1962.

Modifications: Modifications: 1941/42 – side valances removed; 1948 – to 75 per cent cut off; 1952 – ATC fitted; 1953 – long guard irons removed; 1960 – speed indicator fitted.

Boilers fitted: 9031 in 1938, 8951 in 1940, 9024 in 1942, 8960 in 1947, 29283 in 1952, 29270 in 1954, 29295 in 1955, 29300 in 1956, 29311 in 1958, 29333 in 1959, 29327 in 1960 and 27964 in 1962.

Tenders attached: 5639 in 1938, 5642 in 1939, 5332 in 1948, 5325 in 1954, 5640 in 1963 and 5329 in 1966.

Colour schemes: Garter Blue – from new; Black – 9/42; Garter Blue – 12/47; BR Blue – 12/50; BR Green – 8/52.

Sheds: 1938 – Doncaster, 1942 – King's Cross, 1942 – Grantham, 1948 – King's Cross, 1963 – New England, 1963 – St Margarets, 1964 – Aberdeen.

HISTORIES OF GRESLEY'S OTHER STREAMLINERS

Name: Number only, but nicknamed 'Hush Hush'.

Class: W1 4-6-4

Numbers: 10000 and 60700.

Works Number: Not known (when built in 1929 or rebuilt in 1937).

Date to traffic: 21/6/30 in original condition with a Yarrows water tube boiler. 6/11/37 rebuilt as a conventional engine in A4 style streamlined form.

Withdrawn from service: 9/59 and cut up at Doncaster.

Total mileage: No official figure appears to have survived. However, by adding mileages covered between General Repairs scribbled in pencil on Record Cards the following rough totals may be the best available estimates. Original form 1929 to 1937 – 164,823 miles. Rebuilt form 1937 to 1959 – 985,742. Grand total - 1,150,565 miles.

General Repairs/Heavy Repairs: In original form – May/June 1934 In rebuilt form – Feb/Mar 1939, Nov '40/Feb 1941, Feb/Apr 1942, Apr/ Aug 1945, Oct/Dec 1946, Apr/June 1948, July '50/ Jan 1951, Apr/May 1952, Sep/Dec 1955, June/Aug 1957.

Modifications: In original form – 1935 – double chimney fitted & hood fitted at front end.

 In rebuilt form – 1938 – coal capacity increased; 1942 – side valances removed; 1953 – long guard irons removed; 1956 – cylinder diameter reduced to 19 inches; 1957 – to 75 per cent cut off; 1958 – AWS fitted.

Boilers fitted: In original condition – 18193 in 1929. Rebuilt – 9017/ renumbered 29557 (during 1951) in 1937.

Tenders attached: Original condition – 1929 – 763, 1929 – 5484. Rebuilt – 1937 – 5484, 1948 – 5639, 1953 – 5647 and 5639 – 1953.

Colour schemes: 1929 – grey; 1929 – grey/green; 1937 – Garter blue; 1942 – black; 1946 – Garter blue; 1951 – BR blue; 1952 – BR green.

Sheds: 1929 – Gateshead, 1935 – Neville Hill, 1937 – King's Cross, 1938 – Doncaster, 1939 – King's Cross, 1942 – Haymarket, 1942 – King's Cross, 1953 – Doncaster.

Name: *Cock o' the North.*

Class: P2 2-8-2

Number: 2001

Works Number: 1789.

Date to traffic: 22/5/34

Date rebuilt as a de-streamlined Pacific Class A2/2: June 1944 – Sep 1944.

Withdrawn from service: 2/60 (cut up at Doncaster).

Total mileage: 978,597 (in original form – 125,670, streamlined – 362,136, as a Pacific – 616,461).

General Repairs/Heavy Repairs: Dec 1935, May/July 1936, Apr/ May 1937, Sep '37/Apr 1938, July/ Aug 1939, July/Aug 1940, Mar/Apr 1942, Oct 1943.

Modifications: 1935 – new oil cooling arrangement fitted; 1938 – rebuilt and streamlined, plus new middle con rod.

Boiler fitted: 8771 in 1934.

Tender attached: 5565.

Colour schemes: LNER Green from new.

Sheds: 1934 – Doncaster, 1935 – Haymarket, 1935 – Dundee, 1936 to 1944 – Aberdeen.

Name: *Earl Marischal.*

Class: P2 2-8-2.

Number: 2002
Works Number: 1796.

Date to traffic: 6/10/34.

Date rebuilt as a de-streamlined Pacific Class A2/2: Apr 1944 – June 1944.

Withdrawn from service: 7/61 (cut up at Doncaster).

Total mileage: 1,034,854 (in original, then streamlined form – 360,907, as a Pacific – 673,947).

General Repairs/Heavy Repairs: Aug/Oct 1936, Aug/Sep 1937, Oct/Dec 1938, Feb/Apr 1940, Sep/Oct 1940, Mar/May 1942.

Modifications: 1935 – additional smoke deflectors; 1936 – streamlined.

Boilers fitted: 8750 in 1934 and 8797 in 1940.

Tender attached: 5575 (see note below).

Colour schemes: LNER Green – 1934; Black – 1944 (when rebuilt as a Pacific).

Sheds: 1934 – Doncaster, 1935 – Haymarket, 1935 – Dundee and 1936 – Aberdeen.

Note: It appears that five new high-sided tenders (Nos 5575 to 5579) were assigned to P2s 2002 to 2006. Sadly, records of allocations are a little slim and so initial pairings or any interchanges between locomotives are not easily established. Luckily, the Records Cards do provide an occasional clue. As a result, the 'Tenders attached' details shown in these summaries simply show the information a clerk chose to jot down on a particular date and probably do not reflect a complete picture of allocations over a twenty-five year period.

Name: *Lord President.*

Class: P2 2-8-2.

Number: 2003.

Works Number: 1836.

Date to traffic: 13/6/36.

Date rebuilt as a de-streamlined Pacific Class A2/2: Sep 1944 – Dec 1944.

Withdrawn from service: 11/59 (cut up at Doncaster).

Total mileage: 754,781 (in original streamlined form – 246,283, as a Pacific – 508,498).

General Repairs/Heavy Repairs: Mar/April 1938, Sep/Nov 1939, Jan/Mar 1941, Oct/Dec 1942.

Modifications: None recorded.

Boilers fitted:8796 in 1936 and 8785 in 1942 previously on 2002).

Tender attached: 5576.

Colour schemes: LNER Green – 1936; Black – 1944 (when rebuilt as a Pacific)..

Sheds: 1936 – Haymarket, 1936 – Dundee, 1942 – Haymarket, 1942 – North-East Area, 1944 – Haymarket.

Name: *Mons Meg.*

Class: P2 2-8-2.

Number: 2004.

Works Number: 1839.

Date to traffic: 11/7/36.

Date rebuilt as a de-streamlined Pacific Class A2/2: Aug 1944 – Nov 1944.

Withdrawn from service: 1/61 (cut up at Doncaster).

Total mileage: 989,040 (in original streamlined form – 294,243, as a Pacific – 694,797).

General Repairs/Heavy Repairs: Jan/Mar 1938, Dec '39/Feb 1940, Apr/June 1941, Dec '42/Feb 1943.

Modifications: 1937 and 1939 – bypass valve underwent modification each year.

Boilers fitted: 8789 in 1936.

Tender attached: 5577.

Colour schemes: LNER Green – 1936; Black – 1944 (when rebuilt as a Pacific).

Sheds: 1936 – Haymarket.

Name: *Thane of Fife.*

Class: P2 2-8-2.

Numbers: 2005.

Works Number: 1940.

Date to traffic: 8/8/36.

Date rebuilt as a de-streamlined Pacific Class A2/2: Oct 1942 - Jan 1943.

Withdrawn from service: 11/59 (cut up at Doncaster).

Total mileage: 919,747 (in original streamlined form – 246,283, as a Pacific – 673,564).

General Repairs/Heavy Repairs: Nov/Dec 1937, Sep/Oct 1938, Aug 1939, June/July 1940.

Modifications: None recorded.

Boilers fitted: 8799 in 1936.

Tender attached: 5579.

Colour schemes: LNER Green – 1936; Black – 1943 (when rebuilt as a Pacific).

Sheds: 1936 – Dundee.

Name: *Wolf of Badenoch.*

Class: P2 2-8-2

Number: 2006.

Works Number: 1842.

Date to traffic: 5/9/36.

Date rebuilt as a de-streamlined Pacific Class A2/2: Jan 1944 – Apr 1944.

Withdrawn from service: 4/61 (cut up at Doncaster).

Total mileage: 916,200 (in original streamlined form – 287,187, as a Pacific – 629,013).

General Repairs/Heavy Repairs: May/July 1939, Apr/May 1940, Oct/Dec 1940, Sep/Dec 1941, Mar/May 1942.

Modifications: None recorded.

Boilers fitted: 8934 in 1936.

Tender attached: 5578.

Colour schemes: LNER Green – 1936, black – 1944 (when rebuilt as a Pacific).

Sheds: 1936 – Haymarket, 1936 – Aberdeen, 1942 – Haymarket.

Name: *Norwich City and East Anglian*

Class: B17 4-6-0.

Numbers: 2859, 1659 and 61659.

Works Number: Not known.

Date to traffic: 11/6/1936.

Dates rebuilt as a streamlined engine: July/Sep1937.

Dates streamlining removed: November 1950/April 1951.

Withdrawn from service: 3/60 (cut up at Stratford).

Total mileage: Not known.

General Repairs/Heavy Repairs: July/Sep 1937, Jan/Apr 1939, Feb/Apr 1941, Aug/Oct 1942, May/June 1944, Dec '45/Jan 1946, Jan/Apr 1948, May/ July 1949, Nov '50/Apr 1951 (end of streamlining).

Modifications: None recorded, except streamlining.

Boilers fitted: 4716 in 1936, 4708 in 1944, 4045 in 1946 and 5093 in 1949.

Tender attached: 2859.

Colour schemes:LNER Green – 1936, Black – 1941/42.

Sheds: 1936 – Gorton, 1937 – Norwich, 1946 – Ipswich, 1947 – Norwich, 1948 – Ipswich, 1948 – Norwich, 1948 – Cambridge, 1948 – Norwich.

Name: *Tottenham Hotspur and City of London.*

Class: B17 4-6-0.

Numbers: 2870, 1670 and 61670.

Works Number: Not known.

Date to traffic: 13/5/37.

Dates rebuilt as a streamlined locomotive: July/Sep 1937.

Dates streamlining removed: Oct 1950/April 1951.

Withdrawn from service: 4/60 (cut up at Stratford).

Total mileage: Not known.

General Repairs/Heavy Repairs:
July/Sep 1937, Mar/May 1939, June/
Aug 1941, Nov/Dec 1942, Aug/Oct
1944, Jan/Mar 1946, April/Aug 1948,
Oct 1950/April 1951.

Modifications: none recorded except
streamlining.

Boilers fitted: 4728 in 1936, 4035 in
1944, 4706 in 1946, 4727 in 1948.

Tender attached: 2870.

Colour schemes: LNER Green –
1936, Black – 1941/42.

Sheds: 1936 – Leicester, 1937 –
Norwich, 1948 – Yarmouth, 1949 –
Norwich, 1949 – Ipswich, 1949 –
Norwich.

REFERENCES SOURCES

The National Railway Museum (Search Engine)

Records Consulted
Corr/LNER/1 to 6.
Calc/LNER/1
Loco/LNER/1 to 9.
Spec/Don/7.
Spec/LNER/1 to 7.
Test/LNER/1 to 10.
The R Bond Collection.
The E.S Cox Collection.
The R Riddles Collection (donated by author).
The Immingham Collection (donated by author).
The E Thompson Collection.

Other Collections
National Archives
Museum of Science and Industry, Manchester.
Science Museum, London.
Institution of Mechanical Engineers, London.
R.A. Hillier.
D. Neal.
T.F. Coleman/M Lemon.
B. Spencer.
R.A. Thom.
N. Newsome.
R.H.N. Hardy.
A. Ewer.
Paget Archive.

Publications
IMechE/ILocoE Journals
The Engineer
The Gazette various dates.
The Meccano Magazine
Steam World
The Stephenson Society Journal

Allen, J.R. and Bursley, J.A., *Heat Engines; Steam, Gas, Steam Turbines and Their Auxiliaries* (1941).
Bannister, Eric, *Trained By Sir Nigel Gresley*, Dalesman (1984).
Bond, R., *A Lifetime With Locomotives* (1975).
Brown, E.A.S., *Nigel Gresley. Locomotive Engineer"* Littlehampton Book Services (1961)
Bulleid, H.A.V., *Master Builders of Steam*, Ian Allan, (1963).
Bulleid, H.A.V., *Bulleid of the Southern"* Littlehampton Book Services (1977).
Bush, D.J., *The Streamlined Decade*, George Braziller (1975).
Chapelon, A., *La Locomotive a Vapeur* (1952).
Coster, P., *Book of the A3 Pacifics*, Irwell Press (2003).
Coster, P., *Book of the A4 Pacifics*, Irwell Press (2005).
Coster, P., *Book of the V2 2-6-2s*, Irwell Press (2008).
Cox, E.S., *Locomotive Panorama Vols 1 and 2*, Ian Allan (1965/66).
Cox, E.S., *Chronicles of Locomotives*, Ian Allan (1967).
Cox, E.S., *Speaking of Steam*, Ian Allan (1971).

Dalby, W.E., *The Balancing of Engines* (1920).
Dalby, W.E., *British Railways: Some Facts and A Few Problems* (1910).
Grafton, P., *Edward Thompson of the LNER*, Oakwood Press (1971 & 2007).
Hillier-Graves, T., *Gresley and His Locomotives*, Pen and Sword Transport (2019).
Hillier-Graves, T., *Gresley's Master Engineer – Bert Spencer* Pen and Sword Transport (2023).
Hillier-Graves, T., *Gresley's Silver Link*, Pen and Sword Transport(2022).
Hillier-Graves, T., *Peppercorn. His Life and Locomotives*, Pen and Sword Transport (2021).
Hillier-Graves, T., *Thompson. His Life and Locomotives*, Pen and Sword Transport (2021).
Hillier-Graves, T., *Tom Coleman. His Life and Work*, Pen and Sword Transport (2019).
Hardy, R.H.N., *Steam in the Blood*, Littlehampton Book Services (1971).
Haresnape, B., *Gresley's Locomotives*, Ian Allan (1981).
Holcroft, H., *Locomotive Adventure Vols 1 and 2*, Ian Allan (1962).
Hughes, Geoffrey, *Sir Nigel Gresley*, Oakwood Publishing (2001).
Martin, S.A.C., *Edward Thompson. Wartime CME*, Strathwood, Ltd (2022).

McKillop, Norman, *Top Link Locomotives*, Thomas Nelson and Sons (1957).
Nock, O.S., *The Gresley Pacifics*, David and Charles (1973).
Nock, O.S., *Locomotives of Sir Nigel Gresley*, (1945).
Pope, A., *Wind Tunnel Testing* (1947).
RCTS, *Locomotives of the LNER – Vols 2A, 2B & 6B* (1973 & 1983).
Rogers, H.C.B., *The Last Steam Locomotive Engineer*, Allen and Unwin (1970).
Rogers, H.C.B., *Thompson & Peppercorn. Locomotive Engineers*, Allen and Unwin (1979).
Rogers, H.C.B., *Transition from Steam*, Allen and Unwin (1980).
Townend, P.N., *East Coast Pacifics at Work*, Littlehampton Book Services (1982).
Townend, P.N., *Top Shed*, Ian Allan (1975).
Yeadon, W.B., *Yeadon's Registers –* Nos 1,2,3,4,5,8,9,10 and 25 (various dates).

Photographic Sources/Credits
B Spencer (BS), R Hillier (RH), T Coleman (TC/ML), Author (THG), H A V Bulleid (HB), P Atkins (PA), LNER (PR), E Lowden (EL), A Ewer (AE), D Neal (DN), N Skinner (NS), E Thompson/A Parfitt (ET/AP) and BR PR (BR).

Copyright is a complex issue and often difficult to establish, especially when a photograph or document exists in a number of public and private collections.

Strenuous efforts have been made to ensure each item is correctly attributed, but no process is flawless, especially when many of these items are more than 70 years old with photographers or authors long gone. If an error has been made, it was unintentional. If any reader wishes to affirm copyright, please contact the publishers and an acknowledgement will be included in any future edition of this book, should a claim be proven. We apologise in advance for any mistakes. A number of documents held by the NRM have been quoted in this book. My thanks to the museum for permission to do this.

INDEX